WEiRD WISCONSIN

Sterling Publishing Co., Inc.
New York

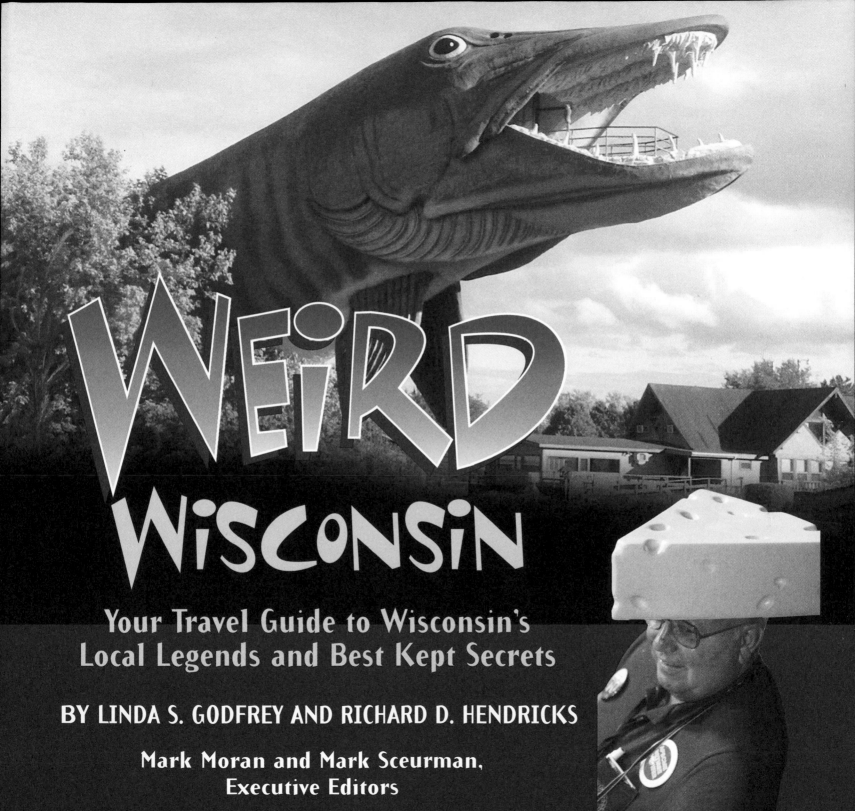

Weird Wisconsin

Your Travel Guide to Wisconsin's Local Legends and Best Kept Secrets

BY LINDA S. GODFREY AND RICHARD D. HENDRICKS

Mark Moran and Mark Sceurman,
Executive Editors

WEiRD WiSCONSiN

Published by Sterling Publishing Co., Inc.
387 Park Avenue South, New York, NY 10016
© 2005 by Sterling Publishing Co., Inc.
Distributed in Canada by Sterling Publishing
c/o Canadian Manda Group, 165 Dufferin Street
Toronto, Ontario, Canada M6K 3H6
Distributed in Great Britain by Chrysalis Books Group PLC
The Chrysalis Building, Bramley Road, London W10 6SP, England
Distributed in Australia by Capricorn Link (Australia) Pty. Ltd.
P. O. Box 704, Windsor, NSW 2756, Australia

10 9 8 7 6 5 4 3 2

Manufactured in the United States of America.
All rights reserved

Photography and illustration credits are found on page 271
and constitute an extension of this copyright page.

ISBN 0-7607-5944-8

For information about custom editions, special sales, premium
and corporate purchases, please contact Sterling Special Sales
Department at 800-805-5489 or specialsales@sterlingpub.com.

Design: Richard J. Berenson
         Berenson Design & Books, LLC, New York, NY

Weird Wisconsin is intended as entertainment
to present a historical record of local legends,
folklore, and sites throughout the United
States. Many of these legends and stories
cannot be independently confirmed or
corroborated and the authors and publisher
make no representation as to their factual
accuracy. The reader should be advised
that many of the sites described in *Weird
Wisconsin* are located on private property
and should not be visited, or you may face
prosecution for trespassing.

CONTENTS

Foreword: A Note from the Marks   6

Introduction   8

Local Legends   10

Ancient Mysteries   24

Fabled People and Places   38

Roadside Oddities   64

Unexplained Phenomena   90

Bizarre Beasts   104

Local Notables   122

Personalized Properties   146

Collected Exhibitionism   182

Roads Less Traveled   202

Badger State Ghosts   226

Cemetery Safari   244

Index   264

Contributors   268

Acknowledgments   269

Picture Credits   270

Selected Bibliography   271

DEDICATION

To my parents, Elaine A. and Roland H. Roberts, who not only bought me *MAD* magazine as a kid but raised me to appreciate the weirder things of this world.—*LSG*

To Todd Roll, for Lovecraftian tales and that little yellow folder where it all began. And to my parents, Theresa G. and Richard A. Hendricks, who, despite their best efforts, gave birth to all this weirdness.—*RDH*

Foreword: A Note from the Marks

Our *weird journey* began a long, long time ago in a far-off land called New Jersey. Once a year or so we'd compile a homespun newsletter called *Weird N.J.* to hand out to our friends. The pamphlet was a collection of odd news clippings, bizarre facts, little-known historical anecdotes, and anomalous encounters from our home state. The newsletter also focused on localized legends that were often whispered around a particular town but seldom heard beyond the town line.

Weird N.J. soon became a full-fledged magazine, and we began doing our own investigating to see if we could track down any factual basis for all of these seemingly unbelievable stories. Armed with not much more than a camera and notepad, we set off on a mystical journey of discovery. To our amazement, much of what we had initially presumed to be nothing more than urban legend actually turned out to be real, or at least contained a grain of truth that had originally sparked the lore.

After about a dozen years of documenting the bizarre, we were asked to write a book about our adventures, and so *Weird N.J.: Your Travel Guide to New Jersey's Local Legends and Best Kept Secrets* was published in 2003. Soon people from all over the country began writing to us, telling us strange tales from their home states. As it turned out, what we had first perceived to be a very local interest genre was actually just a small part of a much larger and more universal phenomenon. So we decided to write *Weird U.S.*, in which we could document local legends and strange stories from all over the country.

Now uncovering oddities in a small state like New Jersey is one thing, but unearthing these hidden mysteries in far-off states was a challenging task, to say the least. We decided that we needed to find like-minded fellow travelers in all of these far-flung localities who could fill us in on just what weirdness there was to explore in their own home states.

During our research into the local legends and oddities of Wisconsin, we became acquainted with the writings of two authors native to the state who seemed to know just what to look for—Linda Godfrey and Richard D. Hendricks. You might say they had what we call the weird eye. Linda had written a book about the Beast of Bray Road, and Richard's Web site, Weird-WI.com, was a treasure trove of articles about Wisconsin lore. Both Linda and Richard generously agreed to contribute material to *Weird U.S.*,

representing their home state as perhaps one of the most bizarre in the entire nation.

In 2004, after *Weird U.S.* was published, Barnes & Noble asked us once more where we wanted to go next. In the year that it had taken us to put together *Weird U.S.*, we had come to the conclusion that this country had so many great tales to tell that we wanted to document it ALL and to do it in a series of books, each focusing on the peculiarities of one particular state.

When it came time to choose the authors for *Weird Wisconsin,* we went back to Linda and Richard. We were delighted to find that they were not only familiar with each other's work, but were actually very close friends and had worked together on projects in the past. We probably should have assumed this, as weird people seem to gravitate toward one another.

Together, the authors have chronicled a broad array of the odd and unique people, places, and stories that make Wisconsin the fascinating and just downright weird place that it is.

So please read on, and let Linda and Richard be your tour guides through one of the most intriguing and bewildering states of them all. It's a place we like to call Weird Wisconsin.

—Mark Moran and Mark Sceurman

Introduction

In *1634*, Jean Nicolet became the first European to land in Wisconsin. Dressed in a flowing Chinese robe embroidered with flowers and birds (alas, he thought he had reached China!), he came ashore near what is now Green Bay firing two raised pistols in an ostentatious display of his majesty. More Europeans followed, importing their wild mélange of folkways and ancestral spirits. All the millions of souls that have since crisscrossed the Badger State have left their history imprinted on the land, but you won't find most of it written about in official textbooks or inscribed on tourism markers or handed out in glossy flyers by chambers of commerce.

We're still creating these strange fragments of private history—an encounter with an eccentric figure at the corner café, a darting shadow coalescing into a monster in our vehicle's high beams, our own mental baggage distorting a forest into witch-entangled nightmares. These will-o'-the-wisp moments become our stories, and ghosts whisper along with us each time we pass these eerie tales on.

Though politicians and the media seem bent on turning Wisconsin into something else, those of us with deep taproots here know what we really are. From the Germanic architecture of Milwaukee to the Polish graveyards of central Wisconsin to the Swiss heritage of New Glarus to millennia-old traditions still observed on Indian reservations around the state, you can't help but think something important happened here—something different, unique, and, yes, weird.

To us, weird is a good thing. It can encompass people, places, things, and stories from the mildly odd to the deeply macabre. Therefore, it was baffling when one or two museums, upon learning the title of our book, sniffed, "We don't know if we could be associated with that." Sigh. Sad, ain't it, not to want to be associated with regular people? What most people call weirdness is often only a sign of originality and nonconformity, which we thought was the whole American raison d'être in the first place. It may imply a touch of the spiritual or paranormal, or it could just describe someone's wacky, individualistic artwork. What's not to love?

Truth be told, there's almost too much too love. In fact, when we learned how much there was, we found it hard to try to fit all of Wisconsin's weirdness between the covers of one measly book. It was like cramming six pounds of ground bratwurst "material" into a one-pound sausage casing or stuffing a

Packers fan wearing a size XXX large into a size small green-and-gold sweatshirt or scooping up all of Lake Winnebago and trying to dump it into a bathtub.

It's not that we didn't try. We traveled the entire state, from Superior to Kenosha. We trudged through northern meadows, got covered in stick-tights, fell into swamps while searching for ghost towns. We tramped city streets photographing funky old murals and haunted buildings; drove down every road that's home to a giant fiberglass mouse, cow, or moose; examined each passing occult glyph for meaning. We rifled so many history files for spook stories that the tales haunt us still.

As for legends, with our ethnic heritage, Wisconsin is so rich in lore that the whole state ought to be installed in the Smithsonian under glass. Trucks in trees, headless nuns, communities of murderous little people—how to choose?

We finally had to accept that this book could not be an all-inclusive encyclopedia of weird culture. Instead, we settled for a carefully selected collection. Just because something isn't included in our book doesn't mean it isn't fabulous, historically important, or weird. It simply means that for some reason we felt we needed to choose something else. And we admit there could be more than a few unturned stones out there that we haven't tripped over yet. Weirdness, we now know, is everywhere.

Consider this book a collective journal of the psychic and historic effluvia that make up the Badger State experience.

Dude, where's our weird?

Turn the page.

–Linda S. Godfrey and Richard D. Hendricks

Local Legends

No one can just let a good story lie, especially if it's tinged with weirdness and involves people and places that are familiar. In fact, entire Web sites are devoted to popularizing such urban myths—those tales that make the rounds both electronically and wherever humans continue to gather in the flesh. Of course, local legends have their naysayers too, and plenty of other Web sites are devoted to debunking the very same myths.

Whether or not we are inclined to believe these stories, it's safe to say that when we hear some tale from our own neighbors about strange happenings in our own backyards, we are much more inclined to believe that story and pass it on. These are the types of yarns *Weird Wisconsin* looks for—hometown tales that keep making the rounds because, as with good vampires, you can't drive a stake deep enough into their hearts to keep them down.

The stories in this chapter are a mixture of current tales and familiar fables that have been told around campfires for decades and even, in some cases, for centuries. Luckily for us, Wisconsin's great ethnic diversity makes for an especially rich witch's brew of myths. But remember, all legends have one thing in common: They strive for emotional impact. They're meant to leave you charged with one deep feeling or another. Terror, wonder, horror, humor, pity, sadness— these are the common reactions evoked by the most enduring and compelling legends. If they didn't deliver, they'd die a quick death.

But beyond their immediate entertainment value, local legends are also our living folk history. As long as words continue to dance on the tongues of storytellers, new and ancient myths will sing on for generations to come, their lyrics sustaining memories of the common past we share with those long gone, some of whom are still with us as spirits and specters and shades from the realm of the dead.

It doesn't really matter if the stories are true or not, except to those who are sticklers for absolute fact or are just plain killjoys. Many legends are impossible to prove. However, in the grand scheme of things, what difference does it make whether Waukesha really was or was not overrun by kangaroos? What matters is that these stories, which inevitably sling twisted ropes around our hearts, anchor us to people and places in our hometowns. Here then are some of our favorite local legends.

Great Waukesha Phantom Kangaroo Flap

Kangaroos are usually lovable and adorable. But sometimes they can be nasty, especially if you've ever stood in the boxing ring and had one put you in a headlock and proceed to pummel you silly, as had once happened to Milwaukee journalist Jackie Louhauis. But overall, they're not the usual kind of monster that raises goose bumps on the flesh.

Yet kangaroos—or something resembling kangaroos—acquire a powerful aura of mystery when they turn up where they're not supposed to. Add to this intriguing situation humans going about their day-to-day business in ordinary suburbia and weirdness inevitably ensues.

Few realize how strange things were in Waukesha County for a brief period in 1978, when stories of kangaroos on the loose hit the national news media. Starting in mystery and wonder, the whole affair soon degenerated into a wacky farce that went down in legend as one of the Badger State's more bizarre episodes, and that's saying a lot.

The episode began on a perfectly normal day—April 5, 1978, to be exact. Waukesha school-bus driver Patricia Wilcox was at the beginning of her morning run on Moreland Boulevard, a busy multilane road, when she reported seeing two kangaroos—one little, one big—hop across the road. "I thought they were deer at first," she related. "People were honking and slamming on their brakes, and finally one guy hit one. But it just got up and hopped off. The skid marks are still there. The guy just got out of the car and stood there, looking."

Seven days later, in the town of Pewaukee, Jill and Peter Haeselich and Peter's mother, Esther, saw a kangaroo in their backyard as they ate dinner. The animal, which was between three and five feet tall, was only fifty feet from their dining-room window. Peter ran outside, but the creature took off very fast toward the south, disappearing over a hill. "It was going pretty quick," said Jill. "It was hopping. We knew it had to be a kangaroo."

That same day, William Busch, a social worker, was returning home from the Ethan Allen School for Boys. It was four forty-five p.m., and he was driving on Highway 83, just south of Waukesha. Fifteen feet ahead, a little creature scampered across the road. At first, Busch thought it was a dog. The creature had a slightly odd–shaped head, two short legs in the front, and two long legs in the back. It stood hunched over and was maybe three feet tall. Busch wasn't sure what he saw. He never called it a kangaroo but reported it in good faith as an example of the crazy local fauna.

On April 16, at three a.m., on County Trunk A about a mile east of Waukesha, Greg and Janet Napientek spotted a creature in their headlights. "We were pretty close, within

Waukesha school-bus driver Patricia Wilcox was at the beginning of her morning run on Moreland Boulevard, a busy multilane road, when she reported seeing two kangaroos—one little, one big—hop across the road.

about thirty to thirty-five yards," Greg said. "It stood up, and I really couldn't believe what I was seeing. It was four feet tall, colored like a deer. Janet thought at first it was a deer, until it stood up on its hind legs, then jumped over a ditch and fled. She said it was a kangaroo."

In Waukesha, people began joking about the so-called kangaroo sightings. The newspaper ran a photo of two children standing beneath a kangaroo-crossing highway sign. Storekeepers put cages out front, advertising $50 rewards for captured kangaroos.

Kangaroo T-shirts went on sale. Weird letters to the editor were printed in the newspaper. The kangaroo cocktail—made of vodka, Southern Comfort, cranberry juice, and grapefruit juice—became the favorite drink around town. As one wag said, "It's guaranteed to keep you hopping." People even started writing bad poetry about kangaroos. One fellow wrote, "Maybe it's like the Bermuda Triangle, man, only it's a kangaroo rectangle." And well-known regional prankster William Woolley, who ran the Woolley Boys Bar, planned a kangaroo hunt on the shores of Pewaukee Lake.

Some fifty hunters gathered on the morning of Saturday, April 22, for the hunt. Many carried long black fishnets, coils of rope, and air horns. Some even wore Aussie bush hats. They were stoked, "primed with beer since Friday night." Their theory was that air horns attracted kangaroos, and since kangaroos were afraid of water, the hunters would use the horns to drive the beasts to the lake, where they'd be netted. Clearly, it was a sound methodology.

Bill Woolley, head kangaroo hunter, led the safari in his 1973 white Caddy painted with black zebra stripes. A seventy-five-foot fishnet was strung across the beach. Then a crazy combo of motorcycles, four-wheel-drive vehicles, and human beaters with poles tried flushing the kangaroos from a nearby wood, all the while consuming beer and blasting their air horns. The only kangaroo they encountered was some guy dressed in a costume, who mugged for the cameras and got a ride on the back of a motorcycle. Even his costume was ridiculous, being a hastily transformed dog getup with large ears sewn onto it. The hunt lasted until four p.m., when the fearsome, weary warriors retired to Woolley's to crack a free fresh half-barrel. A good time was had by all!

Unfortunately, the hunters had been beating about the wrong bushes. Had they been sober enough to wake early the next morning, Sunday, they would have discovered two kangaroos at the Nero residence. Oddly enough, Lance Nero had laughed his head off the night before as he heard about the ridiculous safari on the local television news. During breakfast, however, he was fiddling a different tune as he watched a pair of three- to four-foot-tall kangaroos emerge from the woods, hop across County 22, and traverse an open field before disappearing from sight.

Nero stared, amazed, then ran to wake his sleeping wife, Loretta. She got up in time to see one of the kangaroos hopping away. "Now that I've seen one, I'm wondering if I'm all right," she said.

Lance and his son, Brock, chased them, Instamatic camera in hand, but lost them in the woods. They did find several tracks, however. They were narrow, about six inches long, and V-shaped, with firm impressions of the toe in front and a softer impression in the back. Nero and his son made plaster casts of the tracks, and cryptozoologist Mark Hall (cryptozoology is the study of unknown animals) subsequently traveled from Minneapolis to make his own set of casts. The authorities insisted that the tracks had been made by deer, but they were clearly not deer tracks.

It was at this point that the First National Bank began using kangaroos in its advertising. And that wasn't all. Someone brought a twenty-one-inch-tall wallaby to a Brookfield Volunteer Fire Department meeting and to the Waukesha State Bank, where it posed for pictures.

Then a much more mysterious photo surfaced. Two twenty-three-year-old anonymous Menomonee Falls camera buffs sent the papers a color Polaroid of a kangaroolike creature in a wooded area. The photo was allegedly taken at five twenty p.m. on Monday, April 24. Supposedly, the camera buffs were photographing ducks when they encountered the kangaroo. Their picture appeared in newspapers across the country—proof that a kangaroo was hopping around Waukesha County.

On Thursday, April 27, the Wisconsin Agriculture Department put out a press release warning citizens to beware of kangaroos and to keep all pets away from them, especially horses, because kangaroos could be carriers of equine infectious anemia. To determine whether a kangaroo was diseased or not, the press release explained, you had to examine the inside of its lower lip. If the kangaroo had a tattoo declaring it free of equine infectious anemia, you were safe. However, according to Agriculture Department Secretary Gary Rhode, "The problem is that the absence of such tattoos can mean either that the kangaroo tested negatively or that it was not tested at all."

Tattooed lips on kangaroos? This development had everyone talking for days. Turns out, it was a story created by Edward Jackonamis, Waukesha's Democratic state assembly speaker, who had issued a bogus press release that tricked both the agriculture department and newspapers around the state.

By this point, the mystery was officially a farce. Jokers and pranksters had won out, and most people had lost interest in the kangaroos.

Until, that is, Sunday, May 21, nearly a month later. That's when an Eau Claire woman driving along Highway 12 between Augusta and Fall Creek saw "a figure the size of a man hopping across the highway five to six car lengths in front of her. It wasn't too visible, but it was not a deer, it wasn't a dog, and it wasn't a man."

Kangaroo sightings persisted, even after the famous Polaroid that so many had believed in proved to be a fake. Turns out it was a stuffed wallaby taken from a Milwaukee museum, placed in a cornfield, and photographed. Then in June 2000, some other pranksters confessed to having used a plywood kangaroo cutout, to which they had attached handles. Brothers Randy and Rick Latta and their neighbors, brothers Dick and Jack Schmidt, took credit for many of the kangaroo sightings. They said they would hide in bushes until a car approached, and then they would go bouncing across Barker Road.

However, there were no reported sightings along Barker Road, and it is doubtful plywood kangaroos were getting hit by cars, then hopping away.

Kemper Hall's Headless Nun

Where there are nuns and a five-story tower, there are bound to be ghosts and legends. Kenosha's Kemper Hall fills the bill and then some. The imposing complex of brick buildings set along Third Avenue on Lake Michigan's brooding shore in Kenosha became a private Episcopal seminary for girls in 1871. The campus no longer serves the educational needs of young women. But according to local lore, some former students and at least one ferocious Episcopal nun named Mary Terese have never left the premises of what is now called Kemper Center.

Of the buildings that once served as convent, dormitories, classrooms, and offices, the former science hall at Kemper is the focus of spectral happenings. Outfitted in 1894 with the latest scientific equipment—everything from Bunsen burners to a refractor telescope—this stellar facility was unprecedented in a school for young women, who at that time were usually relegated to teaching or nursing if they were to have any career at all. Even Thomas Edison's great-granddaughter received her science education from the learned nuns of Kemper.

The science hall's crown jewel, the telescope, was housed in a domed observatory with a sliding panel that opened to the stars. The dome was reached via a five-story spiral staircase that doubled as a fire escape and was marked by crimson doors. According to school legend, the dark wooden stairs were the nemesis of Mother Mary Terese. Although no one knows exactly when this was supposed to have happened, the specter of the ferocious nun became tradition and was raised every Halloween at Kemper by older students to frighten the younger ones into submission.

The legends surrounding Mary Terese vary. One version has students pushing her out a window after she had already fallen down the stairs. But the most oft-repeated version depicts Mary Terese as a cruel taskmistress who was hated by the entire Kemper student body. One night, the story goes, the nun climbed to the observatory to fetch some books. To her shock, she found a group of girls lying in wait for her. The girls, eyes dark and glinting with revenge, shoved the despised nun and her armload of books down the deep stairwell. Mary Terese plunged to the bottom in a gruesome spiral of death, the books fluttering around her. Before she hit the ground floor, the violence of the fall had severed her head from her body; the head then thumped down the final few steps, before coming to rest on the bloodied black habit that covered what was left of Mary Terese.

There are no school records that Mary Terese was ever at Kemper Hall, but that hasn't stopped the legends. The building is also said to be haunted by the ghost of a young student who had lunged from the tower in despair over a forced separation from her boyfriend. And another nun is rumored to have killed herself by leaping into cold Lake Michigan.

The school was closed in 1975, and the famous telescope disappeared. Today, the Kemper Center buildings and grounds are a county park, used for weddings, concerts, and other social and cultural events.

The oldest building on the campus is the Durkee Mansion, built in 1861 as the residence of Charles Durkee. It too is said to be haunted. The ghost of a nun who had died in a fire is still reputed to float about the third floor of the mansion, which has been preserved as a historical museum.

Local paranormal investigator David Schmickel took photos of the Kemper Center in 1996 that purported to show ghostly shadows and images in the west second-story windows of what was formerly the science hall. Schmickel even invited Chicago psychic Richard Crowe to visit the center to offer his opinion about whether the science hall was inhabited by ghosts. According to a *Kenosha News* article dated July 15 of that year, Crowe agreed with Schmickel that "there was something going on here." Crowe theorized that the school's strict discipline had caused "pent-up psychic energy" that was now manifesting itself in the form of ghosts.

The *Kenosha News* has also published reports of other weird sightings of ghostly phantoms around Kemper. An article dated October 29, 1995, by Don Jensen described area photographer William Saxby's experience of seeing something blurry fall from the science hall tower as he snapped a shot of the old dome. Furthermore, Saxby's camera inexplicably jammed when he tried to photograph the spiral staircase.

In addition, Jensen cited Laura and Todd Becker, a couple who had performed at the Kemper auditorium. Todd was working alone there one day when his radio began cutting in and out for no reason. He then saw a short figure dressed entirely in black, which subsequently vanished. (The nuns who ran Kemper wore black habits.) And while Mother Mary Terese may not have existed, other nuns who taught at Kemper Hall are buried nearby. Presumably, their heads are still attached.

Screams and Cries at Kemper Center
My friends and I used to hang out in the back parking lot of the Kemper Center almost every night. But one night in September there was something different. Around 11:30 pm we were all sitting on a friend of mine's car when we heard a sound. It sounded like a scream or a high-pitched cry. When we all looked up at the spiral staircase there was a dark figure rolling down the stairs. Then it was gone.

On another night we were all walking around the building and there was an unexplainable shadowy figure crawling around on the grass and up and down the walls of the building.

There are a lot of various yells and screams that come from different rooms when you are in the building. Very cold chills included. There are a lot of weird things that I have read about, but experiencing them is even BETTER!!–*Stefani Ellen Powers*

Curse of the T. B. Scott Mansion

The towns of northern Wisconsin are filled with monstrous houses built to shelter the families and egos of nineteenth-century lumber barons. Most of these men became rich by decimating the state's great timber stands, so it was of little consequence to them to put a small forest's worth of oak and pine into their homes.

Scotsman Thomas Blythe Scott was one such lumber broker (and five-term state senator), who built a hilltop palace in Merrill, overlooking the Wisconsin River. Unfortunately, things didn't go too well for him once the fabulous home was completed. Old-timers in Merrill said he might have done better if he'd only had the sense not to build on land cursed by a Native American chief.

The land had been doomed long before Europeans settled in Merrill, back in the days when French fur traders canoed up and down the rivers, looking to buy beaver, fox, and muskrat pelts. Near what is now Merrill was a village called Squiteo-eau-sippi by the French. One day, a group of French traders came to the village and were received as important guests by the chief himself, who asked his beautiful young daughter to serve the men dinner. Perhaps unable to pronounce her name, the Frenchmen called the young woman Jenny. One of the traders decided he'd like to see more of the comely Jenny, and nine months later the poor girl died in childbirth.

By this time, of course, the traders were long gone, and the chief was unable to direct his revenge at the man who had impregnated his daughter. In his grief and fury, the chief decided she would be buried on the large hill across the river from his village, but he cursed the hill for all time. The curse was recorded in a story by Dolores Chilsen Mielke that appeared in the *Merrill Daily Herald* in 1930. Mielke later wrote a book about the Scott Mansion, which figures prominently in this story. The bereaved chief's prayer was, "O Great Spirit, grant me this peace for my child. Let this ground be sacred to her memory, and let it never do any white man any good."

A settler's village soon sprang up near the hill, called Jenny, and just as the chief had hoped, all who lived on that hill seemed to fall prey to early death and great woes.

By 1884, T. B. Scott had begun building his mansion, and the village, now a city, had changed its name to Merrill. At that time, a small Indian summer camp still occupied part of the hill, and Scott took care to leave it alone. Even so, he died in 1886 at the age of fifty-seven from Bright's disease before the house was finished. His widow, Anna, died the following year. Their son, Walter, sold the mansion, but apparently not quickly enough— he met an early death ten years later, when he was stabbed with

He might have done better if he'd only had the sense not to

build on land cursed by a Native American chief.

a letter opener after a quarrel. None of the Scotts ever lived in the mansion.

The Chicago businessman who bought the house sold it only five days after purchasing it to one Andrew Dunning, who was able to hold on to it for only a few years before passing it on to Edward and Gertrude Kuechle. Edward Kuechle soon lost his shirt in a gold-mine scam, after which the house was owned by a succession of Chicago speculators. A few years later, the Kuechles' fortunes rebounded and they bought the house back. Big mistake. No sooner had they once again become its official owners than they lost everything in a disastrous railroad purchase. Edward Kuechle was eventually declared insane.

The next owner was embarking from Chicago on a trip to Merrill to have his first look at the property when mobsters stabbed him to death in Chicago's Union Station. Another owner died of a stroke at the relatively young age of sixty-two, and in 1912 a one-armed popcorn vendor named Popcorn Dan Coxon, who may have served as caretaker of the house, drowned on the *Titanic*.

Eventually, the mansion was sold to the city of Merrill. In 1923, the city offered it to a Catholic order—the Sisters of the Holy Cross—if the order would build a hospital on the grounds. The sisters accepted, and the grounds now include a modern hospital, a chapel, and other buildings.

Although people still whisper that the mansion is filled with ghostly laughter and mysterious footsteps, there have been no more strange or untimely deaths since the Sisters of the Holy Cross took it over. Townspeople say that's because the religious sisters are the only people the curse could ever allow to live on the hill. Not everyone agrees that there was a maiden named Jenny. Some digging by Dolores Mielke revealed that for some unknown reason an early surveyor had named the town Virginia Falls. Virginia was shortened to Ginny, then corrupted to Jenny, and that is where the town's original name came from.

Whether the curse was real or not, whether there was a beautiful chief's daughter or not, only the river and the hill now remember. But one fact remains: Until the estate was given over to people whose lives were dedicated to God and to healing, it never did do the white men who lived there any good.

La Crosse Nursing Home's Little Boy Angel of Death

Nurses and aides have noticed that deaths in a particular La Crosse nursing home and hospice tend to cluster in threes, occurring within hours or days of each other. But the staff is never caught by surprise, because each time a death cluster is about to happen, a little visitor arrives to serve notice. A young boy wearing a baseball cap and carrying a cat comes to the building just before the deaths and makes his rounds. No one on the staff has ever seen him; the only ones who have are those with Alzheimer's and dementia and, sometimes, nondementia residents who are close to death.

A nurse who spoke to *Weird Wisconsin* on condition of anonymity said that every time deaths are imminent, dementia patients will begin asking staff members who that little boy is or where he went and could they look for him. According to the nurse, there have been reported sightings of the boy at the nursing home for more than ten years. The boy comes at all times of the night or day, and at least two people without dementia have seen him just before their deaths.

"When the little boy has been spotted, we kind of expect that some people are ready to die, or if we've had a death, we know to look for another one," said the nurse. "We had a hallway sighting a couple of days ago, and no one had died, but then a patient who lives on that same hallway that we weren't expecting to pass died a few hours later." And sure enough, a follow-up revealed that two more deaths occurred within days of the sighting.

Some nursing-home employees think that the "angel" was once a little boy who had lived near the site and perhaps drowned. "They think it is a spirit that is at worst ambivalent but could be benevolent," said the nurse. "Or that it might be the Angel of Death. Personally, I think it may be a spirit with a chore. It may be his job."

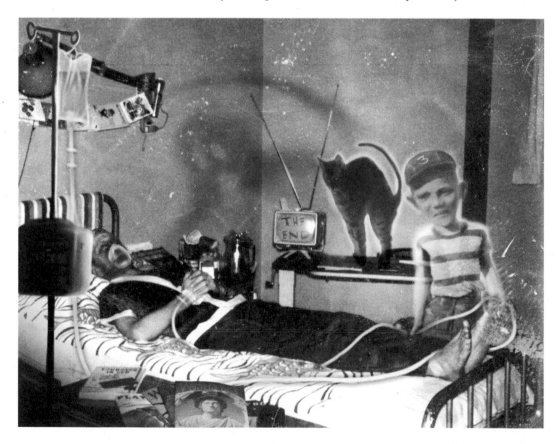

Hell's Playground

Brodhead, Wisconsin, is a tiny town thirty miles from Madison. It is home to just over 3,000 people. Don't let the diminutive size fool you, though. When it comes to creepiness, Brodhead has a handful of legends that has put it on the map with the big boys.

Like most small towns, Brodhead has a local playground. But only Brodhead can lay claim to being the location of Hell's Playground.

Tradition has it that two children and an adult were murdered on the grounds of this otherwise unnoteworthy playground. Since their gruesome slaughter, the playground has been said to be the site of a number of strange phenomena. At night the sound of children at play can be heard even when no children are present. The swings move back and forth by themselves even when there is no wind to speak of. Worse, strange growling noises are often reported. It's said that the area near the slide is particularly cursed, as one of the deceased children was murdered upon it.

So beware of Hell's Playground. Unsettled spirits call it home.—*Chris G.*

Port Washington's Boobooshaw

Whatever it was, the legend of it goes back to the late 1960s through the mid-1970s. It was called the Boobooshaw, or pronounced that way. It was supposed to be a black creature or figure that would lurk in the backyards and roads in Port Washington at night, never seen in the daytime. If little boys and girls did not behave, the Boobooshaw was going to get them!

No one knows where this creature came from. One rumor was that it came off of a coal ship docked by the Wisconsin Electric power plant in the 1960s.

So where is it now? Maybe it died off, or it was just a rumor to scare little children who did not behave.—*Jonathan Scherf*

Appleton Pond Insures Screams

The SECURA Insurance Company has a corporate office in Appleton. The building is nondescript, much like what one would expect in an insurance office complex. It sits on a patch of well-maintained land, surrounded by manicured lawns and numerous trees. There's even a pond behind the building.

If the rumors about it are to be believed, however, that pond is not as tranquil as it appears at first glance. Legend has it that over a century ago, before the land was developed, pipes were installed in the pond's bottom in an effort to keep it well filtrated and more appealing to visitors. Soon afterward, a little girl, enjoying an afternoon of relaxation, fell into the water. Unable to swim, she struggled to get back to the shore but became ensnared in one of the narrow pipes in the pond. As her horrified parents watched from the shore, she disappeared beneath the surface and drowned.

These days, people report strange happenings at night near the innocuous-looking body of water. When all is quiet, one can hear the little girl's screams coming from beneath the dark surface of the water, along with her parents' shrieks and cries coming from the shore. These macabre sounds have been reported for many years. So while the SECURA company sells insurance against injury, the effects of a horrific accident just behind their very building still resonate to this day.—*Chris G.*

Biggest Haunted Farmhouse in Wisconsin

Imagine a house on a hill in central Wisconsin in the mid-1800s. Picture bearded twin brothers, two premature deaths, and a deep grief that won't stop. Let's fast-forward: Now visualize the house as a gangster hideout, complete with whiskey still, at a time when its ghost stories are already musty legends. The small community of Eureka has been fascinated by the huge old mansion ever since the twin brothers Augustus and Argalus Foote built it in 1852. Their country dream house was to be a honeymoon hideaway for the inseparable thirty-four-year-old brothers and their brides, Anna and Adelia.

Set on three hundred acres of farmland just a mile outside Eureka on County Highway K, the cream brick home featured a central hall, with fifteen rooms on each side. The furnishings on both sides were identical and the best money could buy. The men and their brides, all four with the initials "A.F.," made their home a showplace and figured they were set there for life. Life was good.

But the seemingly ideal arrangement proved to be only a setup for tragedy. After a few years, Anna, Augustus's wife, died in childbirth, and their infant daughter died three months later. Augustus, Argalus, and Adelia were too grief-stricken to remain there, so they sold the house to a couple from Chicago—Mr. and Mrs. Herman Powers. They kept up the home's showplace tradition, filling the stable with fine horses and throwing lavish parties. But for some reason, they sold the house after only a few years.

The house went downhill after that. It remained mostly empty, amid rumors of ghosts dating back to the Civil War. Townsfolk claim that during the Prohibition era, Al Capone used the giant basement for making whiskey. And beginning in 1935, the house was used by a local society for "haunted" Halloween tours, complete with a spooky script for the tour guides.

Over the years, the house was occupied by tenant farmers, with some of the formerly fine rooms used as rabbit warrens and for wood storage. Each succeeding owner gave up replacing the glass in most windows, because the local boys kept throwing rocks through them. Today, only the old brick shell of the house remains, and the twins are buried in a nearby cemetery. Perhaps in the netherworld the house is still a honeymooner's dream, but a recent visitor found that trees have grown up around the house so that only the top of the mansion is still visible from the road. A very dead cow was in plain sight from the driveway, and it was evident people are still using the farm area and possibly living in other structures on this private property.

Ancient Mysteries

Above, around expressive vastness reigns,
And nature stalks a giant o'er the plains.
—Ekiega, from *Ojibwa Lodge Stories* by Henry Schoolcraft

Given the comparatively short life spans we humans have, it's easy but discomfiting to see how many things have been on this earth way longer than we have. Weird rock formations and Mesozoic Era fossils fill us with awe and impart a chastened sense of our place in this world. But remnants of the far distant past are even more intriguing when they resemble things we can recognize—like elephants! Those anomalous geological bumps in the landscape are natural magnets for superstitions and legends, which each generation perpetuates.

Mysteries of ancient man intrigue us as well. The thought of civilizations knowable only through the artifacts they left and bits of bleached bone found in tumuli makes us shiver, but then dig for more—more knowledge, that is. How did ancient people think? What were their beliefs? They were people who looked much like us but whose world was completely different. Intuitively, we understand that if we can come to know about them, perhaps we can know ourselves a little better.

In this way, we are all anthropologists, archaeologists, and mystics. We may not be scientifically trained, and we may never get the chance to sift through timeworn soils in search of tiny potsherds or arrowheads or see that misty robed figure appear out of the fog with whispers from another world, but we will never tire of seeking our common past. Ancient giants, visions from heaven—found right here in Wisconsin—have the power to pull us in and reveal their enduring mysteries.

Each time, we think, "Maybe I'll solve the puzzle." But whether we manage to wrest a soupçon of knowledge from these mysteries or, all too often, come out feeling sucker-punched, we always go back for more. The mysteries have that hold on us. They were here before we were, and they will most likely be here long, long after.

"Pre-historic Indian Village At Aztalan"

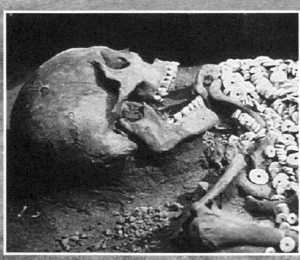

Mystery Woman of Aztalan

Few archaeological sites in the nation can equal the mysterious allure of the ancient ruins near Lake Mills called Aztalan. Studded with huge conical and flat-topped pyramidal mounds built by a Native American community around the eleventh century, the site was once a bustling village of five hundred, surrounded by a massive fortified wall of logs and wattle. Apparently an important trade and ceremonial center, Aztalan was a northern outpost of a much larger city, called Cahokia, which also featured pyramidal mounds. Located near East St. Louis, Illinois, Cahokia once supported about thirty-five thousand people and was easily reachable via the Mississippi River system, hence our name for them—Mississippians. But the site of Aztalan, first discovered by settlers in 1836, received its name because of the idea, now largely discredited, that it was somehow connected to the Aztecs of Mexico.

Aztalan flourished for about two hundred years, then disappeared suddenly around the year 1200 for unknown reasons.

But one female resident, safely deposited in a burial mound, poses perhaps the biggest mystery of all.

Unearthed in 1919 by Dr. S. A. Barrett in a grave situated on what would have been a high point overlooking the Crawfish River, she was dubbed the Princess because of her splendid costume. Her body was lavishly draped in three separate beaded belts, each measuring about four feet in length and six inches in width. The beads, which numbered 1,996, were made from the shells of mussels from local rivers and as far off as the Gulf of Mexico. The shells on each belt were graded from largest to smallest from one end of the belt to the other. Measurements of the skeleton indicated that the woman had stood five feet six or seven inches in height, tall for that time; further study revealed that she had had a spinal deformity. It is estimated that she had been about twenty-five at the time of her death.

Although her burial mound was originally forty-seven feet in diameter and probably rose about six feet above the ground, most of its soil was hauled away over the years. Judging from the mound's original size and the richness of the burial garb, it is believed that the young woman was a member of the ruling class. Some think she may have been a priestess/shaman. Whoever she was, a former historical museum groundskeeper, Don Schuler, made a discovery that indicates she may have been a woman of religious significance to her people.

While clearing a tangle of brush behind the museum, Schuler found a flat, slightly hollowed-out stone slab measuring about two feet square set into the earth. He called in an archaeological expert, who thought that because of the slab's position, it might have been an offering place for the burial shrine.

The offering stone, located about eighty feet from the mound, was later blessed in a special ceremony by a Native American shaman. Schuler witnessed the ceremony. The shaman lit a smudge pot and placed three pieces of charcoal on the stone, lighting one with a stick made of sage and cedar. Although he had lit only one piece of charcoal, the other two pieces immediately leaped into flame as well. "I saw it myself," said Schuler. "He never touched the other two pieces with his fire."

Some archaeologists, however, believe that the woman was not from Aztalan but a member of one of the Woodland Indian tribes, especially since her burial site was found outside the village enclosure; the offering stone may have also been placed by the Woodland people. And the origin of another stone unearthed outside the walls, a boulder wrapped in birch bark, is likewise unknown. The mixture of Woodland and Mississippian artifacts continues to be one of the most baffling features about the site.

It's amazing that anything at all has remained of Aztalan to study. When the site was first mapped in 1850, over forty mounds existed. Only a fraction remained by 1912, when some portions of the site were purchased by area residents and named Mound Park. Farmers hauled away soil from the pyramid mounds to level their fields, and souvenir hunters dug for artifacts.

The archaeological site was originally called the Ancient City by settlers and local Woodland tribes alike. The fact that Woodland artifacts were found throughout the site suggests that some "locals" were on friendly terms with the Mississippians. Not all were, however. The fortified city wall is suggestive of warfare, and bones that appear to have been cracked to remove the marrow were found here. These raise the specter of ritual

cannibalism, a practice that usually involved consuming parts of conquered enemies in order to take on their courage or other desired characteristics.

Strangely, both Aztalan's and Cahokia's inhabitants cleared out around the year 1200. Some people speculate that the Mississippians migrated south to become the Aztec population of Mexico, though few anthropologists think so. But according to Schuler, many tribal members he's talked to, including one Mexican Aztec who claims to be a direct descendant of Aztalan, believe it's true.

Schuler and other historians find further evidence of a link between the Aztalan Indians, the Cahokians, and the Aztecs in the way key elements of the mounds and main buildings of each culture align with one another and with features of the landscape. According to Schuler, a rise near Aztalan named Christmas Hill by settlers, for instance, lines up with the Princess Mound in the same azimuth, or distance in degrees from the North Star, as do similar structures in Cahokia and in Aztec settlements in Mexico.

In 1948, Mound Park

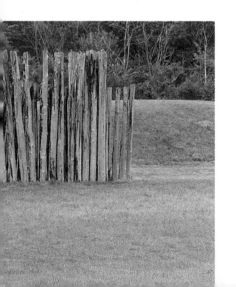

was donated to the Wisconsin Conservation Department, which bought the rest of the site and named it Aztalan State Park. The largest mound, a flat-topped pyramid built on a natural terrace with a series of steps to the top, was rebuilt in 1951. The Princess Mound can be seen directly behind the Baptist church that serves as the Aztalan Historical Museum.

One of the most enduring mysteries of Aztalan is where the other inhabitants were buried. Except for the Princess Mound and a few isolated remains, no other burials have been found nearby.

Aztalan State Park is located three miles east of Lake Mills on County Highway Q. It is open May through October. The area is considered sacred ground by Native American tribes and should be treated with respect. Federal law prohibits any type of digging or destructive acts.

Haunted Aztalan

Have you ever heard about Aztalan State Park being haunted? Well, our group heard rumors about it, so we went there in June. We barely had one picture that turned out normal. Most had orbs, ectoplasm, strange streaks of light, mists, shadows. I could go on! We didn't stay there overnight (wish we would have, and we are going there for an overnight camping trip).

But anyways, almost all of us felt sick there after about an hour. We were dizzy, nauseous, lightheaded. I was getting a horrible migraine, almost like a sinus headache. We found out later, on the way home, that we all had an odd ringing in our ears! A lot more than we anticipated! A few of us thought we saw shadows (and it was still light out—we were there only from about 11 a.m.–2 p.m.). The investigation ended a lot sooner than we anticipated, just because we all felt so yucky.

On the drive home, we all proceeded to feel better after like 10 minutes. We wanted to stay, as we did get crazy feelings of death and suffering, as well as torture, which is weird, because that didn't jibe with Indian burial grounds.

Well, upon research, I didn't find anything about an Indian burial ground, but I did find many stories, fables, or whatever you will call it, that around 1320 A.D., a huge walled pyramid city flourished in Aztalan that gave way to the black side of Cthulhu, a demonic and monstrous entity who is said to lie "dead but dreaming"—their "god" or "titan." Their citizens then delved into human sacrifice and cannibalism, which ultimately climaxed in the destruction of their vast ceremonial center.

But we plan on going back again and will test a theory—that we can use Dramamine, Tums, Pepto, etc. to make sure we don't feel like that again. I hope to remember the exact spot we were at!—*Heidi*

Lost Pyramids of Atlantis?

The southern end of Rock Lake near Aztalan State Park is the site of underwater rock formations that have baffled people for centuries. When European settlers first took up residence in the area, Native Americans told them of "rock teepees" located on the lake's floor. In 1900, their existence was verified when local duck hunters caught site of the massive monoliths from their boat. Entirely submerged, the structures are conical in shape and measure thirty feet high and a hundred feet long.

Explanations for the underwater stone pyramids vary. Some say that they are simply natural glacier formations, while others say that they are man-made, constructed by an ancient civilization before the area was flooded with water.

The following passages come from the Rock Lake Research Society, an organization dedicated to the investigation and documentation of these enigmatic pyramids.

1900. Two local residents, the Wilson brothers, spot mysterious structures underwater while duck hunting. Unusual clarity exists, as it is late fall and rainfall was low for the year, dropping water levels below normal. The two men advise the other residents of Lake Mills and dozens of people in boats converge on the lake to witness the underwater structure. Several boys dive a short distance and touch the pyramidal structure. It is described as a long tent-shaped structure of undetermined height and approximately 100 feet long. The next day water conditions change and the structures are lost to the murkiness and silt of the lake. . . . Lake Mills then becomes a center of statewide attention as newspapers ran articles about the underwater pyramids.

1937. Famous diver Max Nohl, the true inventor of the scuba, tests his equipment in Rock Lake. He comes upon a tall cone-shaped pyramid in the south end of the lake. The structure, made of small stones, looked like an upside-down ice cream cone that was definitely manmade, according to Nohl. Nohl plans to come back to further explore the pyramid legends of Rock Lake. Nohl dies in car crash with wife several years later before he could return.

Owing to murky water conditions, the structures are rarely visible, even with high-tech equipment, but fishermen and divers do catch glimpses of the mysterious structures from time to time, and the Rock Lake Research Society has documented their existence using sonar and aerial photography.

Hidden Dragon

The Elk Mound Tower sits high atop a bald knob overlooking the village of Elk Mound, with commanding views of the surrounding countryside. The tower, built as a memorial to deceased rural mail carriers, is probably the only one of its kind in the country. Visitors, however, have reported experiencing baffling phenomena here unrelated either to postal workers or to going "postal." Howls rend the night. Eerie cries of children disturb the silence. Screams echo through the stands of oaks. Maniacal laughter peals across the valley. Tower climbers report becoming nauseated after leaving the grounds.

Drivers on the road below have witnessed obscuring swirling mists or seen strange lights blinking and dancing around the stone edifice. Few can account for any of these phenomena, although there are whispers of an unknown person—perhaps more than one—perishing in a fall from atop the tower in the 1980s. This malevolent revenant continues to spook the unwary today.

Most inexplicable are rumors that an enormous dragon is buried beneath this castlelike structure. Indeed, scattered stones, embedded in the soil with just a hint of their rounded smooth surface exposed, resemble dragon scales. To date, no one has been able to confirm the dragon's burial or say when or how this story began. Interestingly, European lore is filled with tales of dragons guarding earthen mounds containing treasures or the bodies of kings.

Wouldn't it be passing strange if an ancient dead king lies buried here or an untold fortune is waiting for someone brave enough to face the guardian of the mound? Perhaps there is a dragon beneath the mound—not dead and buried, but still on duty, ever watchful.

IN MEMORIAM
OF THE DECEASED
RURAL LETTER CARRIERS
OF DUNN COUNTY

Hill of the Dead

The west shore of Little Lake Butte des Morts is the site of a well-known Native American burial mound known as the Hill of the Dead, or Petit Butte des Morts. Stories of intrigue and heartbreak have long surrounded this area.

Many years ago, a series of battles between the Fox Indians and the French led to the near annihilation of the tribe. Like most wars, it was political, economic, and involved the pride of both groups of people.

It was common practice for the Indians living along the river to demand a toll for passing by their village. The French, who wanted safe passage for fur traders and for other goods and supplies, did not want to pay those tolls, so they entered into a war with the Fox Tribe.

The series of battles included deadly confrontations, with the French burning houses and crops in an attempt to keep the Fox from making it through the tough Wisconsin winter. The French also tried to get other tribes to help them get rid of the Fox.

The battles ended with the last war effort chronicled on the historical marker located at the entrance to Fritzy Park

in the town of Menasha. It states, "In 1730 the French government decided to destroy the Fox village on the shore of this lake because of the depredations of the Foxes on the fur traders. Captain Morand came up the river with a large force of French soldiers and Menominee warriors. The soldiers were concealed under canvas until they were opposite the Indians gathered on the shore. Then they rose and fired into the crowd. The Menominee, meanwhile, attacked the village from the rear. The village was destroyed and its inhabitants slaughtered. The bodies were piled in a heap and covered with earth, forming the Hill of the Dead."

In 1863, the railroad came through the south side and within thirty feet of the Hill of the Dead. For miles along the right-of-way, bones and relics from the mound were scattered. Other tales include stories of ancient cemeteries and burial firepits being located here, of early area doctors robbing the hill for skeletons to study, and of a native man who murdered two women and was burned to death.

The land is supposedly cursed by the Native peoples. One day, it is said, their skeletons will spring to life and take revenge against the white people. There are also reports of apparitional powwows, with strange sounds of beating drums being heard on a still dark night.

If a quiet day at the park is what you are looking for, there may be more lingering under your feet than you think.

—Rachel Rohloff

Giant Indians and Baffling Burials

The Europeans who settled what is now the United States were always loath to believe that the native population had ever been anything but what it appeared upon the settlers' arrival. So whenever skeletons were unearthed measuring a bit taller than the contemporary indigenous people, a hullabaloo was raised over the discovery of "giant Indians" from what were presumed to be members of ancient civilizations unrelated to contemporary inhabitants. It's true that some of the remains did appear to have physical characteristics that differed from those of the native people of the area, raising legitimate concerns about who these people were and where they had come from.

According to one legend, a Native American skeleton seven feet tall was found buried in a large mound in Theresa. And in March 1911, a discovery on the shores of Delavan Lake in Walworth County made various newspapers, including the *New York Times.* Two brothers, Ernest and Chester Phillips, had purchased the lakefront property known as Lake Lawn and were curious about the great number of mounds located on their farm. They found conical mounds, which often contained burials, and various effigy mounds, constructed in the shape of strange animals and abstract formations.

The brothers toted shovels out to one of the mounds one day and dug a trench seven feet deep. Inside the mound, three feet below the ground's surface, they found a stone pit measuring seven by nine feet. The pit was filled with fourteen skeletons, which the astonished brothers ascribed to a "powerful pre-historic race." The *Delavan Republican* said, "The skeletons appear to be those of warriors of powerful frame and immense size when compared with people of this day and age."

The newspapers described one skull as possessing a very large cranium. The skeletons' breastbones were said to be much more prominent than those in ordinary skeletons, and the skulls were "flat-headed," suggesting these people may have belonged to one of the tribes that shaped the skulls of their infants by binding them to cradleboards.

The grave was meticulously constructed of cobblestones surrounded with gravel. At the base of the burial chamber, layers of white sand and blue clay, "sacred soils," had been added. The bodies all faced south—toward the lake—and had been covered with a foot-high mixture of clay and dirt baked hard by a fire; the process was repeated several times to build the grave to mound height.

No artifacts were buried with the skeletons, but the Phillips brothers decided to take the bones as souvenirs. They coated them with shellac for preservation, then trundled them off to their house in the city of Delavan, according to historian Gordon Yadon. The bones would not prove to be good-luck charms. Chester later committed suicide, and Ernest lived alone in the house until he died. When the contents of the place were sold at auction, the ancient skeletons were nowhere to be found.

For the record, at least one Ojibwa (Chippewa) man, by the name of Ekiega, stood six feet six. So the tall skeletons may have a logical explanation after all.

The Lake Lawn farm is now a resort and golf course, located just west of Delavan on Highway 50. All together, there were over one hundred mounds on the property, but less than a fourth remain. A turtle mound still survives, minus part of its tail, along with oval, linear, and other effigy mounds, and the flagpole at the main driveway once stood in the center of a conical mound. Other burials were found in excavations conducted in 1955 by a Chicago archaeological society, and some of the unearthed artifacts are on display in the resort's restaurant.

The restaurant is constructed directly over what used to be a very large mound, and many of its past and current workers whisper that it is haunted. One nighttime phenomenon mentioned by many is the sound of voices speaking in another language coming from the direction of the lakeshore. The noises have been loud enough to set off sensors, one staffer told us, but when the security people check, nothing is ever found. Perhaps they are hearing the ghostly voices of those sturdy ancient warriors asking the long-gone Chester and Ernest to please bring back their bones.

Odd Skeleton Unearthed

"Cambridge, Wisconsin. The eleventh skeleton that has been dug up in this neighborhood in the last five years was discovered by A. E. Morton while he was excavating for his home on Lake Ripley. The skeleton was entire and is supposed to be that of an Indian. An unusual feature is the double set of teeth in the lower jaw. The skeleton measured six feet three inches from head to base of foot. It will no doubt be presented to the state historical museum at Madison by Mr. Morton."—Eau Claire Leader, *Wednesday, November 27, 1907*

The Stone Elephant and Great Spirit Washbowl

Unusual land formations literally come with the territory around the strange glacier-formed area called the Kettle Moraine in southeastern Wisconsin. Round depressions called kettles alternate with ridges, or moraines, to form a landscape unique to this area. The kettles were considered sacred spaces by the Woodland tribes that had inhabited the territory before the settlers came, and one in particular, just south of Palmyra in Jefferson County, drew their attention. Called the Great Spirit Washbowl by the Potawatomi, the large kettle lies just southeast of a tall hill known as Bald Bluff, which was once a lookout site and probably a ceremonial place as well.

As legend has it, the Potawatomi would build small fires on the bluff and send smoke signals when the wind blew from the south, a direction considered sacred to that tribe. It was believed that the springs that filled the kettle were doorways to spirit life. The Potawatomi claimed that after several days of southern winds, the bowl would fill with water to the top in twelve hours, causing a strong current that flowed from the center to the edges and made it impossible to sink. It was the Great Spirit holding them up, they said, and this signified great favor and protection from their enemies.

However, when the south wind stopped, the water direction would reverse, and anyone unfortunate enough to be caught in the pool would be sucked into the central spring to vanish forever, like an ant down a drain. This made the kettle a handy place to throw war captives into.

Not far from the bluff and the Great Spirit Washbowl lies a rock formation known as the Stone Elephant. It appears to be an elephant buried to its knees—four feet high, twelve feet long, and dull gray, exactly the color of a pachyderm's skin. It was on the Stone Elephant, according to the local legend, that the war captives would be sacrificed before they were thrown into the Spirit Washbowl to disappear forever.

The ancient wonders are all located off County Highway H about halfway between Highway 12 and Palmyra.

That Mona Lisa Smile

In the spring of 2002, Bessie Kmiecik entered the wilderness of central Wisconsin, near the Lemon Rind, to search for a historical legend—an ancient behemoth carved in stone. After a battle with briars and verdant undergrowth, Kmiecik managed to overcome the sentinels that for centuries enfolded the boulder in nature's arms along the upper reaches of the Black River. At last she reached the object of her quest: a carved boulder about ten feet around and three feet high. Some cursory cleaning gradually uncovered an ancient face incised in ages past.

Using a tape measure, Kmiecik found that each almond-shaped eye measured roughly six inches across, with a little more than a foot separating the set. The image's most distinctive feature, a silly-looking grin, stretched twenty-one inches across the stone. Each side of the triangular nose was over a foot long.

Expert opinions about the giant stone face have varied. Dr. James Scherz, emeritus professor at the University of Wisconsin–Madison, examined Kmiecik's photographs and posited that the object most likely was an ancient calendar stone. Noting that the image faced east, Scherz observed that the lines extending from the nose could indicate the position of the sun on the horizon during planting season. Kmiecik also consulted with Professor Robert Boazhardt of the Mississippi Valley Archaeological Center, University of Wisconsin–La Crosse. Dr. Boazhardt admitted that he had never seen anything like it and was unable to offer a scholarly assessment of the find.

Clues concerning the provenance of Wisconsin's Black River boulder might someday be found across the lake, in Michigan. There, in the 1980s, workers unearthed a similar boulder while excavating in the Saginaw Valley. A comparison of the boulders appears to establish a kinship between the images: Both share shell-like eyes, triangular noses, and, yes, the Mona Lisa smile.

An anthropologist from Michigan State University examined the carving and estimated its age at around five hundred years, making it contemporary with the Sanilac Petroglyphs, a series of carvings found to the northeast, in Michigan's Thumb. Like those who carved the smiling boulder, the rock artists at the Sanilac site worked in sandstone. Ultimately, the identity of the prehistoric artists remains a mystery. Did the same culture produce the grinning heads and the glyphs? The similarities between the Wisconsin and Michigan boulders might mean that an as yet unknown culture once ranged the Great Lakes before the arrival of our current Algonquian groups.–*Daniel J. Wood*

Chapel Dedicated to St. Joan of Arc

Quick! Name the oldest structure not built by Native Americans in Wisconsin. Probably some pioneer's cabin or a lead miner's badger hole or the state's first capitol building in Belmont come to mind. But you're wrong. The oldest non–Native American structure is a stone chapel located in Milwaukee on the Marquette University campus. It was built in the early 1400s, if not before.

Though hundreds of years old, the chapel did not originate in Wisconsin. It was built in France in the little village of Chasse, where it was known as Chapelle de St. Martin de Seyssuel. Like many medieval structures, it was not constructed all at once but built in stages over a period of time, and the changing architectural styles can still be seen today.

Beloved by nobles and villagers alike, the chapel stood in the village for centuries. Following the First World War, Jacques Couëlle, a young architect from Aix-en-Provence, passed through Chasse, where he became enthralled by the chapel. Meticulously, he photographed, rendered architectural drawings, and measured and numbered each individual stone. In 1926, Gertrude Hill Gavin, the daughter of the famous railroad magnate James J. Hill, decided to purchase the chapel. It was dismantled stone by stone and, with Couëlle's assistance, transported to Gavin's fifty-acre estate in Jericho, on Long Island in New York.

Stone by stone, the chapel was reconstructed in Jericho. John Russell Pope, a leading architect who designed the National Gallery of Art in Washington, D.C., and the Frick Mansion (later, Museum) in New York, developed the plan. This beautiful chapel was grafted onto a massive French château, which Gavin had also brought to the United States, stone by stone, from France. With enough money, anything can be accomplished.

In 1962, the Gavin estate passed into the hands of Mr. and Mrs. Marc B. Rojtman. Just as they were about to move into the estate, a mysterious fire broke out. The fire gutted most of the château but miraculously spared the chapel. Two years later, the Rojtmans presented the chapel to Marquette, along with numerous authentic furnishings. The chapel was again disassembled, then loaded onto trucks, each carrying a forty-thousand-pound-load, and driven to Milwaukee. Reconstruction was completed in July 1965.

Weirder even than its amazing journey from France to Milwaukee (with a stopover on Long Island) is the Joan of Arc Stone inside the chapel. Numerous legends are associated with this stone. They recount how Joan of Arc (1412–1431) prayed before a statue of the Virgin Mary, which stood on this very stone. At the end of her prayer, she delicately kissed the stone. Ever since Joan's kiss, the stone has been colder than any other stone surrounding it.

Today, you can see the ornate medieval furnishings and fixtures in the chapel for yourself. A helpful smiling undergrad studying in the back will gladly instruct you in the legend of the Chapel of St. Joan of Arc. Go ahead—you can even touch the very stone where St. Joan pressed her lips.

It's up to you to say what those resulting goose bumps mean.

Fabled People and Places

Humans *like to blame cats* for having too much curiosity, but the truth is that many more people than cats have probably met with misfortune as a result of an inborn urge to seek mystery. Warnings fail to deter us. For example, Milwaukee teens have been told they risk arrest, high fines, and a merciless clubbing with dozens of tiny but lethal baseball bats if they dare search rural Muskego for a reclusive colony of little people, and yet scores of young adventurers still look for Haunchyville.

The mysterious midgetlike residents of Haunchyville are certainly among Wisconsin's most fabled people. Then there's the lady who survived being scalped by Indians, the priest who went mad as a result of exorcising the demons from a quaint little house on Lake Superior, and the Episcopal missionary who claimed to be the son of Marie Antoinette and Louis XVI. The stories of these intriguing people, among others, move us to action: We want to take a quick look at the lady's maimed skull, explore—warily—the house that devils once possessed, and learn the truth about the French dauphin.

Although some of Wisconsin's fabled people and places are long gone and can only be known via books, reading about them can be fascinating. Of course, some people and places are all too real. But whether you experience the lore we describe as theater of the mind or as a neighborhood adventure, you're in for an exciting time. So come along. There's a holy grail of weirdness just waiting to be sought around nearly every corner—imaginary or very real indeed.

Spook Temple

Legends of creepy goings-on in Whitewater have been passed down seemingly forever to incoming freshmen at the University of Wisconsin branch there.

It probably all started in 1889 with the Morris Pratt Institute, the nation's only Spiritualist college. The college near downtown Whitewater was funded by an elderly gentleman by the name of Morris Pratt following the discovery of iron ore in Wisconsin after a Madison psychic, Mrs. Mary Hayes, had advised him where to dig. The institute featured regular Sunday lectures on such topics as "Mediumship Explained," and its third floor boasted an all-white room specially designed for séances. The townspeople called the building, located on the corner of Third and Center, the Spook Temple. The "temple" was eventually torn down, but the Pratt Institute still maintains offices in Wauwatosa.

Even before the establishment of the Pratt Institute, however, rumors of witches in Whitewater ran rampant, to the point that the town, according to one newspaper article, was "the second biggest center of witchcraft in the country." The tales vary, but supposedly there existed an active coven in the late nineteenth century that held rituals in tunnels and maintained a sacrificial altar located either in the field behind what is now the university's Wells Hall dormitory or in Oak Grove Cemetery. The sacrificial altar, along with several dead coven members, is said to be buried at the location where the altar once stood. And, it should be added, Wells Hall allegedly has experienced multiple hauntings since it was built in the late 1960s. The ghosts are usually young adults who had died in tragic accidents.

One of the most enduring town legends concerns Whitewater's three cemeteries, which, when connected with lines on a map, form a near-perfect isosceles triangle with the ominous nickname Witch's Triangle. All buildings and the land along the triangle's sides are said to be haunted. Calvary Cemetery, high on a hill above the campus, is rumored to be particularly dangerous, with gates that close on unwitting freshmen dumb enough to have sneaked in at night. According to campus wisdom, an axe murderess, Mary Worth, is buried there, and every Halloween she sallies forth from her grave to vent her rage on new victims.

More recently, in the fall of 2003, while hiking on trails in the same general vicinity as Calvary Cemetery, a university professor and several others witnessed a strange flying object. Thoroughly convinced they had seen a UFO, they posted flyers around town asking people who had also glimpsed the UFO to come forward.

A more grisly piece of cemetery lore dates from Halloween night in 1970, when unknown persons exhumed the coffin of a baby girl from one of the graves and left the sad little corpse on the steps of the university's student center, where it was discovered the next morning. Some linked the deed to antiwar protestors, some to drunken Halloween pranksters.

Not far from Wells Hall and Calvary Cemetery is the old stone water tower in Starin Park, Wisconsin's second-oldest municipal tower still in operation. It has been whispered that various groups had held rituals in the park around the tower, attracting or creating malignant entities in the process. Supporting this allegation was the fact that until 2004, the park was surrounded by an iron fence with pointed spikes that tilted inward, as if to keep things in rather than out.

As for the witches' tunnels, there is something of a tunnel system between a few of the city's oldest mansion-size homes. These tunnels may have served as Underground Railroad hideaways for escaping slaves at one time, but one of them is connected with a truly spooky story. One night in 1981, members of the Alpha Sigma

can burial grounds. The small Indian Mounds Park still exists on the west side of town.

Whitewater Lake, another former home of the area's tribes, has its share of weirdness too. In 1909, large ice floes were found floating on the lake—in June! And in 1923, several fishermen claimed that when their boat capsized, they were pulled underwater by something with long tentacles. The men came back to the surface with great difficulty and with small bite marks covering their bodies. And in 1992, three people renting a house on Whitewater Lake noticed a gathering of black-clad people chanting and dancing on the beach until they "heard a loud gurgling noise and saw something start to come out of the lake." The trio left in a hurry, but the next morning, police found small bones and pebbles arranged in symbolic patterns on the shore where the odd event had occurred.

With this strange blend of fact and fiction to keep the scariness circulating, it's a safe bet that for many years to come, impressionable new Whitewater students will continue to sleep with their lava lamps on.

The Second Salem

I live in Whitewater, and according to legends, the whole town is haunted.

The university that is in town was originally built as a school for mediums and research into the paranormal. I have been told that all possible ways to leave town require going over running water and that the cemeteries form a five-pointed star when looked at from above. There is a hill behind the student dorms that is supposed to be where a coven of witches (evil ones, of course) meet. Also, an apartment building was once the residence of a guy who fancied himself a master of the black arts, and is haunted.

Whitewater has been referred to as the "Second Salem." I can attest that some areas of town just really give me the creeps. The problem is this: There is reputed to be documentation telling about the weird things in town. However, the town council has made sure that none of that exists in town anymore.—*Jeff Woosley*

sorority were sitting down to dinner at their house at 614 West Main when they heard strange noises in the basement.

The young women rushed downstairs to find the basement floor covered with bricks and debris that had popped out from a boarded-up tunnel that was unknown to them. The house is now widely regarded as being haunted.

Some like to say that Whitewater's disturbances stem from the fact that development of the city, built near Tripp and Cravath lakes, destroyed many sacred Native Ameri-

Exorcising Priest of Lake Superior

When I was growing up in these desolate and northernmost reaches of Wisconsin, along the shores of "Gitchi Gumi," I heard many a yarn about ghosts and goblins, UFOs, the supernatural, and so on. But when you're a kid, you don't digest the entire story. You just want to hear about all the eerie and gory details.

Well, that was the case when I was first told of the Bourgo Ghost from right here in Washburn around 1918–1919. I heard the spooky tale from my mother, then from her sister, and finally from my great-aunt. They each told me a similar spooky story, which was simultaneously frightening and amusing.

The Bourgo family lived near the edge of town in the far west end of Washburn, and across the treelined ravine was the home of my grandparents. My mother was told that at first little things started happening, like when the Bourgo dog's demeanor seemed to change overnight. The friendly family pet got mean and would growl and nip even at family members. It would bark constantly and wouldn't let anybody in the yard. At night, its deep, guttural howl kept everyone awake.

Then small objects would move on their own: a spoon, fork, cup, plate. It got worse and totally out of hand. Shoes clip-clopped across the floor with nobody in them; the piano would play, with invisible fingers punching down on the keys. Loretta, one of the Bourgo girls, once told my aunt Verna that all of the living-room chairs were mysteriously tipped over and upside down and that her mother's shoes walked up the stairs all by themselves!

News of these strange phenomena spread quickly throughout Washburn. It wasn't long before some brave souls dared one another to venture down into the west end at night to see what was going on. My cousin and his school chum thought about sneaking into the house, but at the last minute, they got cold feet and chickened out.

Life was becoming a living hell for the Bourgo family. At first, they thought the devil was in the dog, so they shot the dog. Then they thought the devil was after one of the girls. Finally, as a last act of desperation, they called on Father Louis Charron, the Catholic priest at Washburn's St. Louis Church, the same church I attend on Saturday nights each week.

Father Charron was a brilliant speaker and well respected in the community. He established the holy site of Mission Springs in Nash, between Ashland and Washburn. The Bourgos' house was cloaked in a dense pine forest and sat on one of three good-sized hills. We called and still call them "The Three Pines." The priest would stop at my grandparents' house to pray with them and to get a little "liquid encouragement" (homemade dandelion or grape wine). This was before he would go and try to drive the demon or demons from the quaint little house across the ravine where the evil lurked. He told my grandparents and their eighteen-year-old daughter, Clara, about what was transpiring there—the shoes, the dog, the piano, everything. He asked my grandpa to go over to the house with him, but being very leery of such things, Grandpa politely declined.

Father Charron challenged the devil, or whatever was scaring the living wits out of the Bourgo family. He put a holy crucifix on top of a table. He told the evil spirit, or whatever the thing was, that if it was stronger than God, it should knock the crucifix off the table. But if it failed, it was to leave the family and house alone forever. And it had to exit through the same opening it had first entered.

Aunt Clara told me that it sounded like three loud bullwhip snaps, like lightning bolts that struck the blessed symbol of Christ. BLAM! BLAM! BLAM! But the crucifix didn't budge, not one bit. Moments later, the skin-prickling sounds of dragging chains were heard crossing the Bourgos' living-room floor. Then all of a sudden the cellar door was blown open by some powerful and unseen force, and then there was an eerie quiet and calm.

I heard that Father Charron went crazy and cracked up after he exorcised the evil from the house. I didn't know if it was true or not—that is, until recently, when doing research on a book. I saw it on the front page of a February 1919 issue of the *Ashland Daily Press.* The headline read FATHER CHARRON JUDGED INSANE BY TWO PROMINENT ASHLAND DOCTORS.

A few other strange things have happened in the Bourgo house, which is still around today, but nothing compared to what happened there almost one hundred years ago.—*Tony Woiak*

New Berlin's Little Witch

The following article by Jane Hall is reprinted by permission from *Landmark* (Winter 1970, vol. 13, no. 1), a publication of the Waukesha County Historical Society.

It's been over one hundred years since New Berlin's little "witch" caused grown men to tremble with terror, yet the hair-raising tales of her contacts with "the other world" still hang around to haunt us.

As best as can be figured out from early census records and an old letter written in German, translated by J.H.A. Lacher in the Waukesha Historical Society Museum, the "witch" was Jennet Boyd, teenage daughter of McNair and Sarah Boyd. Spiritualism had been sweeping the country westward from New York State for several years following some rather sensational manifestations there in 1848, and in New Berlin, Miss Boyd was "the medium" for the fad. According to her father, the thirteen-year-old girl would lay her hand on a chair and the other side would tip up, and when anyone asked a question answerable by yes or no, the chair would rap on the floor.

This proved quite entertaining to Boyd and neighboring harvest-weary young farmers that fall in 1852, and many gathered at the Boyd home in the evening to watch, ask questions, and ponder whether or not they believed what they saw. After several weeks of chair tricks, the "spirit" let it be known that it would now write by having Jennet's right hand touch letters of the alphabet, which were to be placed on the tabletop. Shades of the old Ouija board!

Now things really began to happen. Following a perfectly innocent question put to "the hand" by a visiting schoolteacher, it spelled out that his dead brother's spirit was near and requested the teacher to be present on a certain night, "fully believing."

On the specified evening, January 26, 1853, the Boyds had a full house. Jennet, "being possessed by the spirit," calmly tied the hands of the teacher, then sloshed a bucket of water over his head "to cleanse him and rid him of evil."

After several questions had been asked concerning heaven and other places, McNair Boyd asked if the teacher would become a believer. Yes, wrote the hand. But he had to remain all night, the next day and the following night, or else everything in the house would be ruined.

"Stay," said Boyd.

"Nothing doing," said the teacher.

"Stay," Boyd demanded, "or pay for the damages."

The teacher stayed, but only until ten o'clock the next morning.

J. K. Meidenbauer, a newly emigrated German neighbor (who understood little English, let alone the thick Scottish burr of the Boyds), wrote to his brother, "I was told that gruesome things occurred during that first night. The window curtains are said to have been torn without anyone having been near them, and fire from the stove was scattered over the room."

The teacher was severely shaken up, but he stubbornly refused to believe. From the security of his own home, he wrote a note to Boyd saying he would come back for another session if Jennet were in another house. By this time, Boyd was in hot water with his daughter's "spirit." He was instructed to get the teacher back or something might happen to his horse.

Since McNair had already driven his two oxen so hard they died, he wasn't about to take a chance on his horse. Off he went in pursuit of the recalcitrant teacher, taking Hansel and Konrad Buchner with him because he was afraid to go alone.

Seeing them coming, the poor teacher took off for the woods.

Boyd really felt he had done his duty, but Jennet's ghostly friend said no. He was to get several farmers to help and bring the teacher back the next day. And at the appointed time, the teacher was there, accompanied by eight or ten husky companions.

Almost immediately, Jennet's hand thumped out the message that the teacher was to rap six times "if he believes." The teacher, whether ready to be done with it or actually believing, replied that he did and was about to make the six raps when Jennet intervened.

"You are not sincere!" she stormed, hurling one man's hat and anything else she could get her hands on at the hapless teacher. It was "the spirit" that did it, of course. Everyone knew that by now.

Neither history nor J. K. Meidenbauer's letter records what happened to the schoolteacher after that night. However, Jennet's séances continued, leading John and Leonard Beeheim down the road of occultism and tempting Konrad Buchner with spirits of his dear brother and sister. Meidenbauer himself claimed he did not believe in it, but he seldom missed a session.

John Beeheim was positive he saw the window curtains drop down and other "such spooky manifestations."

"What I have seen, I believe," he said when upbraided for making such statements. "Who or what causes it, I don't know, but what I see, I believe."

Others were fairly much in agreement that the writing was done by electricity, that other enigma they couldn't explain.

Something good did come of it all. Everyone agreed that Boyd himself had changed from the rude, rough man he had been before. Where he had cursed at religion earlier, he now said grace at every meal. Whenever he didn't, all sorts of disturbances took place.

"It raps somewhere or the table moves about without anybody being near it," wrote Meidenbauer.

Anybody, that is, except New Berlin's "little witch," Jennet Boyd.

Spiritualists of Spook Hill

The craggy hill looms over tiny Wonewoc like a medieval castle wall, its steep backdrop of rocks and trees dominating the village and shading the houses nestled against it.

Even the most casual passerby will notice the magnificent ridge, but only those very familiar with the area will know the outcropping's Halloweenish name—Spook Hill. Anyway, that's what the locals have called it since it became the summer home of a cadre of psychics and Spiritualist mediums in 1877. For their part, the hill's seasonal inhabitants prefer the name Wonewoc Spiritualist Camp, but they cheerfully accept the Spook Hill moniker.

In peak periods, as many as 1,500 people a week visit the camp. Some come to take part in classes or group readings; others make the journey just to enjoy solitude in one of the thirty-nine buildings on the wooded campus. There is even a "healing tree," complete with legends of miraculous cures. Most, though, seek spiritual advice or communication with departed loved ones.

A rotating group of psychics and mediums, certified by various organizations but all adhering to basic Spiritualist principles, conduct thirty-minute sessions on weekends, with each psychic holding up to eighteen sessions per day. Charging $30 for thirty minutes, mediums such as ordained Spiritualist minister Barbara Picha hold court in their simple cabins while clients line up outside. A rainbow of sequins glitters on the pebbled walkway to Picha's small white cottage, and the front steps are accented by two purple

planters, shaped like ladies' boots, which Picha found on sale at Big Lots.

Inside, Picha invites clients to sit at a table, covered with a white cloth, as an indefinable floral scent (Picha says it has no known source) sweetens the air. Like every medium at Spook Hill, Picha puts her own unique stamp on spirit communication. She has a startling way of banging the flat of her hand on the table when the spirits are testifying, and she appears to be able to look at, past, and through the person she's reading—all at the same time. She doesn't just see deceased relatives; spirit guides come too, she says, all clamoring to be heard.

Bradley K. Moore, part African American, part Crow Indian, and part Irish, says that he identifies with the entire human race, which gives him a particular empathy with clients. He has studied Spiritualism with a Native

American shaman, and he is the proud possessor of a tackle box that's filled with a variety of stones. Occasionally, when the spirit moves him, he'll give someone a stone. Moore is an ordained Spiritualist minister and has been a teacher and a reader for twelve years.

A favorite spot for both Picha and Moore is the camp's wood-paneled chapel, decorated with paintings of spirit guides and a portrait of early Spiritualist Andrew Jackson Davis. Davis was Spiritualism's "forerunner," says Moore. "He received the nine principles we adhere to," he explains. "Our creed is called the Magic Staff: Under all circumstances, keep an even mind."

Given the camp's long history, it's not surprising that most of the surrounding community seems accepting of it. As far back as the 1850s, even the sons of an area judge were full-fledged members of the Wonewoc Spiritualists. In those days, the group shared a building with the German Lutherans and other denominations. The Reverend John L. Protter, a medium, served the first flock. Under his direction, the Spiritualists wowed the town with formal affairs, comic pageants, such events as oyster suppers, and the always popular manifestation meetings, which featured table tipping, ghostly rapping, and other antics believed to be the work of spirits. According to a story in the *Wonewoc Reporter*, at a meeting on January 18, 1891, the table was said to have been carried away by unseen forces, jumping wildly until one gentleman leaped on top and rode it around the room in an impromptu furniture rodeo.

Spook Hill has not been without its detractors. In 1884, a plot to burn down the main hall was discovered when someone found wads of straw stuffed into the building's chinks. And more recently, some religious groups have climbed the hill to picket the camp and try to dissuade clients from getting psychic readings. "They really just brought us more people," says Moore philosophically.

Whether the mediums and psychics who give readings at Spook Hill are genuinely contacting the deceased loved ones of their clients is something the clients will have to determine for themselves. But both Moore and Picha emphasize that everyone is welcome at the Wonewoc Spiritualist Camp, no matter what their personal belief system is. "We're an all-inclusive bunch. We love everybody," says Moore.

Here are a couple of Wisconsinites who might have felt right at home at Spook Hill.

Jeane Dixon

When she was just a toddler, says the Web site devoted to the Jeane Dixon Library and Museum in Strasburg, Virginia, little Jeane amazed her mother by asking to "play with a curious-looking letter," a missive that would not arrive at the house until several days later. Born into a wealthy northern Wisconsin lumber family in Medford in 1918, Jeane Pinkert Dixon spent much of her youth in California. When she was only eight years old, a gypsy fortuneteller told her that she would grow up to be a famous seer and that she would give advice to some of the most powerful people in the world. Indeed, after she predicted the assassination of President John F. Kennedy, she became one of the most famous psychics in America, advising, among other notables, President Ronald Reagan and his wife, Nancy.

Jeane Dixon sees peace in 2000, defines mystic talent as 'God-given'

by Kathy Streed

Internationally known prophet-ess Jeane Dixon, in an appear-ance Sept. 12 at Morris Civic Auditorium, spoke of her extra sensory perceptions, the world's future, and man's purpose on earth.

Mrs. Dixon, a Washington D.C. real estate broker whose proph-ecies brought her national attention in the '50's, believes peace will come to the world in the year 2000, but will be pre-ceded by "great trouble" in 1998-99. She says, "Peace will be ours by divine intervention."

A deeply religious woman, Mrs. Dixon advises all men to "use the talents given you by God to make the best of your life. Faith will push you the last inch beyond me-diocrity--God and one is a ma-jority.

Receives 'vibrations'

She classifies her perceptions as "revelations" and "tele-pathy." Revelations come to her from God, says Mrs. Dixon, and are His will, which cannot be changed by man's will. She ex-perienced her first revelation when she was seven.

Mrs. Dixon says she has heard the voices of Christ and angels in her revelations. Her foresight of John F. Kennedy's assassina-tion was a revelation.

Telepathy describes the vibra-tion and thoughts Mrs. Dixon receives from men. Through telepathy, she knew of Martin Luther King's and Robert F. Kennedy's impending assassina-tions.

Through telepathy, Mrs. Dixon has decided that the majority of Americans consider today's most serious concerns to be economic well - being, war, and politics. "This talent is not something you turn on and off like a water faucet," says Mrs. Dixon. She explains that she cannot always, at will, "predict" an event's outcome or some future happen-ing.

'A God - given talent'

Mrs. Dixon regards her "gift of prophecy" as a God-given talent, and feels her life's pur-pose is to develop and use her ability as fully as possible.

Speaking of today's youth, in an

Mrs. Jeane Dixon as she ap-peared last Friday at Morris Ci-vic Auditorium. (photo by Gene Zehring)

Old Hickory interview, Mrs. Dixon said she believes there is "great hope" for most of the younger generation. However, she says "many will not make it because they refuse to listen to and benefit from the voices

(continued on page 3)

He Looks at You and Sees You Dead

Michael Perry is nothing if not multi-talented. He's a registered nurse, a fireman, a *New Yorker* contributor, and an EMT, whose first book, *Population: 485—Meeting Your Neighbors One Siren at a Time,* has received great national acclaim. Perry says he has attained one other, more dubious, ability from his volunteer rescue work in the tiny farm community of New Auburn, Wisconsin. "From seeing so many accident victims, I can instantly visualize how any living person would look if he or she were dead," he explains. It's not something he tries or likes to do, Perry adds; it just happens.

Frank Emmert and the Cheese-Hat Mystique

Sure, people in other states poke fun at the cheesiness: The Wisconsinite dressed for football success with a wedge of faux cheddar stuck on his or her head is the most classic image that comes to mind. Without question, no other state even comes close in the joke chapeau department. But despite rumors of gangs in cheese hats duct-taping Chicago Bears fans to lampposts, wedge-heads are usually easygoing. They don't mind if others laugh. Besides, anyone familiar with recent state history will tell you in a voice hushed with reverential awe that cheese hats are not only warm and pleasing to the eye but have actually saved a man from certain death.

That's according to no less an authority than the Federal Aviation Administration, which made the pronouncement in connection with an incident that has only added to the cheese-hat mystique. In November 1995, Frank Emmert of the town of Superior survived a plane crash largely because of his cheese hat. He keeps his lucky headgear, which is still smeared with blood and engine grease, enshrined in a glass case on the wall of his home. After all, you don't risk wearing a holy relic to Lambeau Field, where it could be splashed with Miller Lite or ketchup from a stray bratwurst. Emmert remains humble despite his status as a living legend. "I'm just another Packers fan," he told *Weird Wisconsin* in a recent phone interview.

Emmert was flying home from a Packers–Browns game in Cleveland when the accident occurred. He was cruising along near Stevens Point with his flying instructor when ice began choking the rented Cessna Skyhawk, and the two pilots realized they were heading for the frozen turf below. Thinking fast, Emmert, who was thirty-six years old at the time, clutched his genuine Foamation Cheesehead hat and burrowed into it. There was another foam hat in back, said Emmert, but his instructor was a Steelers fan, so he chose not to use it.

The plane was a total wreck, but the two men walked or, in Emmert's case, limped away. Emmert's section of the plane took the brunt of the crash, and the FAA told him he most likely would have been killed if not for the cushioning effect of the cheese hat. As it was, Emmert's right foot was twisted into almost a complete circle by the impact. And the (almost literally) diehard Steelers fan suffered a sheared scalp and a smashed jaw.

"The ironic thing was," said Emmert, "that before the flight, my sister had told me to go break a leg."

The incident made Emmert an instant celebrity, getting him his fifteen seconds of fame on various television shows, including Jay Leno's and Geraldo Rivera's talk shows and an NFL Films show. There have been additional perks too. "I've been to Brett Favre's house," said Emmert, "and had a lot of good times over the years." For a while, he became a sort of cheese-hat "spokesmodel" for Foamation, Inc., the St. Francis company that makes all manner of foam-cheese paraphernalia. And for a short time while he was recuperating from his injuries, he even ran his own cheese-hat store in Superior.

The crash didn't sour Emmert, now forty-five, on flying, though. "It was the airplane's turn, not ours," he told us. But to this day, he never flies without a cheese hat within easy reach.

Home of the Cheesehead Hat

Ralph Bruno, head of Foamation, Inc., is considered the official father of the Cheesehead hat. His company churns out cheesy hats in all sizes, as well as other items. Between Foamation and its competitors, it's even possible to acquire classy cheesewear, like cheese sombreros, cheese bras, and cheese butts—all of which begs the question, How did the idea of wearing fake cheese apparel get to be so huge in Wisconsin? Bruno credits his customers rather than his own flair for dairy couture. "The success of Cheesehead revolves around the type of people Wisconsinites really are," he says. "It's the hardiness and the heartiness of the people. We put our hearts on our sleeves, and we're not afraid to say where we're from."

Initially, not everyone thought Bruno's idea would be a success, but he stubbornly refused to cut the cheese hats. "Something key to my success has been my own stupidity and not knowing when to quit," he explains. "People would say, 'When are you going to get a job?' and I'd say, 'Huh?' "

Bruno has inspired others. Bill Hansen and Dan Hanson, who are both from Beldenville, had an idea in 1997 for a keyring fancied up with a small wedge of cheese. They named it the Packifier, got a patent and copyright, and received a license from Foamation to manufacture it. It was an instant hit and is now sold in non-Packers states.

Burlington's Whopper Trail

One of Burlington's most famous attractions is the Tall Tales Trail, which commemorates seventeen of the award-winning lies collected since 1929 by the Burlington Liars Club.

The trail also offers a trip through the city's historic center as visitors look for the lies, preserved on bronze plaques mounted on buildings. A good place to begin is the chamber of commerce on East Chestnut Street. The office is Tall Tales Trail central, where visitors can pick up a map and other information about the city's lying past.

The first competition, in 1929, got its start when two local reporters, Otis Hulett and Manuel Hahn, fabricated a story about a lying contest between the city's police and fire departments.

They wrote that firemen and police officers were sitting around the police station on New Year's Day and decided to see who could tell the biggest fib. The judges were about to award the championship when someone asked the police chief if he wanted to compete.

"Me?" replied the chief. "Why, I never told a lie in my life." By unanimous consent, the judges awarded the chief the medal.

The reporters filed the story with news services and before long, lies were pouring in to their newsroom.

Hewlett formed the Liars Club and expanded the quest for lies to every state in the Union and, eventually, to every country in the world. He charged $1 per entry fee.

Nowadays, the Burlington Liars Club receives more than three hundred lies per year. The tall tales come from all over the world. Judges are particularly astute during election years, and say that listening to politicians' promises is "good training for judging lies." (Politicians, by the way, are considered "professional" liars and aren't eligible to enter the contest.)

A sample Trail of Lies plaque, honoring the winner of the 1979 contest, C. A. Laurie of Eckland, Missouri, reads IT WAS SO COLD IN MISSOURI LAST WINTER THAT I SAW A POLITICIAN STANDING ON A STREET CORNER WITH HIS HANDS IN HIS OWN POCKETS.—*Julie Von Bergen*

Seeking Cornucopia

The Cornucopia Yacht Club was something people would whisper about in envious tones, but no one really seemed to know much about it. Every once in a while, you'd spot someone swaggering around in one of its trademark jackets. Heads would turn; conversations would stop. "Where'd you get that," the boldest might ask, gulping a little. Usually, the wearer would only smile. He was wearing the satiny Cornucopia Yacht Club jacket, after all. Let the rest of the world wonder and weep.

Weird Wisconsin just had to go to Cornucopia and find out the truth about the club—the only yacht club in the world, it was rumored, that didn't require its members to own a rowboat, much less a yacht, the only yacht club in the world that might let boatless Seekers of the Weird in as members!

The town of Cornucopia, on the shore of Lake Superior, boasts the distinction of being home to Wisconsin's northernmost post office. The town was named by an early settler for its great abundance of wild berries. In the summer, the harbor shelters a motley assortment of Great Lakes–worthy vessels; it is also the site of an old clubhouse that used to be the headquarters of the famed Cornucopia Yacht Club. The clubhouse happened to be hosting a barbecue the day we visited, and it was just our luck that a few members of the Cornucopia Yacht Club were behind the counter, serving up hot dogs. Well, former members, actually.

Turns out that the Cornucopia Yacht Club, started in 1972 by Ryan O'Malley, died, along with its founder, in 1991. O'Malley had established the club so that he could get admitted to a yacht club in Mexico, said former member Jim Keyes. "The club was supposedly located at Pier 99 in Cornucopia, but of course, there was no Pier 99," Keyes told us. "People joined from all over the world, and at one time, we had three to four hundred people. We had red jackets and, later, blue ones. People either came here to join, or their friends enrolled them as a joke. Even President Gerald Ford was a member."

To join, applicants had to answer one qualifying question: What is the name of your boat, and if you don't have one, what would you call it?

Keyes was one of the nonboaters. "I live in Nebraska," he explained.

The group did have one big activity every year: a picnic presided over by "harbormaster" O'Malley. It was held every August at the lakefront, paid for by club dues, which were about $5 a year. As for the coveted jackets, Keyes said they still turn up at rummage sales around Cornucopia now and then. There's one in the Cornucopia Historical Society's Green Shed Museum by the harbor. At any rate, the once-elusive dream of belonging to the Cornucopia Yacht Club is now an impossible dream, since the club exists only as legend. But to some, its non-existence only increases the appeal—a club that no one can join is the ultimate in exclusivity.

Elvis Presley, Peacemaker

It was shortly after midnight on June 24, 1977. The King of rock and roll had just arrived in Madison for a performance at the Dane County Coliseum. A limo picked him up at the airport, and by one a.m. Elvis was rolling down East Washington Avenue toward the Edgewater Hotel, where he'd be staying the night. This was less than two months before his death on August 16, 1977.

The limo pulled to a stop at the intersection of East Washington and Stoughton Road. Elvis, staring out the window, witnessed two hoods hassling Keith Lowry, Jr., a seventeen-year-old La Follette High School student working at the Skylane Standard Station.

"Look at those two punks," growled Elvis. "I don't buy this two-on-one deal."

Ever a good man, he asked the driver to wait to see what would go down. When the three started fighting, Elvis—with dyed jet-black hair, bloated, and still squeezed into a sequined blue jumpsuit from a Des Moines concert a few hours earlier—scrambled out of the car, ready to rumble. He assumed a kickboxing stance. "If you want to fight, let's fight," he challenged.

It was powerful mojo. The punks' jaws hit the pavement. Stunned in the presence of the King, any fight in them instantly dissolved. They stood humbled, downcast, embarrassed.

"Is everything settled now?" asked Elvis.

It was.

His work done, Elvis delivered a classic line: "I found you as enemies; I leave you as friends." Is it any wonder Elvis inspired a new religion?

With that, as cameras flashed all around him, the King shook hands with several bewildered onlookers, climbed back into his limo, and was whisked away.

Viva Elvis, peacemaker! He'll always be the King.

Scalped Lady

In Prairie du Chien, there once lived a woman who was scalped by Indians as a baby and who would, for a fee, sometimes exhibit her head. The woman, Marie Regis Gagnier, was born in Crawford County on August 15, 1826. Her father, Registre Gagnier, was of French and African ancestry, and her mother was French and Sioux. According to the *History of Crawford County,* Gagnier and his four brothers were highly regarded citizens of Prairie du Chien. Registre had a farm three miles from town, where he lived with his wife and two small children, Frank and Marie. Gagnier was known for his kindness toward all the local indigenous people, which made what happened all the more shocking.

The whole thing was started by a false rumor told to a Winnebago chieftain named Red Bird, who was well respected in the area. In June 1827, some visiting Sioux informed the Winnebago that the Long Knives, or whites, had killed and cut to pieces two Winnebago men. The Winnebago, who were known for their unrelenting policy of blood vengeance, chose Red Bird to carry out the revenge, and Red Bird decided that a minimum of two whites would have to be killed in order to avenge his people's honor. He evidently felt that the Gagnier family would do, and he took several men, including one named We-kaw, or Little Sun, to the Gagniers' isolated cabin, where he had often been a guest.

After welcoming the visitors, Mrs. Gagnier became suspicious. Still, she busied herself preparing food. Also present were Registre Gagnier and his young half-brother, Pascal Menoir, and an elderly soldier named Solomon Lipcap, who lived with the Gagniers. At a prearranged signal, We-kaw shot Gagnier. Another Winnebago fired at Pascal Menoir, who was sitting next to an open window. He missed. Menoir fell backward out the window and was able to escape into the woods. The room filled with gunsmoke. Mrs. Gagnier grabbed little Frank and ran out of the house. She raced to a neighbor's for help, but the neighbor had run away. By this time, the Indians were outside in pursuit of old Lipcap, so Mrs. Gagnier returned to her cabin. She could not find Marie, who had crawled under the bed, and her husband was barely alive. He gestured for her to leave, so she took Frank and ran for the woods. Mother and son hid in some brambles that had grown around an old, uprooted maple tree, crouching in terror as Lipcap was finally caught, killed, and scalped within twelve feet of their hiding place.

We-kaw and the others then returned to the cabin and found baby Marie. We-kaw kicked her, hit her with the butt of his rifle, and was about to behead her in front of the anguished eyes of her dying father when word came that a large group of settlers, alerted by young Menoir, was approaching from the village. We-kaw decided to scalp her instead, taking part of the occipital bone. He then scalped Gagnier.

People later remembered that We-kaw and Gagnier had had a previous altercation over We-kaw's disrespect for a Catholic church procession, which may explain his brutality toward the Gagniers.

By the time help came, Registre Gagnier was dead and Marie lay in a pool of blood. She was taken to town and was being

washed for her funeral when it was realized that she was somehow still alive. Miraculously, she survived and lived the rest of her life in Prairie du Chien. She married twice and had thirteen children, some of whose descendants still live in that town. People remembered that she always wore a sort of lace cap over her injured head.

The killing of Registre Gagnier and Solomon Lipcap led to what became known as the Winnebago Wars in southwestern Wisconsin. Both Red Bird and We-kaw were eventually taken into custody. Red Bird died in prison, but We-kaw and another Indian who had been at the cabin were subsequently pardoned by President John Quincy Adams with the provision that $50 a year was to be paid to Mrs. Gagnier by the Winnebago for fifteen years (to be deducted from the Winnebago's annuity) as compensation for the tragic loss of Registre. The only other recompense for the tragedy suffered by the Gagnier family would be the small fees collected by Marie now and then for showing people her scars from that bloody day in June 1827.

Little Boy Lost

Cases of missing children are always tragic. They are especially so when no clue ever surfaces regarding a child's fate. One such incident occurred in Sheboygan Falls and involved a little boy named Frankie Bond. Most startlingly, after Frankie's funeral, it was claimed for years that he was still very much alive.

It happened on April 19, 1852. Two-year-old Frankie, the son of Dr. and Mrs. M. A. Bond, walked through the open gate of his family home in broad daylight and vanished.

There were relatively few facts. A Mr. Mead, calling on Dr. Bond for some medicine, allowed Frankie to exit the gate. Guests at Brown's hotel, near the corner of Pine and Broadway, watched the young boy pass by. One woman saw a child wearing a black-and-red-checked flannel shirt following a man toward the bridge over the river. She was watching the street from her dinner table but was distracted when her own child fell off a chair. By the time she looked up again, the little boy was gone. She could never say with certainty that it was Frankie.

The bridge had been swept away by the river following heavy rainfall, and a temporary one with no railings had been installed. Based on the slim evidence, many people naturally concluded that Frankie had fallen from the bridge into the turbulent river.

Despite heroic search efforts, no sign of Frankie was ever found. His parents sadly accepted that he had died in a fall from the bridge and held a formal funeral without the body. A few years later, they moved to Fox Lake and eventually returned to their native Vermont.

It was more than just grief that drove them away from Sheboygan Falls. For over twelve years after Frankie's disappearance, people claimed that he was still alive, though far from home. Some assumed the man Frankie was following had kidnapped him. A woman jailed in Manitowoc insisted that Frankie had been abducted by Indians and then spirited away to Michigan. It turned out she was lying in an attempt to gain release from prison.

Another story that circulated was of a dying impoverished Hillsdale, Michigan, woman who was convinced that she could not pass on until she revealed a dark secret. As friends gathered around her as she lay on her deathbed, she pointed to her young son, standing in the corner. She claimed that the child was not hers. Laboriously, she gasped out the story of how she and her husband had been passing through Sheboygan Falls and had stolen the boy as he came through a gate. At this point, the woman collapsed, unable to continue the story. She died two hours later without revealing her entire secret. There were several other alleged deathbed confessions about Frankie's fate.

Over the years, E. Frank Barrows, a personal friend of the Bonds', tracked down all of the confessions and rumors concerning Frankie. He discovered no foundation in fact for any of them, but he detailed his search in a series of articles called "After Twenty Years!" published in the *Sheboygan Times* in 1875.

Barrows ended his debunking of this "urban legend" with the following paragraph: "And now, 'After Twenty Years' of fitful agitation, we sadly and tenderly recommit our little friend to the silent embrace of death, hoping that henceforth he may peacefully rest in his unknown tomb, until the final resurrection, and that the hearts of his sorrowful parents may never more be pained by false hopes or unsubstantial rumors."

Whether that ended the stories, we do not know. But if there was ever a fabled character in Wisconsin, Frankie Bond, a young boy presumed dead but kept alive by rumor in multiple states, was surely one.

They Lived to Tell the Tale. . . . Or Did They?

Did the long-lost heir to the throne of France once live in De Pere, Wisconsin? In 1853, an Episcopal minister named Eleazar Williams stunned America with the claim that he was in fact Louis XVII, the son of Louis XVI and Marie Antoinette, the monarchs beheaded during the French Revolution. No matter that their son, Louis, who was eight years old at the time his parents were guillotined, was supposed to have been an "imbecile" and was imprisoned in a tower, where he died. However, it was rumored in France that the prince, or dauphin, as he was known, had been spirited away from the tower and another child put in his place. The dauphin, it was alleged, was sent to safety in America, to be raised among the St. Regis Mohawk tribe on the shore of Lake Champlain in New York State.

To those who wanted to believe, it didn't seem to matter that Eleazar Williams was at least five years too young to have been the dauphin. But they did have a few good reasons to think that this educated missionary might be the lost prince.

The scheme that brought Williams to Wisconsin in the first place was hardly any less strange or grandiose than his later claim to French royalty. His plan had been to create an "Indian Empire" in the Fox River area, of which he would be the sole dictator. He had been a missionary to the Oneida in New York State and had talked several bands into coming with him to start this amazing enterprise. (There was also pressure on the Oneida to leave New York because the state had its eye on their lands there.)

Williams arrived in Wisconsin in 1822, and the following year he married a young girl of fourteen who was part Menominee. Once in Wisconsin, he continued to work with those Oneida who had followed him west. He set up a school and translated hymns and parts of the Bible into their language, in which he was fluent. Williams and the Oneida also purchased acreage from the Menominee and Winnebago (Ho-Chunk) nations. But things didn't go well.

Williams's grand scheme was brought down by fighting and mix-ups between the settlers from New York and the original owners of the Fox River land, and it wasn't long before Williams was held in some disregard by people from all the groups involved in his "empire."

Then something strange happened. In 1841, the Prince de Joinville, the son of Louis Philippe, the latest occupant of the French throne, came all the way across the ocean to visit Eleazar Williams. Louis Philippe sent Williams a gift of expensive books, and according to Williams's diary, which is preserved in the State Historical Society of Wisconsin, the prince told him of his true identity and offered him a huge sum of money if he would give up his claim to the French throne. Williams refused.

Other sources say it was a lawyer who first advised Williams of a facial resemblance to the lost dauphin. However, all sources agree that the Prince de Joinville really did visit Williams in Wisconsin. Either way, it was enough to convince the missionary and several prominent members of his church that he was indeed the lost dauphin. In 1853, an Episcopal clergyman wrote a book called *The Lost Prince* to convince the world that Eleazar Williams was truly the son of Louis XVI and Marie Antoinette, and Williams developed something of a popular following. Evidently, he did bear certain scars that matched those of the dauphin, and several doctors testified that Williams was of European, not Mohawk, ancestry. Interestingly, according to a Wisconsin Oneida story, Williams's Mohawk parents were given a very sick baby boy to adopt by two white men. However, the lost dauphin was hardly a baby when he purportedly would have been brought to America.

Williams took advantage of his newfound celebrity status to return to New York, where his followers built him a French-style château. He spent all his time studying French documents, trying to prove his origins and becoming more and more unhinged in the process. He once offered to sell the journals of the French explorer Jacques Marquette, which of course he did not have, to New York State. Toward the end of his life, Williams succumbed to paranoia, believing that unknown assassins were after him. He died in 1858 in his New York château, far from his great Indian empire, in a room where he had hung a fancy silk ball gown on the wall. On his deathbed, he told those attending him that the gown belonged to his mother, Marie Antoinette.

Williams's wife remained in their Wisconsin home, which had a sweeping view of the Fox River below. Today, the cabin's flagstone foundation can still be seen in what is now Lost Dauphin Park, on the west bank of the Fox on Highway D. There's a historical marker in the park that asks, WAS HE THE LOST DAUPHIN? DNA analysis technology could probably answer that question now; maybe someone will take on the challenge and find out whether Louis XVI and Marie Antoinette's son really did walk among us along the Fox River.

Small Wonder—The Short Story of Haunchyville

As much as Weird Wisconsin *loves* unsolicited e-mails, we're not always enthusiastic about the correspondents who come across as know-it-alls. We, as self-identified experts, are expected to know everything, and when we don't have a ready answer, the typical know-it-all tends to be snide. Despite this annoying trait, however, know-it-alls often spur us into launching new investigations. The e-mail that started this line of research was, "Surely you've heard of Haunchyville."

Our response: "What, like we're supposed to know everything? No, we haven't heard of Haunchyville. And stop calling us Shirley."

Intrigued, we asked around, "What's up with Haunchyville?" We discovered it's a colony of midgets living in the woods near Muskego. Furthermore, these midgets are said to be armed, even deadly. Supposedly, a lone "normal-sized" man is their protector. And the Haunchies are reputed to be prolific, spread across a huge area from southeastern Waukesha County into Milwaukee County, through Franklin, St. Francis, and into Grant Park in South Milwaukee. It's one huge midget infestation—at least according to our e-mail correspondents.

Haunchyville is a legend known to teens throughout the Greater Milwaukee area. What makes it a legend is that the stories defy common sense. The so-called facts aren't consistent, the location of the colony changes based on who's telling the story, and only teens seem to know about it. Thanks to the Internet and rumor, teens from as far away as Fond du Lac have heard the wild tales.

Of course, fascination with miniature versions of everyday things seems to be part of human nature. This is nowhere more evident than in our interest in miniature people. Little people, or midgets, have always been showstoppers, from General Tom Thumb in P. T. Barnum's circus to the Munchkins of Oz to Mini Me in the Austin Powers movies.

It's no wonder, then, that each year carloads of teenagers make the pilgrimage to Muskego, hoping to find Haunchyville and score an encounter with this tribe of tiny folks living in the woods and brandishing baseball bats. Or maybe the midgets live in the cornfields or in a house or in a village. The stories vary.

The legend goes back to at least the 1950s. Thanks to reliable types—fathers, uncles, grandfathers, older brothers—the Haunchyville mystery is passed down from generation to generation. In the old days, wise old people used to send kids on snipe hunts in search of that mythical bird—or of a hodag. Now wise elders send teens on midget hunts. It's a strange rite of passage.

The teens descend on Muskego looking for Mystic Drive, a real street name, hoping to rile up a village of midgets in the name of good clean fun. Alas, there are no Haunchies. There are no midgets. The legend has become a cash cow for the city of Muskego, though, as hundreds of trespassers have been caught and forced to pay fines of $276.

However, when it comes to Haunchyville, it's best to let the true believers tell their own stories. They're far more entertaining than anything we could provide.

Searching for the Li'l Guys

The infamous Haunchyville I've always heard about is located on Mystic Lane Drive in Muskego, which is about a twenty-minute drive from Milwaukee. I've been there myself, and I didn't see anything of major interest. However, there's a fenced-in or gated home or farm where the "acclaimed" midgets are. I've never attempted to get a closer look; I've talked to people who have, though. Some say yes, they've seen the li'l guys, and some say no.—*Sarah*

Wacky Thing

Haunchyville is the nickname for a community supposedly inhabited by midgets. They try to keep away from everyone else, and there's one normal-sized man who acts as a guard for them at night. I don't know if there's any truth to the legend, but I do have friends that have been out there and have seen stop signs that are only waist-high, and some of them would even know how to give directions. I'm from West Allis, and this legend is well known among kids. So how's that for a wacky thing, eh?–*Jon*

Haunchies Are Just Simple Farm Folks

The version I heard was that it wasn't a village, but a farm that was being worked by a bunch of midgets who had retired from show business. Story is that the farm is surrounded by cornfields and has a long drive up to it. The residents are not kind to strangers and will run them off if bothered. Of course, nobody could give me directions, but the person who told me the story assured me he knew people who had been there. *Todd Roll, Wausau Paranormal Research Society*

How Do I Get There?

I recently heard about Haunchyville. I'm from the Fond du Lac area and would really like to go to Haunchyville—if nothing else, just for fun. But midgets have always freaked the beegeezers out of me. If you could by any chance send some directions, that would be great.–*Chad*

Waist-High Stop Signs

Have you ever heard of Haunchyville? Supposedly it is a town of midgets. I have heard that the stop signs around this town are waist-high, and if you get into the actual town, the midgets come after you with bats. If you have heard of it, could you tell me where it is? I would very much like to see if the story is true.—*Michelle*

Lord of the Cornfield

I did talk to a guy today who told me he was at Haunchyville a couple of years ago, and he told me not to go there. He said that it's in Muskego and that it's surrounded by a cornfield and there is this man who lives in a farm house and once he sees a car go by he calls the cops and runs out with a rifle. I've heard several stories similar to that, so I believe him. My friends and I are going to check it out this weekend, so I will let you know if we can find it.—*Casey*

They May Be Little, but They Have BIG Guns!

One of my friends has actually been there. This is the story he told me: "One night me and some friends were cruising around and went through this little town. It was really weird. There were little houses and little stores and even little people walking around. Well, I guess they didn't like big people, because one of the little guys in a truck was trying to run us off the road. He even had a shotgun he was pointing at us. We didn't expect him to try to shoot us, so we just flipped him off. Then he shot at us! It went right through the windows, barely missing us. After that, we slammed on the gas and got the hell out of there.—*Muziclvr85*

Signs, Signs, Everywhere Signs

My friends and I went out to Haunchyville tonight. We saw the signs and the gate. All the signs strictly prohibited us from going onto the property; it was very weird. There were three different roads, and we went straight, ignoring the signs. About halfway down, we noticed what we thought might be the gate to Haunchyville, but then three men appeared. They walked towards our car and threw something at us. At that point we just sped off.—*BJM1982*

They Attack with Their Little Knives

I'm from Bay View, and the legend of the Haunchies has been around since I was a kid. Supposedly, the Haunchies live in the woods around the lakefront in Grant Park, and Sheridan Park around Bay View, Cudahy, St. Francis, and South Milwaukee. They wait for the big people (that's us) to park their cars and make out. Then they attack, wielding little knives. They have their own society in the woods. I was seriously scared of them when I was a kid and still retain a little of that fear today.—*Zatty3*

Large Fines in Small Haunchyville

Okay, I have been to Haunchyville with two carloads of friends, and I'm not sure, but I think we went the wrong way. But either way, we never saw any midgets, and we ended up with a big fat $276 trespassing fine. Sooo . . . if you decide to go to Haunchyville, which I thought was pretty creepy, make sure you go the right way and don't flash your headlights in someone's driveway.—*Paige*

Mutilated by Little Creatures

I first heard the story growing up in Greendale about thirty years ago. We were told that the area was once home to a group of midgets who had worked in the circus. Years later, after the area had been abandoned, a teenage couple parked their car in the cornfields to make out, and they were attacked by "little creatures" that left scratch marks on the roof of the car. The teenagers were found dead, mutilated in the car.

We used to skip school and drive out there into the cornfields, and strangely, there were little roads going through the fields and small shacks and little boats. I never went back there as an adult to put it all together, but I'm sure what I saw had some rational explanation.—*Rich Maringer*

There's Nothing at All to Haunchyville Except for the Time . . .

This whole Haunchyville thing is completely outta control—there is nothing there. I have lived in Muskego all my life. I've been to Mystic Drive, like, a million times. I know people who live there, and there is no Haunchyville. There's a big mansion out there, and that's it. My friends know who owns the mansion. Anyway, there's nothing Haunchie-like about the area, the house, or the family who lives in it. There is no Haunchyville. This myth got out of control in the eighties. My dad knows a police officer in Muskego who has been around for many, many years. He says it's a shame that there have been so many people trespassing for something that's not even true. It's just a made-up rumor. I've taken my bike on the bike path that goes right past there so many times in both day and night, and never once have I seen anything, been attacked, or anything like that.

Now, about some of the stories I've heard. There's one about there being a large, large man guarding the entrance to Haunchyville, who's the only "normal-sized" person there. I've also heard that there has been a massive killing back there. The people who were killed were normal-sized people.—*Jess*

There You Have It

Of course, your friends would never lie to you about midgets popping up out of the corn. There's also another legend that a farmer, out plowing, ripped a giant oak stump out of the ground, exposing the Haunchies' secret underground cavern system. Their underground world exposed, the Haunchies had to silence the farmer. They killed him—strung him up with a rope and hanged him in his barn. If you drive by a certain barn along Mystic Drive, you can still see the ghostly silhouette of a man dangling at the end of a rope. Some say this hanged man is like a permanent stain on the side of the barn and that you can see it in daylight. We've lost track of all the hanging ghosts in Wisconsin, but there's probably enough to fill a small city, like, well, Muskego.

We're told that traffic became so bad that residents on Bass Bay Lane, off Mystic Drive, eventually installed a private gate complete with keypad entry, which only served to fuel the legend. Such a hi-tech device, of course, could only mean that something supersecret was hidden there. In an October 2000 newspaper article, Detective Lieutenant James Budish of the Muskego Police Department estimated that hundreds of

trespassing citations had been issued since he had joined the force twenty-nine years earlier.

"When they find Paul Bunyan and Babe, his blue ox, then they might find the Haunchies," he said. "I'm not the prince or king of the Haunchies, so I'm not trying to protect them. There are only one or two guys in this department who are actually short enough to be considered real Haunchies."

As one of the residents of the Mystic Drive area said, "A young boy once asked me if we have seen the Haunchies, and I responded, 'Yeah, we feed them raw meat.' The terrified boy ran away as fast as he could."

Weird Wisconsin has yet to uncover where the name Haunchyville comes from or even what it means. But we do know that a similar legend plagues Totowa's Norwood Terrace in New Jersey, where convoys of teens in expensive cars cruise up and down the streets, honking horns and flashing lights to draw out the shotgun-toting inhabitants of Midgetville. Apparently, Midgetvilles are also located in Virginia, Kentucky, and Florida. We suppose little people have to live somewhere.

Miracle of the White Buffalo

She came unannounced, as most miracles do, but not completely unexpected: Two thousand years before, a white buffalo calf had been promised by the White Buffalo Woman to the Lakota Sioux. The female calf was born on August 20, 1994, on a farm in Janesville. Surprisingly, she came not to a Plains state, but to southern Wisconsin, known more for Holsteins than for buffalo.

The owners, hobby farmers Dave and Valerie Heider, were astounded that two ordinary brown buffalo could have created a calf with pure white fur. Dave admits that at first he also saw green. He thought the calf would bring a million dollars. But within a few short weeks, he was experiencing something else—a whole new sense of spirituality, brought home by the steady pilgrimage of thousands of souls who came to see the calf. He would later turn down large offers to buy her. How could he sell the fulfillment of a prophecy?

Chief Joseph Standing Horse of the Lakota Sioux traveled from Rapid City, South Dakota, to Janesville to visit Miracle. He told the story of the White Buffalo Calf Woman that his grandfather had told him. She had come to his ancestors bearing a sacred bundle called the White Buffalo Calf Pipe; then she turned into a white buffalo calf and then back into a woman. She taught the people many things and told them that as long as they took care of the peace pipe and respected each other and the earth, all would be well with them. She said that when a white buffalo calf was born, the whole world would know about her message of peace.

The prophecy also said that the buffalo would turn yellow, red, black, and brown to signify the unification of all the races of man. Miracle did turn all those colors as her coat darkened over the years. By August 2004, when her tenth birthday was celebrated with a giant party, she was a dark brown. The fence surrounding her pasture was

covered with gifts and tokens brought by visitors, who never stopped coming to see her.

Miracle's longevity was one thing that the prophecy never addressed, however, and not long after her tenth birthday, the Heiders were shocked when Miracle died on Sunday, September 19, 2004. Buffalo can live to be twenty-five, so the death was unexpected. She was buried next to her sire, who had died soon after she was born.

Miracle was sacred not just to the Lakota, but to many other cultures. People gathered from around the country to give Miracle a traditional farewell with drums, prayer, songs, and offerings. The farm is still open and free of charge on weekend afternoons for those who want to see Miracle's birthplace and pay their respects and is located on the south side of Janesville, on South River Road.

As for the Lakota Sioux, they have seen an ancient prophecy fulfilled in their lifetime. And they now look for the promised healing to come.

Garden of Eden in Wisconsin?

For decades, residents in the Greater La Crosse area referred to their environs as God's Country, due in part to the towering bluffs overlooking the Mississippi River, the abundant wildlife, and other beautiful natural wonders found there. Even brewers of Old Style, that former La Crosse beer, coined the phrase "Pure Brewed in God's Country" as its advertising slogan. But few remember how the name had originated.

It began in 1886, when the Reverend D. O. Van Slyke published his theory that the Garden of Eden was located in Trempealeau County. His tract was titled *Found at Last: The Veritable Garden of Eden, or a Place that Answers the Bible Description of That Notable Spot Better Than Anything Yet Discovered.*

While Van Slyke was much revered, he was also viewed as a bit of an eccentric. He boasted in his diary that he had read the Bible twenty-five times and felt he was onto important things. In his book, Van Slyke identified specific local landmarks with those mentioned in the Bible, noting hanging gardens, apple orchards, serpents in the bluffs, and numerous other parallels.

Today, a statue of Van Slyke greets visitors on the city's south side, and organizations such as the Garden of Eden Preservation Society and the Garden of Eden Visitors Center perpetuate Van Slyke's vision. Whether you agree or not, the view of Marinuka Lake is breathtaking from the lofty heights of the Pine Cliff Cemetery in Galesville, where Van Slyke is buried. Before he shuffled off this earthly paradise, Van Slyke left an unanswerable challenge to future generations: "Nobody can prove that this is not the Garden of Eden."

Mary Ann Van Hoof and the Virgin Mary

"Mrs. Fred Van Hoof Reveals What the Mother of God Said and Did When She Appeared on Their Farm Near Necedah, Wisconsin." That little quote from a brochure for the Queen of the Holy Rosary Mediatrix of Peace shrine packs a wallop if you were unaware that the Virgin Mary appeared on November 12, 1949, in Necedah, Wisconsin, to a farmer's wife named Mary Ann Van Hoof. The appearances were controversial from the very start and serve as fodder for dueling Web sites to this day.

The Lady first showed up as a silent figure standing in Van Hoof's bedroom doorway. She visited again five months later, on Good Friday, April 7, 1950, after Van Hoof noticed her wall-hung crucifix glowing. A voice told her to "pray hard." The voice also instructed her to tell her priest and parish that they should all pray the rosary every night at eight p.m.

On May 28, Van Hoof was brushing a mosquito off her leg at her front door, about to call her family to dinner, when just above four ash trees in her yard she spotted a blue mist that turned into a vision of Mary. Van Hoof stepped outside toward the apparition, which told her to eat a twig from one of the bushes in the yard. It then gave her devotional instructions and insisted she mark the spot with a cross. (Today a statue of the Virgin stands on the spot.) The apparition appeared seven more times, according to the shrine's brochure. By August 15, the vision had promised to show a "Miracle in the Sun." A crowd of a hundred thousand people gathered and was told to stare directly at old Sol, potential cornea damage notwithstanding. Some said they saw a cross in the sun; some claimed it was spinning or changing colors. Most saw nothing.

Van Hoof told the crowd all the things the vision had told her, from instructions to pray the rosary daily to warnings about danger to Pope Pius VII and "darkness spreading over America." Many of the exhortations were for prayers for the "conversion of Russia," but she also made ominous references to Russian submarines attacking Alaska and the Pacific Coast and hinted that a darker, worldwide conspiracy was behind it all.

The visions did not really stop, however. Van Hoof continued to see angels and saints, six-inch-tall messengers, and other things that no one else saw, and began talking about a spaceship guided by someone named Alex who would come to save believers before "the chastisement."

Writer Kevin Orlin Johnson noted in a recent issue of the online Catholic magazine *This Rock*, "Until her death in 1984, it was all Commie plots hatched by a Council of Elders, mind control through fluoridation, and global nuclear conflict that would destroy everything outside a thirty-mile radius of Necedah, where a spaceship would come to take them to a paradise inside the hollow Earth."

The official church, not too surprisingly, was having none of it. The local Catholic bishop pronounced Van Hoof's visions to be "false claims" and ordered her activities to cease in 1950. Another bishop ordered the shrine closed in 1969, but Van Hoof refused, and in 1975, all those connected with the shrine in any way were excommunicated. In 1983, the shrine was condemned by the Vatican, and most followers finally were convinced to leave.

So who was this chosen messenger of the Mother of God? Interestingly, Van Hoof's mother was a Spiritualist and was said to have held séances in Kenosha. She and Mary Ann frequented the Spiritualist Camp in Wonewoc. Mary Ann's personal life was unstable; she had several husbands, lacked an education, and even her official publications noted that the grammar used in visionary messages was that of Mary Ann, not of the Virgin Mary, who would be expected to speak more correctly. Mary Ann was also rumored to be unnaturally strong, with the ability, when in a rage, to throw an adult across a room.

Van Hoof's farm has been turned into a shrine that continues to draw visitors to this day. There are enclosed devotional statues for pilgrims to walk among, as well as what are arguably some of the least aesthetically pleasing statues of George Washington, Abraham Lincoln, and Jesus Christ ever created. The shrine complex, which includes a church and school, can be visited at W5703 Shrine Road, Necedah. For the sake of modesty, wrap skirts are provided for women wearing slacks or shorts.

Roadside Oddities

This is a mobile society. Hand us a cell phone, stick some tunes in the CD player, and we're freewheeling down the highway. But here's a caveat: So many of us now drive with one ear glued to a tiny chunk of metal and our minds on the person we are talking to that we've stopped looking at the amazing things that are strung along our Wisconsin freeways.

Wake up, roadsters! Get that phone off your ear, hang your head out the window, and really look at what you're driving past: giant lumberjacks, big goofy mice, even a truck in a tree. There's also a whole category of the world's largest things—from the biggest penny to the biggest corkscrew, all put up just because someone dared to think huge. In Wisconsin, the weirdness is everywhere.

The alarming part is that much of the good stuff is fading fast. The eccentric signs and roadside props once designed by mom-and-pop businesses are gradually being replaced by slick global McVillage-like chains.

From the stupendous to the humbly insane, we mean to document Wisconsin's rich cache of roadside treasures before too many more highways are widened and more icons are consigned to the landfill. Wisconsin really does have it all—from incredible natural scenery to a badger head the size of a woolly mammoth sticking up out of the ground. And sure, most of these unnatural wonders were created as advertisements, but at least they have attitude and distinctiveness. We've accepted them as state landmarks, and they deserve to remain a part of our heritage.

So hang on, free yourself from all distractions, and ready your eyeballs for some good, old-fashioned rubbernecking. And if you ever find yourself stuck behind a lollygagging vehicle on some black-topped county road, please hold back on the rude gestures; it could be *Weird Wisconsin*. You'll know from our bumper sticker: WE BRAKE FOR WEIRD.

Sparta's FAST Corp.—Birthplace of Roadside Giants

"Yow! Are you one of those giant, wheeled beings from th' Planet Wisconsin?"
—Zippy the Pinhead, *Zippy Comics Annual 2001* © Bill Griffith

Every comic-strip fan knows Zippy the Pinhead, Bill Griffith's clownish yet philosophical character. Each year, Griffith publishes a collection of the year's comics, and for those of us from Wisconsin, the 2001 annual will always be special. On the cover with Zippy are cartoon drawings of giant fiberglass roadside attractions, all made in Wisconsin. There is the Octopus Car Wash of Madison, the Bicycle Man of Sparta, and even apocalyptic-looking drawings of downed statues spread over the grounds of FAST Corp. in Sparta, where gargantuan fiberglass lawn art is fabricated and sold.

Weird Wisconsin arrived at the headquarters of Fiberglass Animals, Shapes & Trademarks Corporation— or simply FAST Corp.—on a blistering Sunday afternoon.

Giant replicas of everything imaginable were strewn around the building in various stages of construction. Some were bright and shiny, ready to be trucked off; some were awaiting a coat of paint and a gob of lacquer. Acres of evergreen-ringed fields behind the building served as an outdoor showroom. Among the oddities we saw were a six-foot-tall honey bear with its stomach wide open down the middle. Nearby, a shark's head pushed up through the sod, and for those who find sharks unappealing, there was the oversized ice-cream cone. The whole scene was a landscape from another planet.

A sign invited visitors to walk around the grounds and take pictures, but it also warned against touching, climbing, or otherwise desecrating the massive artworks.

One famous FAST Corp. statue occupies a permanent spot in Sparta's bicycle-trail park. It's a well-dressed gent seated high atop an old-

fashioned bicycle. In the Zippy comic strip, Zippy has a conversation with this fellow. "I don't know why, Wheelman, but you fill me with a deep sense of ironic detachment," says Zippy wistfully.

Not us. *Weird Wisconsin* felt a sense of ironic attachment. These are the icons of the urban environment we've all grown up with, and their instantly recognizable forms are somehow comforting. We reluctantly concluded that we couldn't fit any of the fiberglass giants into the trunk of our car, and so we left the enormous creatures to comfort one another in their mutual strangeness.

The Tall Tale of the Lakewood Paul Bunyan

Back in 1962, in an era when advertising was unselfconsciously flamboyant, a café on Route 66 in Flagstaff, Arizona, commissioned the Prewitt Fiberglass Company of California to make a giant statue of Paul Bunyan. Prewitt's cowboy owner created a magnificent twenty-foot-tall fiberglass lumberjack. The statue proved so successful at attracting customers to the café that when the company was bought by International Fiberglass the following year, the new owners decided to go into the giant statue business big-time. They used the same mold with a few modifications to create Texaco's Big Friends, Phillips Petroleum cowboys, various Indian figures, and the famous Muffler Man, among other fiberglass giants. Today, all these permutations are referred to as Muffler Men by a quasi-cult of roadside seekers who travel the country hunting and documenting remaining examples.

There's a great Muffler Man in Lakewood, Wisconsin. It's a miracle, though, that the statue is still there, since the bar to which it was attached, the Paul Bunyan Corner Pub, burned to the ground on February 16, 2004. We'd been told that the lumberjack was still on view, in front of the Lakewood Hotel. However, we drove through Lakewood's abbreviated downtown, on Wisconsin Highway 32, five or six times without spying Paul Bunyan, and two-story statues are usually hard to miss. Finally we walked into the Schmidt House tavern, adjoining the Lakewood Hotel, and asked the bartender, "Where's Paul Bunyan?"

"Oh," said owner Lin Schmidt, "he's out on loan for the county parade, dressed up as a cowboy."

Lin's son, Tim, and Tim's wife, Karen, had owned the Paul Bunyan Corner Pub and lived in the building. They had barely escaped with their lives after an electrical fire gutted the building. Tim had suffered

"Babe" the Blue Ox

painful burns on his back, hands, and face while rescuing a dog. The Muffler Man Paul Bunyan was a bit luckier. "All Paul got was a burnt butt; it was just all black," said Lin. It was easy enough to repaint Paul, so there was nothing to keep him from wearing a mammoth Stetson and helping out a local parade.

Tim and Karen hope to rebuild their tavern and have Paul remounted at his rightful home base before too long. They plan to rename the tavern the Paul Bunyan Hot Spot, in honor of the fire.

Meanwhile, Paul has new lumberjack gear and waits patiently at the Lakewood Hotel, where passersby can still see him. If you notice a look of longing in the old muffler-jack's eyes, it might be because his mighty blue ox, Babe, has been relocated to the Maple Heights Campground on Highway 32 just north of Lakewood. It's tough when an attraction and his sidekick are separated. However, as a fire survivor Paul Bunyan seems to lead a charmed existence. Who's to say he and Babe won't some day tromp the northern woods together again?

The Statue That Will Not Die

The statue of chinless wonder Andy Gump in Lake Geneva's Flat Iron Park is one of the city's most recognizable landmarks. But most of the tourists who snap Andy's picture have no idea of the battles this brave comic-strip character has endured to keep his big foot firmly planted on the globe. In the cartoon strip created by Lake Geneva artist Sidney Smith for the *Chicago Tribune*, everyman Andy Gump's most famous line was a yell for help to his wife: "Oh, Min!" If statues could talk, this one would have screamed many times for Min over the last eighty years.

The original statue, made of plaster and coated with bronze, was presented to Sidney Smith by the *Chicago Tribune* to commemorate the cartoon character's run for U.S. president in 1924. It was unveiled at Smith's lakeside estate, Trudehurst, in a ceremony attended by more than one thousand people. The statue's pose, with one foot on the globe, represented the deluded self-importance of the common man.

After the death of his first wife, Smith moved, taking the statue with him to his new digs, Robinswood. Then, tragically, at the height of his career, he was killed in a car crash. Robinswood passed to a new owner, who returned the statue to the *Tribune,* which, in turn, presented it to the city of Lake Geneva in 1947. Andy Gump was promptly installed in Flat Iron Park atop a bronze pedestal donated by the *Tribune.* However, plaster is not a permanent outdoor material, and the harsh Wisconsin winters began to take their toll on Andy. Then, in 1952, someone stole the bronze plaque. It was missing for two weeks before a Lake Geneva mother found her young children playing with it in a vacant lot.

That was just an omen of things to come. In 1967, the small resort community endured a Fourth of July invasion by three thousand marauding teenagers, who

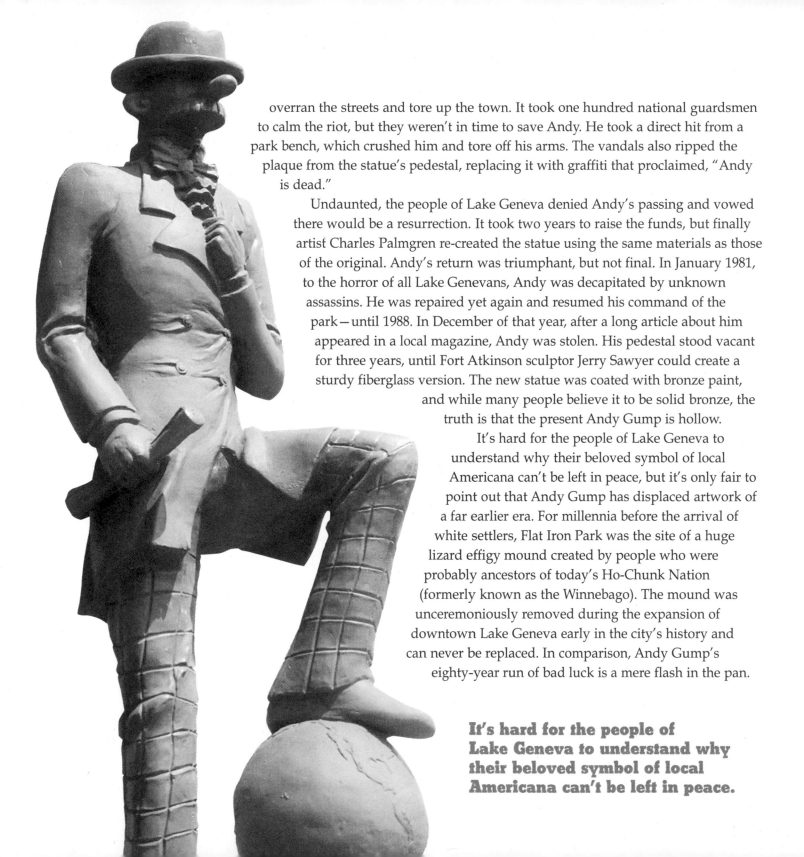

overran the streets and tore up the town. It took one hundred national guardsmen to calm the riot, but they weren't in time to save Andy. He took a direct hit from a park bench, which crushed him and tore off his arms. The vandals also ripped the plaque from the statue's pedestal, replacing it with graffiti that proclaimed, "Andy is dead."

Undaunted, the people of Lake Geneva denied Andy's passing and vowed there would be a resurrection. It took two years to raise the funds, but finally artist Charles Palmgren re-created the statue using the same materials as those of the original. Andy's return was triumphant, but not final. In January 1981, to the horror of all Lake Genevans, Andy was decapitated by unknown assassins. He was repaired yet again and resumed his command of the park—until 1988. In December of that year, after a long article about him appeared in a local magazine, Andy was stolen. His pedestal stood vacant for three years, until Fort Atkinson sculptor Jerry Sawyer could create a sturdy fiberglass version. The new statue was coated with bronze paint, and while many people believe it to be solid bronze, the truth is that the present Andy Gump is hollow.

It's hard for the people of Lake Geneva to understand why their beloved symbol of local Americana can't be left in peace, but it's only fair to point out that Andy Gump has displaced artwork of a far earlier era. For millennia before the arrival of white settlers, Flat Iron Park was the site of a huge lizard effigy mound created by people who were probably ancestors of today's Ho-Chunk Nation (formerly known as the Winnebago). The mound was unceremoniously removed during the expansion of downtown Lake Geneva early in the city's history and can never be replaced. In comparison, Andy Gump's eighty-year run of bad luck is a mere flash in the pan.

It's hard for the people of Lake Geneva to understand why their beloved symbol of local Americana can't be left in peace.

Kenosha's Dairy Palace

Based on the assumption that the first thing flatlanders want to do upon crossing the border into Wisconsin is to acquire some decent cheese, the Mars Cheese Castle is conveniently located on I-94. And don't worry—with its crenellated towers at each corner and its brassy retro sign dating from 1947, it's impossible to miss.

The outside walls of the building are adorned with insignia that feature a flying saucer hovering over a castle. Inside, the decor is dominated by knights in armor and by dairy symbols. Rows and rows of Holstein-patterned salt and pepper shakers fill a corner of the gift shop, which also features a near-life-size statue of Bossy. There are cow objets d'art of every possible form and utility to drive home the dairy theme, but strangely there are no castles or UFO replicas for sale. For Badger State fashionistas, there's a large selection of T-shirts promoting milk, cheese, cows, and, of course, the Packers, along with foam cheese hats and other cheesy baubles.

The big draw is the very edible real cheese. It comes shaped like Wisconsin or cows in every variety, from Limburger to Colby. A Packer fan could get carried away and buy enough cheese to make a real cheese hat. There's a little restaurant too, down a hallway that's guarded by two suits of armor.

What, you may wonder, are the implications of this UFO/medieval/Holstein potpourri? As we see it, the curious blend of symbolism can only have the following interpretation: Cheese is a valuable treasure, worthy of a castle's protection from Martian invaders, and the dairy cow is an animal that is deserving of our devotion and whose black-and-white markings should be proudly replicated in home furnishings and wardrobes. It's a creed Wisconsinites can live by, and there are some we know who do.

Giant Mice with Cheese

We're not sure who first decided that massive likenesses of the rodents that defile our pantries would make good sales props for cheese, but the idea caught on so solidly that, next to cows, mice are now the most abundant giant fiberglass animals along Wisconsin highways. But unlike the cows, many of which are clones, cast from the same mold, the mice have their own looks and personalities.

One of the most famous is Igor, the mascot of Fennimore Cheese on Route 61 in Fennimore. He was named after the composer Igor Stravinsky, who died on the same day the mascot was delivered. "Actually, he's more of a rat than a mouse," admits Fennimore Cheese owner Steve Bahl. Igor's original name was Yum-Yum. A friend of Bahl's had commissioned Yum-Yum the Rat for a chain of cheese stores, but the store never opened for business. Bahl's family had been making cheese in Fennimore since 1943, so when he discovered Yum-Yum in his friend's ditch, Bahl offered to

"Hi There...I'm IGOR" FENNIMORE CHEESE CHEESE MORE CHEESE

buy him. "I hooked him up behind the van and brought him home. He paid for himself the first month he was here." Igor has been to college too, says Bahl. "He was invited to be in the homecoming parade at UW-Madison."

Schettl's Freight Sales

Everything is weird, everything is big, and there is a lot of it at Schettl's Freight Sales outdoor lots. Six-foot pink flamingos stalk Betty Boop; Michelangelo's David stares a giant bunny in the eye; and angels hover over mannequins of a sailor and an island girl. Salvador Dali never painted anything so surreal. And yet, even after a hard blink and a sobering shake of the head, it's all still there, near Winneconne, spread out over several acres four miles west of Highway 41 on County Road S. But this flea market of the gods is not a museum—almost everything is for sale. Allow yourself plenty of time, though. The array is overwhelming, and it can take a good hour to walk around the grounds and see everything. There are also several buildings, where smaller items are sold.

The thing you have to wonder is where all this stuff could possibly have come from. How does one company acquire such diverse items as sculptures of charging buffalo, fleeing deer, rowdy bikers, even a careening

stagecoach? You duck instinctively from a massive chicken flapping its wings atop a shed. Where else do Serta-mattress sheep graze next to a tiger? And could there be another place where Jesus Christ shares a greenhouse gazebo with Marilyn Monroe and where a vintage Elsie the Cow takes up the whole front of a barn?

Owner Mel Schettl gets these things from all over the world. "We've been around for a while," he says, "and people call us if they have something weird they want to get rid of." It doesn't strike Schettl at all strange that the universe would dump its oversized misfits on his property in the middle of Wisconsin. Schettl is in the game of extreme salvage, where something odd jumps through the looking glass and lands on his lawn every other day. To passersby, it's road theater. To Schettl, it's business.

If you have some bucks and a very large vehicle, you could take one of these behemoths home with you; if not, you will still have a good time looking at them and pondering their origins. And if you hear strange faint repetitive music as you walk around, listen closely: It's probably the theme from *The Twilight Zone*. And only then, as you scream, will you notice Rod Serling smirking at you from behind the zebra.

Endres Manufacturing

The city sign—WELCOME TO THE WORLD'S ONLY WAUNAKEE!—hints that something out of the ordinary might be expected, and what you find does not disappoint. Just down the road on Highway 19 stands a tribute to Bavaria and to . . . goats. Easiest to spot from the road is a giant statue of a Bavarian maid, which welcomes people to Endres Manufacturing Company, a fourth-generation family business that fabricates structural steel. The Bavarian theme is in honor of the family's German heritage.

The Bavarian-themed Kappel Park, which is open to the public, is just to the right of the driveway. It's a perfect spot to enjoy a walk and to stretch road-weary legs. Most sensational is a tall metal fence crowned by a giant cowbell and decorated with cutouts of Bavarian people and goats; a sign atop the fence reads FOR EWE AND THE KIDS. Nearby, there's a weird whirligig. At its center is a man in lederhosen hoisting a beer; above the man perches—what else?—a goat, of course, plus a rocket-shaped doodad. From Memorial Day to Labor Day, live goats romp in a nearby pen.

Most of these wonders were designed by Larry Endres, who stepped down as president of Endres Manufacturing in 1990. Also worth a look is the company lobby, which features a chandelier with another of those giant cowbells. Yodeling is optional.

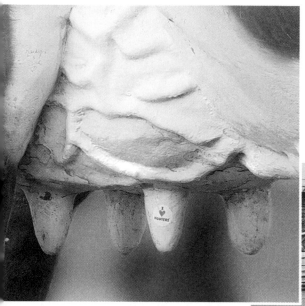

WisCOWnsin—Come Smell Our Dairy Air

There couldn't be a bigger stereotypical image than that of cows and Wisconsin. But for once, the cliché is justifiable. Even though the family farm is fast disappearing as mega dairies take over, the cow— especially the giant roadside variety—is still queen of the Wisconsin landscape. Although painted to represent different breeds, at least six of them come from the same mold at the Sculptured Advertising Company, the forerunner of Sparta's FAST Corp.

One of the most famous is Janesville's Bessie, which has stood at the Oasis Restaurant on Highway 14 for decades. In the 1960s, *LIFE* magazine included her in a photo essay, "America's Ten Ugliest Roadside Attractions." Restaurant owner Ollie Natter was proud of the distinction and kept a framed copy in his office. Bessie also starred in a Fruitopia commercial. She suffers from an occasional bout of udder graffiti these days, but

otherwise the old girl has aged very well.

Neillsville has long been known for Chatty Belle, the world's largest talking cow. You'll find she has a one-track mind, though, focused exclusively on the merits of milk. She's easy to locate with her silent son, Bullett, at the Wisconsin Pavilion at 1201 East Division Street.

Plymouth's cow, Antoinette, stands in front of a dairy store. Not long ago, when nearby Sheboygan hosted the PGA tournament at Whistling Straits, Antoinette was dressed in tartan plaid in celebration.

Since the city of New Glarus invited local artists to decorate fiberglass cows several years ago, it probably has the most cows per capita of any Wisconsin city. The imaginative and colorful bovines now grace the downtown area, offering a refreshing break from the standard-issue Holsteins you see elsewhere.

Big-Top Leftovers

Seeing the statue of the giant giraffe and its companion elephant, Romeo, on Highway 11 in downtown Delavan, you might start looking around for a circus. However, you'll find only the ghosts of circuses past, still lingering from the years 1847 to 1894, when Delavan was the winter home of twenty-six circuses and many big-top families. The Romeo statue memorializes a real elephant, whose murderous rampages resulted in the deaths of five trainers. Romeo died in the summer of 1892 in Chicago. However, another circus elephant, Juliet, had died less conveniently during the winter of 1864 in Delavan. The ground was too hard to dig a big grave, so she had to be dropped through the ice into Lake Delavan. Although fishermen pull up an occasional rib now and then, most of Juliet's skeleton remains at the bottom of the lake—along with her ghost.

Chevy on a Silo and Truck in a Tree

Men tend to put their motor vehicles on a pedestal, but in Wisconsin some do that literally. There's a Chevy set atop an old grain silo on Highway 13 south of Marshfield. And just outside Clinton, visible from Interstate 90, eagle-eyed travelers can spot a pickup truck set into a tree outside a quarry. Quarry owner Mark Madson has said that the tree branches were naturally shaped to hold a truck, so he obliged, using a crane to hoist the truck up into the tree. He recently celebrated the tree truck's tenth anniversary! Madson has converted a 1974 Cadillac Coupe de Ville into a boat and has appeared on the TV show *Monster Nation* with some of his other outrageous contraptions.

Where Food Is Road Art

Those who prefer veggies to Wisconsin's omnipresent cheese can find their road-trip nirvana at Peck's farm stand on Highway 14 in Spring Green. Peck's sells Mother Nature's best, but mammoth produce of the inedible kind is also featured here. A giant ear of corn beckons people into the driveway, which is flanked by two massive watermelons. Kids can hide in a playhouse-size pumpkin. Behind the store is a zoo that includes an alligator, a prairie-dog town, and a white-tailed deer, a Japanese sika deer, and other assorted critters intended for petting, not eating.

Size Matters

Build an object—any object—make sure it's the world's biggest, and people will flock to see it. The object doesn't have to be the actual thing, just a reasonable facsimile. It's doubtful, for instance, that the world's largest corkscrew could open the world's largest bottle of Merlot, but that doesn't matter. It's still fun to see a fifteen-foot corkscrew sitting in a liquor-store parking lot. It's at Corkscrew Liquors, naturally, on Highway 2 north of Hurley.

Claire de Loon, named after an old tune found most often these days in music boxes, stands sixteen feet high and weighs two thousand pounds. That's a lot of loon, but don't tell the folks in Mercer that there's actually a larger one on a lake in Minnesota. Mercer already called itself the Loon Capital of the World when Claire was deposited in 1981 next to its chamber of commerce building off Highway 51.

Okay, so it isn't made of copper, but it still looks like a penny. It's the world's largest replica, and it was created for a good cause—the Million Penny Parade. Back in the early 1950s, Woodruff's Dr. Kate Newcomb wanted a hospital for the area. When funds ran out for her project, local children started a penny drive. They had been planning to collect a million of something for their math class anyway. A million pennies might not have been enough, but in 1954 Dr. Newcomb was a guest on the TV show *This Is Your Life.* After she told her story, sympathetic viewers from all over the United States sent money, and the funds were raised at last. The ten-foot concrete penny was created to commemorate Dr. Newcomb and the Penny Parade. Its monetary value is unknown, but it weighs 17,452 pounds.

What has to be the world's largest badger or, more accurately, badger's head and claw does not derive from as noble a cause as Woodruff's pennies. The woolly-mammoth–size badger head used to be seen atop a hollow log next to the Badger Country filling station in Birnamwood. When the business changed hands a few years ago and the gas station was converted to a dance club, the badger was lowered to ground level, where it now shills for Badger Country's exotic dancers. A huge squirrel still frolics on the log behind the badger.

Leave it to an institution of higher learning to lay claim to one of

the world's largest letters of the alphabet. It's the letter M, and it's located on County Highway B west of Platteville on a hill that is now part of the University of Wisconsin Pioneer Campus, formerly the Wisconsin Mining School. Not surprisingly, the M stands for "mining," the former school's specialty and at one time a huge local industry. Devised in 1937 by a group of engineering students, the letter has existed for many decades, partly because the annual paint job needed to keep the granite stones visible is the perfect freshman hazing activity. The M measures 214 feet across and 241 feet from top to bottom. There are over 260 steps winding up the hill to the M's crown. Twice a year, at homecoming each fall and for the annual spring M Ball, the M is lit up with kerosene in coffee cans.

Fontana Frog

Just outside Fontana, on Highway 67, stands a giant green frog with a door in its belly. The frog has been a local landmark next to Fontana Outdoor Sports since 1964, when it was part of a miniature-golf course. Fontana used to be known as Frog Hollow because of its marshy location, which made it the perfect home for billions of frogs, and so the fourteen-foot-high green amphibian is still appropriate for its location even though it no longer has to work for a living.

Culvert Man

Resembling a crinkly version of the Tin Man from *The Wizard of Oz,* Culvert Man, on Highway 13 just north of Park Falls, displays all the best metal-fabricating skills of the Koshak Construction Company. And if he ever rusts apart, he can still help reinforce someone's driveway.

World's Last Humpback

Locals call her a humpback, but the S. S. *Meteor* should technically be referred to as a whaleback ship. Permanently berthed on Barker's Island, just off Highway 53 in Superior, the *Meteor* was built in Superior in 1896 and is the last ship of her kind in the world. No question, she does resemble the basic shape and color of a whale. You can tour this humpback's belly—from the pilothouse to the engine room—between May and October.

WORLD'S LARGEST SIX PACK
(22,200 BARRELS OF BEER OR
688,200 GALLONS OF BEER.)
★ **ENOUGH BEER TO FILL 7,340,796 CANS.**
★ **PLACED END TO END THESE CANS WOULD**
RUN 565 MILES.
★ **WOULD PROVIDE ONE PERSON A SIX PACK**
A DAY FOR 3,351 YEARS.

World's Largest Six Pack

The roadside attraction of Homer Simpson's dreams, the World's Largest Six Pack in La Crosse is actually a group of massive storage tanks in the form of giant cans of beer. The "six pack" once held 22,200 barrels of Heileman's Old Style beer. After Heileman's sold the business to City Brewery a few years ago, the giant beer-can tanks were repainted to resemble a six pack of La Crosse Lager. City Brewery gives free tours Monday through Saturday. There is, of course, a gift shop, where you can pick up a portable and potable facsimile of the six pack for about $9. Right across the way, at 1111 South 3rd Street, is another famous La Crosse landmark—the fifteen-foot statue of King Gambrinus, the patron saint of beer. Gambrinus, a knight who probably lived in the thirteenth or fourteenth century, is said to have invented hopped malt beer. Most European breweries feature a statue of Gambrinus, and the tradition continues in a larger-than-life way in La Crosse.

Turkey in Every Way

In southern Wisconsin in the 1970s, there was only one place to go for a really big night on the town. Whether you were a couple of well-scrubbed kids out for a lavish prom feast or Aunt Mabel celebrating her seventieth birthday with a magnificent bash or jaded city dwellers longing for a circular dining room with country views, Hartwig's Gobbler just off I-94 in Johnson Creek filled the bill. The turkey bill, that is. The whole place, according to its brochure, was intended to make you think of its specialty—turkey. The windows were shaped like turkey eyes, and the entrance carpet was woven with bright gobbler designs.

With its circular floor plan, rotating bar, pink-purple interior, and live music every Saturday night, the Gobbler was the area's casbah. People flocked there from Chicago and points beyond and stayed all weekend at the adjacent motel, also round and stuffed with shag and mirrored everything.

Weird Wisconsin experienced the motel only via brochures, but we do remember dining at the restaurant on a few special occasions. You could have turkey just about any way you wanted, but it was the decor that truly struck us: The futuristic roundness of the place combined with its pink, white, and lavender rugs and upholstery made an unforgettable impression—sort of like finding yourself inside a giant peony blossom set in a modern vase. The Gobbler was all about atmosphere; you sensed you'd suddenly been transported to someplace far from small-town Wisconsin.

If the ever-turning bar and luscious colors weren't dizzying enough, diners could climb the purple stairways to the hanging balcony over the bar, known as the Roost or the Royal Roost. With tables

surrounding the Roost's perimeter, the parquet center floor was left free for dancing to the big-band sounds of Jimmy Hartwig's Orchestra. It was the hottest nightspot around.

Sadly, not even the most unusual turkey-centered restaurant can last forever, and after owner Clarence Hartwig died, the place began to fade. The motel has been demolished, but the restaurant is still there. However, it has suffered from a succession of unsuccessful owners, and the turkey eyes have an empty, forlorn look about them these days.

The Gobbler was built in 1966–1967. According to Helmut Ajango, its architect, the turkey resemblance was only coincidental; the Hartwigs simply wanted something unusual. Ajango describes his design as based on the prairie style of architecture, which features low, sloping buildings meant to meld harmoniously with the surrounding landscape. The Gobbler's single story and sinuous curves snuggle into what was once a rolling landscape that is now filled with a large outlet mall and other developments.

Ajango had to deal with unusual design requirements inside the building, including the rotating bar. "Normally, you don't find that done in a one-story building," he said. "We didn't know for sure how fast to go. We started with one rotation every forty minutes; then we geared it down to once every hour and twenty minutes, which is reasonable. You don't even notice." There was one problem with

"My mom and my dad just both liked the color pink," explained Clarence Junior.

the rotating bar: Once it started, the bartender couldn't get out until the bar swung around so that its gate lined up with the doorway again, eighty minutes later.

According to Clarence Hartwig, Jr., one of two Hartwig children still living in Wisconsin, his parents had very specific ideas concerning the restaurant's decor. The interior color choices, including the color of the turkey carpet, were made by Mrs. Hartwig and her interior decorator. The 1970s pink shag carpet was used wherever a suitable surface arose. "My mom and my dad just both liked the color pink," explained Clarence Junior. "Some people like green. Some like blue. They liked pink. My dad had a pink Lincoln Continental too."

This 1970s kitsch will forever shine a frothy pink and white in the memories of those who knew the place in its heyday, whether the building finds a new use or not. As Clarence Hartwig, Jr., said, "As far as we're concerned, it doesn't really matter. It's history."

rine for Something Big

The name Glarner Stube means "the Living Room of New Glarus." But based on its most popular asset, this New Glarus bar and restaurant should probably be called something that translates as "Bathroom of New Glarus." Locals flock to the Glarner Stube for its delicious cheese fondues, but it has achieved fame elsewhere as the home of the world's largest urinal. Measuring forty-two inches in height, twenty-five inches across, and sixteen inches in depth, the urinal isn't exactly gargantuan, but it's still pretty big for a urinal. Over the years, owner Debbie Anderegg heard so many customers come out muttering that this was the biggest urinal they'd ever seen that she finally decided to have postcards made and give it a title. "We only call it the Midwest's Largest Urinal," she cautioned. "We don't really claim to be global."

And she doesn't know how or why the supersized piece of porcelain came to be in her establishment. It has no brand on it. "I think it was put in when the building was built in 1901," she said. "Probably someone just got a good buy on a big urinal." Over the years, the building has housed a cigar maker, a pool hall, a blacksmith shop, and a phone company, so it wasn't necessarily installed as a commodious receptacle for beer-swilling patrons. However it got there, though, it's the pride of New Glarus, and Anderegg rests secure knowing her men's room can handle whatever comes its way.

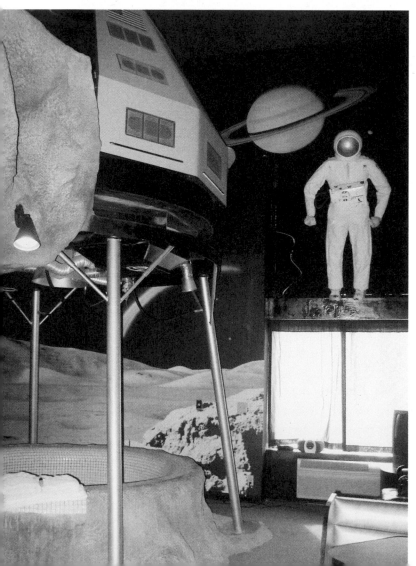

Don Q Inn

It used to be marked by a sixty-seven-foot-high tower of four hundred wagon wheels welded together into one huge, shining "tree." The tree tower grew over the years, as customers provided wagon wheels in exchange for free drinks. Alas, the wagon tree no longer stands, but you can't miss the Don Q Inn near Dodgeville. It has to be the only resort in the country with a Boeing 377 Stratofreighter—the onetime mainstay of the Strategic Air Command airborne refueling program—serving as its highway sign. Once the largest plane in the world, it's still big enough to catch the traveler's eye from State Road 23.

The Boeing 377 is only the beginning of the strangeness that is the Don Q Inn. Opened by the enterprising Don Quinn in a barn he had purchased from a local farm family in 1964, the resort is probably now best known for its exotic FantaSuites, where adventurous guests can sleep in everything from a real hot-air-balloon gondola to a bed in a tree house. If these two settings don't appeal to you, you can snooze the night away in a simulated lunar landing module tucked high up near the ceiling of a two-story room, with a suited astronaut leering down at you from above the window. There's also a Jungle Safari room, with a thatched hut, and a popular den called Mid-Evil that you may not want to write home about. Free tours of unoccupied FantaSuites are given daily at three p.m.

These fantasy rooms didn't come about until 1979, after Quinn had sold the place to Roger Dehring of Minnesota. What Quinn had already done, however, was far more inventive than the suites. Quinn was an uber-salvage-meister, and he started adding local history to the Don Q in 1972, when he bought a steeple from an 1872 Methodist church in Dodgeville and turned it into a two-story love nest. He had already nabbed a real train station from the Chicago and Northwestern Railroad and converted it into eight sleeping rooms. The resort's oak entrance pillars came from a church in Peoria, and the big wooden entrance doors once graced the same Methodist church as the steeple. Another set of doors—these in solid brass—formerly guarded Madison's First Wisconsin Bank. Many of the lobby's ceiling rafters come from the Schick Army Hospital in Clinton, Iowa, while other lumber made its way north from the Douglas Aircraft plant in Chicago.

Not content with just plain mortar in his hotel, Quinn studded all suitable areas with old tools and implements, along with as many Model-T Ford parts as he could acquire. The main lounge cossets its loungers in fifteen barber chairs and one—shudder—dentist's chair. Quinn found most of these chairs in Fennimore, but he acquired two of them from the prison barbershop at Iowa's Anamosa State Penitentiary.

Don Quinn died in 1988, but the new owners have kept their word to maintain the eccentric structures and furnishings the way Quinn had intended. Today, only one of Quinn's dreams remains unfulfilled. His original idea was to mount the Stratofreighter on tall supports so that it would seem to hang above the resort's parking lot. He had also envisioned a ramp that would extend from the inn's restaurant into the Boeing's tail, where a coffee shop would be located. But even without having the Stratofreighter hovering above it, the Don Q Inn is still way over the top.

Unexplained Phenomena

Showers of worms, angel hair, and plummeting blue ice;
bolts from the sky and 188-year-old coin finds; aliens bearing
pancakes and people who glow with a misty white light; meteorites
crashing through Geo Metro windshields; crop and tree circles;
swirling black shadows alive with menace—Wisconsin offers all
these and plenty of other enigmas besides. We are blessed with a
plethora of unexplained phenomena. How many states can boast
three UFO capitals of the world?

Of course, some experiences just defy explanation.
We're often asked, Why is Wisconsin so weird?
Read on and find out.

Things Falling from the Sky

Angel Hair from the Heavens

In Wausau, at five forty-five p.m. on October 17, 1983, a pleasant partly cloudy day, eighteen-year-old Todd Roll was sitting in his living room, enjoying a book, *Mysteries of the Unexplained,* a Reader's Digest tome about weird phenomena. Roll was reading about a stringy white substance that sometimes falls out of the sky. This substance even had a cool name—angel hair. Weird, he thought. What would falling angel hair look like?

He looked up from his book and out the window. Remembering the scene, he said, "I looked out the front window, and I saw these big blobby strands of white, stringy stuff falling out of the sky." It was just like in the book!

Startled, he ran outside to discover that the strange substance was falling everywhere—on his entire block and in the park across the street. Clumping in globs and sticky to the touch, the stuff was blanketing lawns and draped over houses and power lines; garlands of it were hanging from trees. Seven or eight other people were outside, watching the blobby shreds fall. Roll scooped up a sample, sealed it in a plastic bag, and took photographs. He still has the sample, over twenty years later.

At the time, there were no planes flying overhead. A short while later, the material, which was as evanescent as its name, evaporated from the neighborhood and was no more.

By way of contrast, on Thursday, October 27, 1881, Milwaukee's *Evening Wisconsin* carried a story headlined NOT MANNA, BUT SPIDER WEBS. A STRANGE SHOWER ALONG THE LAKE SHORE IN MILWAUKEE AND ELSEWHERE. NO ONE CAN SATISFACTORILY ACCOUNT FOR THE PHENOMENON. THE TEXTURE OF THE WEBS UNUSUALLY FIRM.

There is no discounting . . . that the fall was as genuine as was the fabric of the webs . . . brushed from the clothes of one party who witnessed it and was impressed with the sight, but failing, like all others, to give any satisfactory reason for the phenomenon. The webs seemed to come from over the lake and could be seen a distance of fifty feet, filling the air as they were gently wafted to and fro. They apparently came from the upper air strata. . . . The fall . . . continued for some time, the webs varying . . . from two feet to several rods. . . . Milwaukee was not the only city in which this strange shower was observed. . . . At Green Bay the fall was the same, coming from the direction of the bay, only the webs varied from sixty feet . . . to mere specks and were seen as far up in the air as . . . the eye could reach. At Vesburg . . . Ft. Howard, Sheboygan and Ozaukee, the fall was similar . . . in some places being so thick as to annoy the eye. In all instances the webs were strong in texture and very white.

Worm Shower

Things fall from Wisconsin's skies with alarming regularity. Most of us are familiar with rain, hail, snow, and the various incarnations of water. However, some falling objects don't conform to usual expectations and are totally unpredictable.

If you were lucky enough to live in Palmyra in 1897, you would have seen this headline in the *Enterprise* newspaper on Thursday, April 29: A SHOWER OF WORMS. Early risers several days before, on Friday, April 23, had found the ground beneath their feet covered with worms. They were everywhere—crawling in the dirt, crawling in tubs set out to catch rainwater, crawling in pans full of chicken and animal feed. According to the *Enterprise,* "The worms on examination proved to differ from our native angle worm, and Captain McDonald, an expert fisherman as well as gardener, declared them to be 'gilt-edged, so named because of yellow or golden spots or yellow rings on the end of the worm.' "

McDonald claimed expertise because he had used the same exact worms to catch trout in Ireland. The newspaper article continued: "The question arises, where did they come from? Did they drift in a cloud across the deep blue sea?"

Alas, no one responded to this inquiry. The mystery of the worms' origin was never solved, and within a short time they had all disappeared into the earth.

Flying Fish

In late 1972, eighty-year-old Richard Hagstrom of Zig Zag, Oregon, wrote to *Dear Abby:* "I had a farm three miles from Ashland, Wisconsin. A storm broke suddenly, and afterwards I saw tiny little fish in the cow tracks around our barn." Hagstrom assumed the fish had fallen from the sky.

Thirty years later, on Tuesday, November 5, 2002, at seven p.m., a Combined Locks woman and her son were unloading their car after grocery shopping, when the woman noticed something in the driveway. It was a fish. Odd, she thought. There were no marks on it. It was fully intact, and weirder still, it was fresh, though the woman lived a quarter mile uphill from the Fox River. She found another fish on her front step. Both fish were silver shiners, some five inches long. She idly wondered if some birds had dropped them.

After they finished unloading the car, the woman and her son went out with flashlights to search for more fish. In a short time, they discovered five more: three scattered in the front yard, one on the neighbor's drive, and one on the back lawn. The next day, during daylight, the woman discovered three more fish on her roof and another two on her lawn! This incredible incident received coverage in the prestigious journal *Scientific American.*

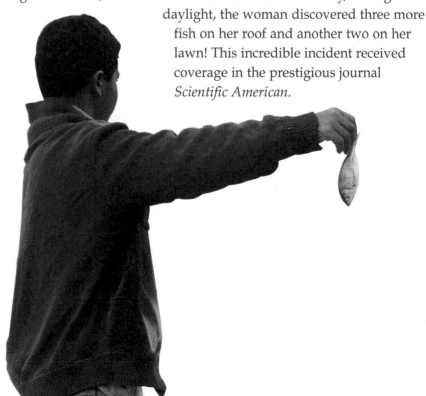

Unexpected Space Junk

Reports of fiery flying saucers were called in from across northern Wisconsin on the night of September 4, 1962, predominantly from Eagle River, Tomahawk, and Merrill. The next morning, at five forty-five, two police officers on patrol in Manitowoc found a chunk of metal on North Eighth Street. The officers initially ignored it, thinking it was a piece of crumpled cardboard. But an hour later, the object was still there, and at that point they realized it was metal. Since it was too hot to touch, they kicked it to the side of the road and waited for it to cool down.

The object turned out to be a twenty-pound piece of Russia's Sputnik IV spacecraft, which had broken up over northern Wisconsin. During the next few days, treasure hunters and homeowners found pieces of the craft in Mishicot, Two Rivers, Wittenberg, West Bend, and various places around Manitowoc, including the Lake Michigan shoreline and the roof of a Lutheran church.

In October, the city of Manitowoc got into a tug-of-war with the U.S. State Department, the Smithsonian Institution, the Soviet authorities, and, most inexplicably, Mayor Henry Maier of Milwaukee for ownership rights to this metal space junk. But in a peculiar twist of fate, a minor contretemps that later came to be known as the Cuban Missile Crisis intervened, and the fracas dissipated. The Sputnik junk was eventually returned to the Soviets, but today, you can view a realistic replica of it at the Rahr-West Art Museum in Manitowoc. Also, for the price of admission, it can be viewed at the Tommy Bartlett Exploratory display. Times do change!

Red-Hot Metal Chunks

On Wednesday, August 21, 1974, a sixty-five-pound chunk of hot metal came to rest near the home of William B. Murray, thirty-three, of 5972 North Eighty-fourth Street, Milwaukee. The object first punched a hole in the street at the intersection of North Eighty-fourth and Florist Avenue. It then ricocheted off the pavement, bore a second hole in the tarmac, and bounced over a four-foot fence to make a large hole one foot deep in the earth. But it still wasn't finished! It rebounded out of the hole, hitting the Murray home and popping a hole through the aluminum siding before finally coming to a halt near the children's swing set.

When the police first looked at this bounding chunk of metal, they thought it looked man-made. It was two hours before the metal had cooled down enough for the police to handle it. They explained away the incident, saying the sixty-five-pound chunk of overheated metal had been shot out of a metal shredder and through the roof of the Wisconsin Metal & Chemical Corporation, which was next door to the Murray house. It is up to you whether you believe a superpowered can crusher is able to heat metal like this, launch it with incredible energy, and inflict so much damage.

Meteorite Back at Ya

Luckily for Rick Wirth of Clayton, the rock that had crashed through his Geo Metro's windshield on Monday, October 21, 1996, did so when the car was sitting empty in his driveway. It was no ordinary rock, as subsequent tests revealed. The rock proved to be a chunk of meteorite over 4.5 billion years old that had not burned up upon entering the earth's atmosphere. The meteorite split in two on impact. The two pieces together weighed three ounces and were two inches long, with a gray interior and an ash-black exterior.

Red Snow and Blue Ice

According to reports at the time, red snow fell across Wisconsin on February 5, 1875. Then a little more than a quarter of a century later, on December 16, 2003, a reddish-brown mud rained down across much of the Greater Milwaukee area. This turned out to be dust carried in from New Mexico.

On Monday afternoon, January 29, 1973, Herbert Krug, eighteen, of Route 1 in Vesper witnessed a ball of blue ice weighing fifteen to twenty pounds crash into a field about two hundred yards away from him. It shattered, leaving a fifty-foot debris field surrounding a one-foot-wide depression in the frozen earth. Speculation over the blue ball caused a media sensation across the country. "I haven't been getting any sleep in the last two days," Krug told reporters as people called him from California and New York to discuss his find. An analysis of the blue ice conducted at St. Joseph's Hospital in Marshfield revealed that the ball contained urine and disinfectant—most likely waste from a commercial airliner. However, Federal Aviation Administration officials dismissed this idea, saying that they had never heard of airline waste falling from the sky. Besides, Krug's farm was outside the usual flight paths, and subsequent investigation found that no airplanes had been in that area at the time. Interestingly, officials at the North American Air Defense Command in Colorado Springs requested information about the sample's analysis.

A similar dark blue icy glob landed near the Ron LaGran residence just west of Spring Valley on May 19, 1984. According to LaGran, "We were in the yard, taking pictures and getting ready to go to graduation when it seemed like it was the Fourth of July. We heard a whistle and a bang, and whatever it was hit the ditch, breaking into pieces. It came down fast and made an indentation in the ground. If it had hit somebody, it would have killed them."

Bolt from the Blue

In August 1976, eight-year-old Michael Kiolbasse of Milwaukee was one lucky kid. One day, after a lightning storm, Michael was playing in his backyard when he found a coin next to a hole three or four inches in diameter and some six inches deep. The hole was a few feet away from a large tree, which had suffered wind damage during the storm. Michael went running to his father, Henry, shouting, "Daddy, look what I found!"

Henry Kiolbasse rubbed away the dirt to reveal an oversized copper penny in pristine condition. It had been minted in the Massachusetts Commonwealth back in 1788, some 188 years before. Appraisers estimated the coin's value at between $50 and $100. What made the discovery unusual is that Henry Kiolbasse believed that lightning had struck the coin and unearthed it. "There was a hole, and we figured lightning made the hole. I think the coin attracted the lightning. You have to accept the story or reject it. Believe me, it's true. I'm not about to make something up. I'm not that type of person."

The discovery had the family digging for other coins in the backyard, but no more were ever found.

The Black Swirling Thing in the Basement

I am a twenty-eight-year-old Waukesha woman who has been immersed in the study of spirituality for ten years. I have a B.A. from Carrol College in religious studies, with a minor in psychology. Currently, I'm going for an M.Div. Obviously, I am very familiar with various spiritual claims, am educated in diverse religious practices, and know how the psyche interprets such experiences. However, I am left agreeing with the theological view of atheism. I shall not go into why, except to say that I find no empirical evidence to prove otherwise.

Nonetheless, like most, I still have theistic longings. I chalk this up to desire for survival beyond my own death. But I don't often discuss metaphysical topics, because this makes me feel hypocritical. And I don't often reveal the incident I experienced a few short years ago. It's paramount that you understand I don't believe in the supernatural. It's equally paramount you understand that I am simultaneously compelled, repelled, and embarrassed by this incident.

Two years ago, I resided in an apartment building on 900 Scott Street in Waukesha. I lived there for quite some time with no incident. Occasionally I'd hear footsteps but attributed them to the fact that it was a sixteen-unit building. I often felt nervous in the apartment when alone, but again, I explained it away with logic.

Though I chalked up those feelings to normal existence, in truth my foreboding was caused by something else. I was sick in that apartment quite often, something rare for me. I figured it could have been the nearby city dump, yet I'm still close to it and don't have that sense today. Something was odd about the building. Even today I can't articulate a reason for that odd feeling.

Regardless, what is at issue is what I experienced physically. There were coin-op laundry machines in the basement. One night, I went to retrieve my basket of newly dried clothes, then made my way to the staircase to walk up. The staircase jutted into the center of the floor. There were deep recesses (at least fifteen feet long) on either side that were lined with storage areas. Both sides lacked proper lighting, so my focal point was the stairs. I noted both sides were dark, but paid no real mind, because I was used to the setup.

In the recesses, you could see the first ten feet, but beyond that it was dark. As I made my way toward the stairs, it seemed that the dark recess in the right corner actually moved towards me. This darkness instantly filled up the entire corner running along the staircase. A part of it even flowed into the room, covering over my right extended arm that held my laundry basket.

I froze. I thought my eyes were surely playing a trick on me. My first instinct was, "Stop, analyze, check your senses, this is normal." That is what I did.

I stopped, blinked, and looked down towards my arm. I could see my hand, my chest, yet this blackness lay across my forearm.

I stopped, blinked, and looked down towards my arm. I could see my hand, my chest, yet this blackness lay across my forearm. I remember thinking, "It's your eyes," so I looked at my other arm but could see everything clearly. I looked back at the right arm, saw the blackness again. Suddenly overcome by an overwhelming dread, I screamed like I never have before. I stood there, shrieking at the top of my lungs because I felt as if I couldn't move. Then suddenly, the darkness retreated from my arm, swirling instantly backwards into the corner. I took off up the stairs, dropping laundry everywhere in my haste.

The next couple days I refused to retrieve my laundry. I was frightened of the basement, but I was

simultaneously berating myself: "What kind of atheist are you? You had tunnel vision. No, I could see clearly on the other side of me." Back and forth I fought with myself, trying to make logical sense of my experience.

On the third day after the incident, the apartment manager came to visit and asked if I was going to get my laundry. I said something in the basement freaked me out; I didn't want to go down there. She asked if she could come in. She sat at my kitchen table, looked me straight in the eye, and asked, "The black thing?"

I just about wet my pants. I refused to answer. I made her draw the story out of me. Every few minutes, I interjected, "This was just my imagination, right? I mean come on, I don't believe in this stuff." Yet as I proclaimed my disbelief, I found myself getting more and more confused. Here was the manager telling me she had experienced the same thing. Our feelings, the

Suddenly overcome by an overwhelming dread, I screamed like I never have before. I stood there, shrieking at the top of my lungs because I felt as if I couldn't move.

way the black thing looked, the way it moved, were the same. She told me that we weren't the only ones—an upstairs neighbor saw it too.

Ever since that night, I felt VERY uncomfortable in that building. Just walking past the stairs made me physically ill. It wasn't just the memory of it, for I have had bad experiences before. I know what psychosomatic feelings are. I felt physically ill, bordering on dry heaves, with a sense of portentous omen and, simultaneously, a sense of extreme curiosity about what it was. I didn't even feel that these were my real feelings, but that they were being intruded upon me.

I moved out several months later, not just because of the event, but because I got into a spat with the manager. Regardless, something weird happened in that basement, and I want it explained. I have considered everything, from it being a hallucination or illusion caused by the gases from the dump to tunnel vision and more. Nothing resolves my confusion.—*Charlotte*

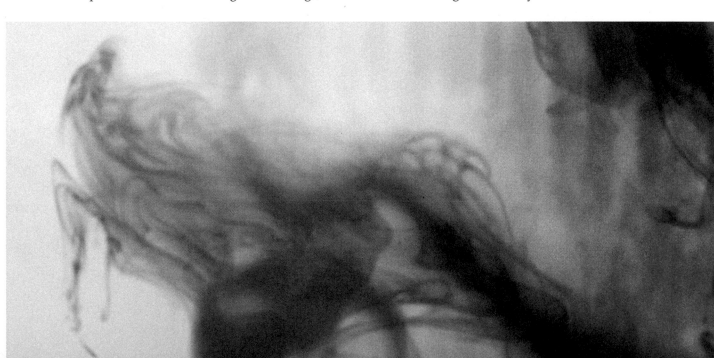

Orange Ghost Ball

April in northern Wisconsin is when the snow gods finally, reluctantly, and slowly retreat from the frozen marshes and piney woods. It's when hardy northerners like to get out, take a walk, and remind themselves what it's like not to have to trudge through ten-foot snowdrifts just to get to the mailbox.

It was early April in 1938 when farm lad Alven Marcott, enjoying the clean spring air, strolled home past the old Forest Home Cemetery just east of tiny Fifield, on Old Highway 70. As he passed the cemetery grounds studded with tall pines, he was startled to see what looked like an orange ball of fire about two feet in diameter descend from the trees and hover a few feet off the ground. To his amazement, the ball then traveled down a lane to a nearby farm, circled the barn, and returned to the cemetery, where it disappeared. Of course, no one believed the startled Alven—until his father, Arthur, saw it, too.

One night a few months later, Alven and a friend named Peter Jeneyick were driving past the cemetery when the orange ball rolled across the road forty feet in front of them. Alven's uncle Leonard was the next to catch sight of the mysterious globe. Word soon got out.

Soon the cemetery became the secret nighttime destination of most of the town's high school students, as teenagers heady with spring fever rendezvoused to try their own luck at spotting the light. A local newspaper reported on April 14, 1938, that Ida Koshak, Sally Bennett, and Camilla LaVoie saw the orange ball at nine p.m. as they waited by the front gate of the cemetery. The girls told a local reporter that the ball was about as big as a billiard ball and that it floated to within five feet of them, "rolling all around."

The girls ran back to the village in fright, but eventually they wound up returning to the cemetery many times. Ida Koshak, now in her eighties, recalled the incidents

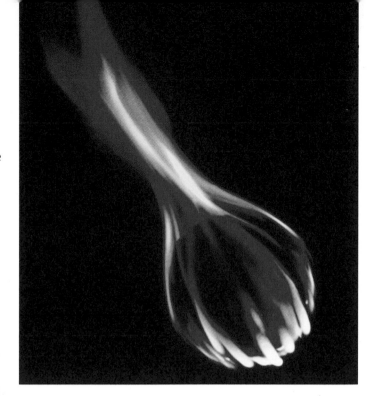

clearly in a recent phone conversation: "I was sixteen. We seen it more than once, maybe three, four times. We'd walk up there on the hill. It went right in the middle of the main road of the cemetery; it kind of danced around, went up, down, up, down. We looked forward to sneaking away and doing that. There were other kids that said they seen it, too, maybe a dozen."

Eventually that summer of 1938 the light stopped appearing. Koshak said the nonbelievers in the village charged that someone was sitting in one of the trees with a flashlight, but that wouldn't explain how the light could be seen rolling across a road or flying around a barn. It also seems unlikely that, with so many groups of teens, not to mention curious out-of-towners roaming around the cemetery, anyone could have sat in one of the pine trees for so many nights without being seen or caught. Among the theories offered by town scoffers to explain the orange light were that it was Saint Elmo's fire or luminous natural gas. But Ida Koshak knows what she saw, and sixty-six years later, she's sticking to her story.

Hairy Flying Saucer Pilot?

William L. Bosak was returning home from a Frederic Farmers Co-op Exchange meeting on a rapidly cooling night in 1974. It was December 2, and he was driving slower than usual because of unusual patches of fog on Highway W, some six miles east of Frederic. Light snow covered the ground. It was ten-thirty. Less than a mile from home, he received the fright of his life—his headlights illuminated a strange disc-shaped contraption sitting amid swirling fog in the westbound lane.

It had a curved front of glass, and inside I could see a figure with its arms raised above its head. The figure had a square face with hair sticking straight out from the sides of its head. Its ears were long and narrow and stuck straight out. Its arms were brown and furry, and there was fur or hair on the top part of its body. It looked a good deal like a man, but it had a different-looking face than you'd see. It had a kind of cow-looking face.

I couldn't tell if the figure was wearing a tight fur suit or had fur itself. I only could see the top half of the body, but the figure appeared to be a little taller than a tall man. The eyes were very large and protruding, and it seemed to me to be afraid. But it wasn't nearly half as scared as I was.

I was so gol-darned scared, I was afraid to go out at night for a few days. I'm over the shock now, but I was pretty shook up for a couple of weeks. I wish I had had somebody with me in the car. When you see something like that and you're all by yourself, you don't know what to do. What would anyone else do in a situation like that?

A good question! Bosak didn't talk about his experience until a month and a half later and then only "so that anybody else who sees something like what I saw will maybe know what to do and maybe even try to communicate with it."

In one of those spooky twists of fate, Bosak was found dead in his home at the age of ninety on December 2, 1996—exactly twenty-two years to the day of his strange encounter on that foggy winter night. As his obit noted, he "was a man who was very concerned about the future of his country and he tried to make a difference." He remained a prolific letter writer to his final days, when he kidded that President Clinton "probably had his name on a crackpot list."

UFO Daze and Flying Saucer Capitals Galore

UFO sightings are so numerous in Wisconsin that there are three different towns battling over the title of "UFO capital of Wisconsin." This can get a little confusing for space pilgrims seeking the ET experience.

Each of the would-be capitals claims the honor of alien visitation. Elmwood, in Pierce County, got started in 1975, when a local police officer observed a ball of fire as large as a football field over the town quarry. Belleville, on the southern edge of Dane County, also caught saucer fever after a police report came in about an object flashing red, white, and blue overhead in January 1987. Dundee, on Highway 67 in Fond du Lac County, officially entered the UFO capital trifecta with the first UFO Daze festival in 1991, but the area had a long tradition of weirdness to build upon. Nearby Dundee Hill was called Spirit Hill by Native Americans, says Bill Benson, owner of Benson's Holiday Hideaway tavern and host of the annual festival.

"We also had a sort of crop circle in '47 or '48 on the Jersey Flats, five or six miles southeast of here," he says. "My mother's cousin owned the property, and people saw a big ship come down there and take off again. In '89, a farmer east of us, on Vista Drive, saw a ship hovering to the southeast of his barn. A couple I know very well watched it, too, from the road. They said it was circle-shaped and had windows."

Then there was Benson's neighbor, a man in his eighties, who said he saw a UFO hovering over nearby Long Lake in 1959. He claimed it lit the water so clearly that he could see right to the bottom of the lake. "People have seen lights zipping up and down under the ice in the winter, too," adds Benson, who used to be called Martian Bill around town. "I think we have these [sightings] either because of the water, the way the magnetic energies are under the earth, or both."

As further evidence that this area has long been recognized as a place for spectral happenings, Benson tells of a farmer four miles south of Dundee who has an ancient formation of large red stones in one of his fields that archaeologists say had been set up to mark the solstices. And early settlers from Ireland used to insist that the Dundee area, located in what is now the Kettle Moraine State Forest, was inhabited by "little people," much like the leprechauns they'd left behind in their homeland. Long Lake was even said to be home to a forty-five-foot lake monster.

But the biggest boost to Dundee's UFO heritage has probably been UFO Bob, a retired landscape architect otherwise known as Bob Kuehne. Kuehne, seventy-three, claims to have undergone repeated alien abductions and says he frequently works with ETs on various projects, such as preventing the Y2K disaster. He hosts his own Fond du Lac radio show called—you guessed it—*UFO Bob*. And he was one of the featured guests at the 2004 UFO Daze seminar.

Speaking to a packed room in the back of Benson's tavern, UFO Bob held the rapt attention of the crowd of fifty or more, some of whom wore headbands sporting boingy antennae with silver balls on the ends. He had made a special request to the aliens to show up that night, he told the audience, and they told him they would. "They want recognition—I know that," said UFO Bob. "So take your flashlights outside tonight and shine them around at the sky."

The alien Bob talks to most is a female named Eve. "And an angel whose name is Max," he adds. "Angels and ETs don't hit it off that great. One woman met an ET, and she also had an angel. She asked the angel if the ETs would help us, and the angel said that remains to be seen."

Bob also sees other creatures besides aliens and angels.

He noted that about a week before the festival, while visiting his former hometown of Lomira, he had observed a two-foot chupacabra hanging onto a horse's neck, drawing blood. "They are more humanoid than animal," he declared. He also related the slightly more comforting news that "ETs are not going to let a big terrorist attack happen again. If anyone is running around with a suitcase bomb, their mind will just go bonkers."

While UFO Bob galvanized his audience in the back room of the tavern on that warm July day, an equal number of people sat at tables outside, chowing down on hamburgers served up by the local Lions Club and exchanging their own UFO stories. A tent had been set up nearby specifically for those wanting to share their personal experiences. Noah Voss, owner and CEO of GetGhostGear.com and UFOwisconsin.com, did a brisk business selling T-shirt, books, and raffle tickets. The prize

was an electromagnetic detection device designed for ghost inspections.

Meanwhile, inside Benson's, a third contingent filled the bar, taking time to examine the blend of alien- and fishing-themed decor, as well as the many framed photos and drawings of different types of aliens and spaceships. A few of the patrons were nervous about the future of the festival because Benson's tavern is for sale. However, Bill Benson, whose family also owns the state's oldest campground nearby, is hoping that whoever buys the bar will continue with the annual tradition.

He admits that even if they don't, people would still come. That's because the aliens seem to show up on cue over Long Lake. The faithful arrive with lawn chairs and cameras and sit outside long after dark, waiting to catch some ET action overhead. Many also observe local tradition, bringing boxes of aluminum foil, from which they create

Hershey's Kiss–style hats to prevent the aliens from reading their minds. Dave Pait of Fond du Lac and Greg and Dee Calvey of Armstrong had their brains protected by eight p.m. for the UFO Daze event.

Over the years, attendees have been well rewarded with interplanetary flyovers. It happened again in 2002, when a string of enigmatic lights appeared directly over the lake and were captured on several home videotapes. The following year was a washout, but in 2004, UFO Bob proved that he still had some pull with the space invaders. They showed up at about eleven-thirty p.m., said Bill Benson, not too long after UFO Bob—as well as *Weird Wisconsin*—had unfortunately given up and gone home. "A big something came over the lake with a whole bunch of lights on it," Benson said. "I have it on video. You could see

the star lights right through it. It was about seventy-five to a hundred feet wide and fifty to seventy-five feet long."

But thanks to the other two would-be UFO capitals of Wisconsin, the year's ET excitement wasn't completely over. The true enthusiasts could still visit Elmwood's festival on the third weekend in July and then stay on a few more months until the Halloween weekend blowout in Belleville.

Benson's tavern has an advantage, however, in being open—literally and figuratively—to UFO seekers all year round. Benson, who admits to having had a "missing time" experience that may mean he was beamed up somewhere between Plymouth and Kiel, is always ready to talk UFO turkey with interested customers. And he keeps well abreast of whatever is happening in the skies around Dundee. "There was a sighting on Artesian Road three weeks ago," he said. "A lot of people have seen things, but most won't divulge this unless they know you understand strange things."

Bizarre Beasts

If there is one animal synonymous with the Dairy State, it would be the placid cow, chewing her cud in front of a carnelian-hued barn. White-and-black-spotted Holstein hide is the state's proudest design cliché, daubed on countless souvenirs, from salt and pepper shakers to baseball caps. But as any dairy farmer knows, old bossy can kick when she wants to. And Wisconsin has a second nickname—the Badger State, after a down-and-dirty carnivore that not only claws tunnels reminiscent of early lead-mining shafts, but whose snarl can scare a junkyard Rottweiler.

True, this state-animal dichotomy may make Wisconsinites seem conflicted, but it's only a symptom of the deep truth understood by everyone who lives in this region of wildly varied terrain: There is, within the state, a menacing menagerie beyond bovine and badger—a freakish zoo that inhabits the outskirts of civilized places. Its denizens are everywhere, sometimes as shadow, sometimes as flesh. They skulk and lurk and hunker on prairie and on rock cliffs, along lakeshores and in deep piney woods, even in the dark alleyways of our cities. Traditional biologists would be hard-pressed to define many of these bizarre critters: small, hairless entities that pop out of the bushes, a glimmer of blue brushing past a trail hiker, or—on the opposite end of the spectrum—brown, furry, manlike things that walk, run, and leap with Olympic agility past fear-stricken roadside observers, then disappear in the blink of an eye into cornfields and forests. Not bears, not wolves, these scary pelted things leave footprints and return our curiosity with their own fearless stares. Wisconsin has even become world-famous for a Wolfman doppelganger—the Beast of Bray Road.

Some of the participants in the bestial parade might have lived here long before mankind; others might just be passing through. In fact, it's been suggested that southeastern Wisconsin is a "window" area, a place where it's possible for beings from other worlds to enter and exit at will.

In the pages that follow, we'll dissect some of these weird creatures as best we can without benefit of pickled laboratory specimens or DNA fur analysis. In most cases, eyewitness descriptions will have to suffice. At the very least, you'll never again look at a cow without imagining what beastie might be skulking behind her picturesque barn and without pondering just why it is that barns in Wisconsin are painted the color of blood.

Creature Miscellany

Hairless Creature Attacks Dog

In March 1992, the family beagle's barking drew the attention of Ed Hora and his nineteen-year-old son, Brian, as they were feeding cattle on their Hillsboro farm. Suddenly they saw a bizarre hairless little beast—two feet long, with a nine-inch tail—jump out of a pile of hay bales and attack the beagle. Ed beat the creature off with a metal pipe as it was about to kill the dog. Experts from the Department of Natural Resources later insisted that the creature was simply a raccoon the Horas had mistaken for something else, but these longtime farmers remained dubious.

Lodi's Blue Mystery Thing

The Ice Age Trail snakes through Wisconsin from Green Bay south to Janesville, then north again to Adams and Langlade counties, before ending in Polk. The trail can be accessed in many spots along its six-hundred-mile length.

One access point is on Riddle Road, near Lodi. On August 22, 1999, a Madison resident named Michelle was hiking back to her car through woods near the Lodi Cannery. Ahead on the trail some fifty feet away a quick blue flash with a hint of gray caught her eye.

A bike rider, she thought, even though the trail was off-limits to bicycles. Angry, she moved aside, ready to shout at the cyclist when he passed. He was gliding along so smoothly, she couldn't imagine anything but a cyclist.

Suddenly the gliding blue thing made a hard forty-five-degree turn to Michelle's right, angling off into a dense stand of trees and vanishing into the thicket. Behind it, a long blue plume wafted from its head. Was it a scarf, feathers, or hair? Michelle couldn't tell. One thing was for sure, though—it was no bike. But whether an animal, a spirit, a wraith, or something far stranger, she could never decide.

Highway 13's Reptile Man

It's highly appropriate that Highway 13 originates in the Wisconsin Dells, that notorious locus of weirdness. From there, Highway 13 runs mostly due north, through the heart of Wisconsin, before terminating in Ashland. Along its route, superstitious types are likely to have any number of twilight-zone encounters—from various sightings of Bigfoot to an encounter with a reptile man.

One day, in the mid-1990s, a Department of Natural Resources warden was driving south of Medford when he saw a figure standing in the road. He slowed down. Staring back at him was a shiny, green-scaled, man-size figure—a reptile man.

As the warden got closer, wings suddenly snapped out from behind the creature's back. The creature zoomed straight up and over the warden's vehicle and landed on the road behind him.

A short while later, a group of highway workers in a truck were heading south from Medford along Highway 13. Something was in the road ahead—green, shiny, scaly. They slowed. It was a reptile man—the same or another, who knows? Wings shot from behind its back. It went vertical and flew off into the trees.

Mauston Birdman

In 1980, I was ten years old. We lived in the country, on the side of a bluff five miles west of Mauston on Highway 82. It was a very isolated place, with lots of trees surrounding the house. My grandparents lived in a trailer right next to our house. One day my grandma started screaming. We went to see what was going on. She was hysterical, screaming about a "birdman" looking at her through the window. She got up to see that there was this tall birdman looking in at her. It was six feet tall, covered with yellowish feathers, with a very long beak.

It had the body of a man, complete with arms and legs—very human-looking. Its feathers were yellowish, big and round, not long and skinny, like on most birds. They covered its body. The feet were just like bird feet except that they were really big and thick, with claws on the toes. Its head was a huge bird head, covered with feathers, like on the body, with a long yellow beak. The head came right out of its shoulders.

A few years before that, my sister insisted that "Big Bird" came to visit us one night. She said he took us outside and showed us all kinds of neat stuff and played with us. Then the next morning, we went outside and found big yellow feathers. I don't remember ever seeing or playing with Big Bird in the middle of the night or ever finding any big yellow feathers. My sister talked about it for a year, insisting that it happened. Then she just never talked about it anymore.

We never heard of any other birdman sightings. I searched the bluff for years looking for anything that could possibly be connected to it, but I never found anything out of the ordinary.—*Spooky Robinson*

Big Hairy Ape-Man of Rome

This happened in the town of Rome in northern Adams County. We were traveling down Apache Road between Highway 13 and 8th Avenue, as we do often, trying to catch frogs and salamanders for fun. I said, "Hey, looks like someone is doing cartwheels across the road." I slowed down. Then we realized that the person doing cartwheels was under the arms of a larger person covered in black fur.

At first we laughed and thought, good prank, since it is near a lot of houses, not some remote spooky place. Then suddenly it hit us both how big the hairy guy was. I tromped on the gas, and we sped away.

No children have been reported missing, so I don't believe it was abduction.

It happened so quickly, there was no time to make a good description other than an ape suit. The hairy guy ran quickly into the woods without looking back, so we could not see the face, which would have made it easier to tell if it were an ape costume, since they have that plastic that looks fake. But without a flashlight, how could a guy run around in a clumsy ape suit through brush, tall weeds and trees? Again, it was so quick, it is hard to really say what was going on. Also, unlike other Bigfoot reports, this seemed to be totally black and afraid of the truck.—*R. W. Wolff*

Brookfield Thunderbird

It was late afternoon on September 21, 1988. Twenty-five-year-old Kevin W. was staring out a bay window on an upper floor of Brookfield's Elmbrook Memorial Hospital. He was alone, pacing, waiting for his wife to give birth to the couple's first child.

The hospital sits high on a bluff, with a commanding view of the surrounding countryside. Suddenly a black form dipping in and out of the cloud bank arrested Kevin's steps. Was it an airplane? No—it was a huge bird! It glided closer.

Its eyes locked on him, the prey, plainly visible behind a huge sheet of glass. "I wanted to run out of the room," Kevin says, "but I couldn't move. It was bigger than a full-size pickup truck but smaller than a Piper Cub plane. It was no blue heron."

· Kevin estimates the wingspan at twelve to fifteen feet across, with a similar distance from head to tail tip. The bird didn't flap its wings, but glided in and out of cloud cover. Then abruptly it headed back into the clouds and vanished.

It was only then that Kevin realized even weirder aspects of the bird—its size, the pointy, aerodynamic head. It looked like a pterodactyl. "I couldn't make out any feathers. It was more batlike."

Native American stories abound of enormous birds in the sky over Wisconsin. Was it one of these—a time hopper or something that never became extinct? For Kevin, as with many other expectant fathers, what arrived that day wasn't quite what he had expected.

Lower on the Food Chain

I feel taken to tell you about the Thunderbirds that used to frequent the skies in the dense wooded areas near the town of Stangelville. Between 1990 and 1994, the sightings were commonplace but not talked about. The sight of these avian giants is so unbelievable, you think your mind is playing tricks on you!

When I was a kid, I remember hearing about one of the monster hawks that attacked a man. The frail old man who told the tale of a big hawk clutching his shoulder made me fully aware that what he saw was real. The man sat in the local bar fully sober and smiled at us kids, asked us if we liked playing outside. Being the kids we were, growing up with woods surrounding us, the answer was yes.

His face turned very serious as he looked at our parents. He told us, "Now, you kids, when you play outside and you see a big bird circling the sky and you're the center of that circle, make sure you make yourself look big. Big like a bear. Make your arms wide and protect your face. I don't want you getting a good pinch like I did."

He showed us his shoulder, and we all gasped at the sight we saw. His entire deltoid region was gone! A huge series of claw scars lined the front and back of his shoulder. The shoulder itself was flattened, the muscle apparently torn away. His arm was of little use from the damage this big hawk had caused. He told us how his doctor at first thought a bear attacked him by the look of his injury. As he talked, fear overcame me, and I knew he was hiding some prime details about this bird. I knew what he was talking about. My parents also were fully aware of it. We all suffered from denial and would not speak of the sightings, would not speak of the big shape that glided in the sky over our yard now and then.

The first time I saw it was in the summer of 1990. My stepfather and I were doing yard work. The sun was shining; the sky was clear. Then a shadow played across the ground. I looked up, frozen. There was a bird so high up, yet it looked as if it were as big as a large hawk. This just can't be, I thought. It circled, never flapping its wings, never calling.

I pointed up and asked my stepfather if he was seeing it too. He looked up, looked at me, and winced. He told me in a very shaky voice, "Let's go inside and get some water to drink. It sure is hot."

I asked throughout the day if he saw the hawk, but he acted like the sighting never occurred. Throughout the next four years, the recurrent sightings of this big bird would stir up a fascination in me. It came lower when I took too much time to watch him, but my fear of being his dinner always told me to go inside after a few seconds. Then one year, it just disappeared. Did someone kill it or cage it, or did it finally get enough wind gusts to move to a new location? I wonder.

Through binoculars, I spied on this natural wonder—so high, so huge. I myself felt like a rabbit being circled by the big bird. We humans may indeed be lower on the food chain than we think.—*Glass Angel*

Stranger in the Night: Beast of Bray Road

It's something that cannot be, and yet, there it stands. The paradox quickly overwhelms any rational mind.

A quick drubbing of two heavy feet on the pavement behind you, an impossible movement of hairy limbs to one side, and suddenly two lemon eyes fearlessly search your own with uncanny, brazen mockery. You're transfixed, chilled, and completely bewildered. Once those lemon eyes have transfixed you with their cogent stare for a few eternal moments, the creature's head snaps away, fangs glinting, leaving you dazed as its hulking form leaps into the brambles or hurdles a stone fence to drop twenty feet onto a creek bed. After a parting glimpse of matted dark fur, all you want is to be anywhere else. As your foot jams on the accelerator or you stumble into a run, willing your legs to hightail it in the opposite direction, you are desperately grateful to have survived this unholy meeting of strangers in the night.

And the night really is stranger if you live in Walworth County or Jefferson County.

The dark hours, the witching hours, are when the creature dubbed the Beast of Bray Road most often shows itself. This enigmatic "thing," as most witnesses tend to call it, was named after a country lane east of Elkhorn, a small town squarely in the center of Walworth County, where it was seen by the first witnesses to go public. Over the past six decades, it has shocked as many as three dozen area residents with its sudden, sporadic appearances.

The first known sighting was in 1936, when a security watchman at a convent and home for the developmentally disabled in Jefferson County made an unsettling discovery one night as the clock neared midnight. Straining to see in the shadows, Mark Schackelman thought he made out something digging in an old Native American burial mound behind the main building. Thinking it must be a dog, he trained his flashlight on the animal. With a shock, he realized that it was not a dog but a man-size, shaggy creature with pointed ears and three long claws on each hand. Years later, he told his son, Joseph, he considered it to be a "demon from hell."

Other sightings occurred throughout the '60s, '70s, and '80s in Jefferson and Walworth counties, with puzzled and frightened witnesses sometimes calling local police in an effort to find out what exactly they had seen. Unbeknownst to one another, surrounding communities whispered for years about a creature known by the local names Bluff Monster or the Eddy.

The whisperings became public for the first time in December 1991, when rumors began to circulate around Elkhorn. People claimed that a shaggy, manlike, wolf-headed creature was haunting the cornfields and woods around Bray Road, a country byway

People claimed that a shaggy, manlike, wolf-headed creature was haunting the cornfields and woods around Bray Road, a country byway several miles long and lined with farms owned by the same families for decades.

several miles long and lined with farms owned by the same families for decades. Eyewitnesses were calling this creature a werewolf.

Jon Fredrickson, the county's animal control officer, used the "W" word on the manila file folder in which he stored all the queries trickling into his office. One story was from witness Lori Endrizzi, who saw the "manimal" kneeling by the side of the road and holding what looked like roadkill in its paws. Fredrickson speculated that perhaps the witnesses were seeing a "deformed coyote." But Endrizzi insisted that if werewolves existed, this creature would be one.

As other witnesses began to speak up, it became apparent that the hairy phenomenon was not limited to Bray Road. In fact, the sightings went back decades and crossed county lines, meaning either that a reproducing family of such creatures existed or that the "thing"

was very long-lived and able to travel great distances.

The witnesses, with one or two exceptions, seemed trustworthy. Most were reluctant, and many felt fear when recalling their encounters. There was no single "type" of witness either. The witnesses were male and female, children and the elderly, white-collar and blue-collar, and local folks as well as those just passing through. Almost all said something like, "I know what I saw, and nothing is going to change that."

The descriptions were similar: height between five and seven feet; hair shaggy and often extremely wild; coloration dark brown, sometimes with gray or silver streaks or tips. Those who had had a good look usually reported the creature as being like a wolf or German shepherd, with pointy ears, although some have claimed the head was apelike. The creature was sometimes seen standing on two feet, other times being on all fours. The most compelling characteristic, however, was its aggressive stare.

One witness, Williams Bay businessman Marvin Kirschnik, who came forward in 2003, was able to corroborate the other sightings with one of his own in 1981. His was unusual in that it had happened in broad daylight. Driving along Highway 11 near Bray Road one August afternoon, Kirschnik became aware of a creature staring at him from behind a fallen tree. He pulled over and scrutinized the creature from the window of his van for a good minute, he estimated, as it returned his gaze. Finally, totally unnerved by its stare and by his

Does the Beast still prowl? Stories keep rolling in. However, most of the recent sightings have been in places other than Bray Road, which hasn't had one since the early '90s. A woman saw the creature in Washington County in the summer of 2003, and in May 2004, a Madison man saw a strange dog-ape beast prowling a sidewalk about one a.m. in a dimly lit residential area. Some Illinois residents have also reported seeing it in four different places in recent months.

One woman who regularly saw what she called the Bluff Monster while growing up in southern Jefferson County gave a description that makes the Beast sound more like Bigfoot than Wolfman. There have been other witnesses who felt that the creature bore Yeti-like traits. A professional couple from Kenosha both saw a seven-foot-tall, almost classic Sasquatch-type creature hurl a bridge rail into Honey Lake in eastern Walworth County. Some cryptozoologists—those who study unknown animals—have speculated that the Beast may indeed be a smaller species of Bigfoot.

Of course, there have been sightings of various bipedal canines around the world and elsewhere in the United States, including the Michigan Dog Man flap in the mid-1980s. But the Beast of Bray Road

inability to identify the beast, Kirschnik sped off. But he made a drawing of it as soon as he got home. Its resemblance to the descriptions of other witnesses is remarkable, although Kirschnik's drawing was made ten years before the newspaper story broke.

remains unique for the number of sightings and the worldwide attention it has received. As to the true nature of the Beast, probably only time and perhaps a video or a lucky capture will solve the mystery to everyone's satisfaction.

Tupperware Partygoer Spies Knuckle Dragger

My wife and her mother saw something on their drive home one night on Highway DM near Highway 1 south of Arlington in Columbia County. It happened on December 30, 2003. Around nine p.m. something ran across the road. She said it was hunched over and ran on its back legs and knuckles, sort of like an ape. If it were standing upright, it would have been around six feet. It looked doglike and was covered with hair. The color was black and brown. They had to slam on the brakes to avoid hitting it. It ran across the road and into the field. My wife was very shaken when she arrived home. She is not one to make up stories. You are told your whole life things like this don't exist until you see one for yourself. *–Anonymous*

Northwoods Bigfoot a Supersized Werewolf?

I am probably not the only person that has claimed to have had sightings of "Bigfoot," which I believe are actually werewolves, also known in lore as loups-garous. I believe all of them are the same species, just subgenera. In May a few years back, me and a small party in two separate vehicles were headed down 51 between Wausau and Stevens Point. A very large animal about the size of a black bear crossed between the two separate cars. The speed that this animal had was incredible. Me and my friend were in a small RV, and the other two passengers were in front of us in a car. By all rights and laws, at the speed we were going, we should have hit it. By the time we saw it, it was in the headlights. However, we didn't get a good look at it. I watched a four-legged, very dark creature jump a four-foot fence with ease after clearing the RV. I have lived in the North-woods for sixteen years and have never seen a bear jump that high a fence. I am a hunter. I know it wasn't a deer. I know it wasn't a dog. I am not the only one who saw it either. The driver of the RV did.

Then this year, someone hit something in the Minocqua area. They didn't kill it, and it wasn't a bear—but as big as one. It also was on four legs. I have heard that they got hair samples from the bumper and sent them into the DNR. There's been nothing since, which doesn't surprise me. I just think that with added exposure, it is going to drive them further from sight as people get out their dogs and rifles. *–A friend of creatures*

Cabin Creature

My friend's uncle lived back in the woods, and he had a severe problem with an unknown creature around his cabin. He had two large dogs that were never afraid of anything. But when my friend's uncle would be up at night, he could sense and sometimes hear this creature just walking around his cabin. His two dogs would get scared and stay by his side. It got to the point where he would have to carry a rifle with him whenever he went outside. It became such a problem, he had to move. —*Jon, Bruce, Wisconsin*

Dumpster-Diving Canine in Madison

It was the day after Christmas in 2003, and I was sitting with my husband's family, just finished exchanging Christmas gifts. I was telling his sister about the strange animal I had seen. Before I was finished with my story, she interrupted with a story of her own. She said it would have been in '93 or early in '94. She was living on a cul-de-sac about ten minutes southeast of the capitol building in Madison. Late in the evening, she was watching TV. She heard a lot of banging outside by the garbage cans. There were two enormous animals sniffing around the garbage. She said they were as big as a Rottweiler, with long tails similar to a German shepherd's. She was shocked at the size and shape of their heads, saying they looked far too big for the bodies. She also noted that under the streetlight, she could clearly see the fur color (light gray) and the canine teeth. She said the teeth were also "too big-looking for the mouth." The head was huge and flat, and the snouts were longer than the snouts of any animal she had ever seen before. The ears sat on top of the head and were pointy. She said the idea crossed her mind that they might have been wolves, but the snouts were far too long for even a wolf. And she said they definitely were not coyotes. I asked about a possible mix-breed dog. She ruled that out as well, saying the heads were not doglike.

So, ruling out dogs, wolves, and coyotes, what else is there? This is a very levelheaded lady who doesn't drink or do drugs, works a full-time job, has a kid and a happy marriage. Not a nut looking for attention. I believed her right away when she told me about the animals. —*Kim*

Lake Monsters

Lake monsters torment our imaginations with their possibility. Prior to 1920, it seems that any lake of respectable size had its resident lake monster. Even unrespectable lakes boasted monsters. Monsters flourished beneath the surface—a watering hole was thought unfashionable without one—and their demise from the current scene is much lamented.

Man has done his best to change the landscape and thus the lake monsters' habitats. We've diverted waters, stoppered freshwater springs, introduced alien species, destroyed wetlands, created boat traffic jams, and dumped chemicals in the monsters' breeding grounds. You can only imagine what all this has meant for the monsters who called Wisconsin's lakes home. Even mundane creatures aren't immune to what man has done, as evidenced by a dog that had died of toxic shock in Lake Kegonsa after swimming in blue-green algae in June 2004. Another poor pooch suffered seizures.

Hope springs eternal for the monster hunter, though. Perhaps by frequenting spots where they once flourished, someday soon one will flap a flipper or cast a blazing eye your way. Most to date have been affable, but after the havoc we've wreaked, don't expect a warm welcome. However, if you do see one, send a hip hip hooray its way and a postcard our way—we could all do with a bit of cheerful news.

Some Classic Lake Monster Encounters

Folklorist Charles E. Brown was an inveterate collector of monster tales. Many of the following stories are derived from his classic work *Sea Monsters*.

Elkhart Lake

A creature with "big jaws" and "flashing eyes" pulled a fisherman end over end into Elkhart Lake in the mid-1890s.

Lake Mendota

The scales of a sea serpent were found on Lake Mendota's Picnic Point in 1917. That fall, a fisherman angling off the point was startled when a "large snake-like head, with large jaws and blazing eyes" popped up from the depths less than a hundred feet away from where he was standing. And in that same area, a University of Wisconsin coed tanning on a dock reacted with a speed she didn't know she possessed when she turned over to yell at her boyfriend to stop tickling her feet, but instead witnessed the head and neck of a huge serpent whose long tongue was lapping at her toes. Bozho, as the marine anomaly was known locally, had a reputation as a prankster, overturning canoes and piers, chasing sailboats, and scaring swimmers half to death. Back in 1899, a group of ladies had spotted Bozho while they were out boating on the lake. They reported that the serpent's head, which reared some distance out of the water, was ten inches in diameter and that the end of its tail, decorated with two big horns, lashed the water into a frothy foam as the creature dove beneath the waves.

Lake Michigan

During one winter in the late 1990s, Kim, thirtysomething, was riding on a bus near Grant Park in Milwaukee when a movement in Lake Michigan caught her eye. Weaving in and out of broken chunks of ice was a dark object resembling the submerged roof of a Volkswagen Beetle. Kim immediately signaled for the bus to stop. She got off and, despite wearing a skirt and inappropriate shoes, went running through the snow to the water's edge to get a better look. The object appeared to be feeding as it moved farther out from shore.

Lake Monona

In June 1897, Eugene Heath of the Garr-Scott Company fired two rifle shots at a twenty-foot serpent plying the waters of Lake Monona, near Madison. The marine monster may have been responsible for swallowing a swimming dog a few days earlier.

Lake Waubesa

An Illinois resident who went rowing on Lake Waubesa in the 1920s claimed to have seen a serpent "sixty to seventy feet in length and of a dark green color" apparently sunning itself on the surface of the lake. In the same period, a couple swimming off Waubesa Beach were terrified when a creature with glittering eyes surfaced near them.

Lake Kegonsa

A "dragon" was frequently sighted during the 1920s in the waters of Lake Kegonsa, off both Colladay and Williamson points. Unlike the mild-mannered Bozho, this habitué of the deep was characterized as vengeful and destructive.

Pewaukee Lake

In the 1890s, a "huge green thing traveling like a gray streak" and "spouting water" was frequently reported near the resort hotels that at the time dotted the shores of Waukesha County's Pewaukee Lake. One man claimed he'd tried to spear the green leviathan, but his "weapon bounded back as though it had struck a rock or iron plate."

Red Cedar Lake

The famous sea serpent of Red Cedar Lake in Jefferson County was first seen by fishermen in 1891. One witness said it had a "very large head with protuberances like saw teeth on its back." It was fifty feet long.

Rock Lake

Not to be outdone by other Wisconsin lakes, Rock Lake in Jefferson County is the lair of a monster named Rocky. Although he became more benign with age, Rocky started his career much like the vengeful dragon of Lake Kegonsa. It was in August 1882 that rowboat racers Ed McKenzie and D. W. Seybert spied what they thought was a floating log. However, as they approached the "log," it suddenly "manifested life," thrusting its "head about three feet out of the water" and opening "its huge jaws about a foot or more" before diving out of sight. McKenzie screamed in terror as the creature resurfaced near his boat. Seybert yelled, "Strike him with the oar!" But McKenzie, terrified out of his wits, called in desperation to a group onshore. A Captain Wilson, shotgun at the ready, came to the rescue, but by then the monster had vanished, leaving the air "heavy with a most sickening odor."

That was not to be Rocky's only sortie. Passing boaters reported being hissed at by the monster from the rushes near the shore.

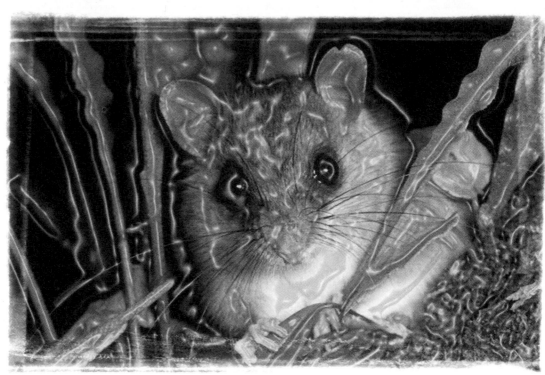

No one had ever seen anything like it either, so they called it a whatsit. In captivity, the whatsit gave birth to two baby whatsits.

The Central American Whatsit

The year was 1939, and the most recent freight train into Elkhorn had just brought in a bumper crop of bananas from Central America. As the grocer picked through the tightly packed bunches of bananas, separating the good fruits from the rotten ones, something inside one of the bunches caught his eye. The something was brown and furry, and it jumped and chirped. The grocer grabbed the furry beastie. But once he had it, he had no idea what it was. He described the critter as larger than a chipmunk but smaller than a squirrel, with big black eyes, a ratlike tail, and light brown fur. As far as the grocer could tell, it ate only bananas. It had to have come from Central America, he figured, along with the bananas.

He took the little beast out to the farm of a man named Adams. No one there had ever seen anything like it either, so they called it a whatsit. In captivity, the whatsit gave birth to two baby whatsits. The *Elkhorn Independent* noted that "every other animal on the farm was black and white, so these did not fit the color

scheme." The newspaper didn't mention if the tiny creatures were banished from the premises for clashing with the Holstein cows.

Although no one could identify it at the time, the stowaway may have been a vesper rat, one of the more attractive squirrel-like members of the rat family. In their native Central America, vesper rats spend virtually their entire lives in fruit trees, almost never coming down to the ground. Whether the three on the Adams farm died or escaped to attempt survival in the Wisconsin wilds is unknown, but their arrival in Elkhorn does prompt the question of how many other species, small or large, have been inadvertently brought into the state hidden in giant fruit crates on old steamships and freight trains.

Skeptics may well want to keep in mind that when strange things are spotted darting out of cornfields or swamps, they might not be mere figments of the imagination or solidified swamp gas. They could be the descendants of Central American whatsits.

Bigfoot Is Dead—Long Live Bigfoot!

Bigfoot has had some difficult times lately, with the media around the country declaring him dead.

When people think of Bigfoot, they primarily think of the Pacific Northwest, but Bigfoot-like creatures have been reported in all fifty states except Rhode Island and Hawaii. Still, when noted hoaxer and prankster Ray Wallace died at the age of eighty-four on November 26, 2002, his family felt it was time to let the world know that Bigfoot's coffin was nailed shut. As his son Michael put it, "Ray L. Wallace was Bigfoot. The reality is, Bigfoot just died." While Ray's widow, Elna, slipped into a gorilla costume to sport for the camera, other family members recounted how Ray had carved sixteen-inch plywood footprints and left fake tracks. The newspapers ran headlines proclaiming Bigfoot's death. It was obvious that the media loved the story of two crusty old-timers pulling the wool over the true believers' eyes, just as Doug and Dave, two geezers with too much time on their hands, had supposedly created thousands of increasingly elaborate crop circles in the United Kingdom.

Despite all the media spin, Wisconsin's Bigfoot population knows enough not to believe everything it reads in the paper. Bigfoot continues to pop in and out of the public's attention, much as it always had before its exaggerated demise.

Wisconsin has a long history of Bigfoot sightings in every corner of the state, particularly up and down the Wisconsin River valley, from Rhinelander to Prairie du Chien. Paula, a Madison schoolteacher, vividly remembers her own experience. "In 1997, I lived on the dead end of Bluff Drive between Pittsville and Marshfield," she says. "One night around eleven p.m., I took the dogs out, and there was a large 'animal' on hind legs thrashing around. It was at least eight feet tall and had long arms and hair. It had come out of the woods, crossed the road, and was coming up the ditch. The dogs went crazy, and I had to physically drag them inside."

Paula's account is similar to dozens of others, and it seems entirely possible that many sightings purported to be the Beast of Bray Road could be Bigfoot rather than a werewolf.

The oldest written account we've uncovered is from the *Milwaukee Sentinel* dated August 17, 1867. The headline reads A "WHAT IS IT" NEAR MILWAUKEE. The article goes on to describe the sighting, which had occurred in Oak Creek, near the Milwaukee–Racine

Wisconsin has a long history of Bigfoot sightings in every corner of the state, particularly up and down the Wisconsin River valley.

county line. After experiencing a series of chicken-coop raids, as well as finding partially devoured lambs in nearby woods, one farmer decided to take matters into his own hands. One night, he got a rifle, hid in the woods, and watched his henhouse. Around eleven, he saw something creeping toward the henhouse, sometimes on all fours, sometimes erect. Unable to determine what it was, the farmer, being a sensible Wisconsinite, figured he'd solve the mystery by shooting it.

As the *Sentinel* described it, "A piercing shriek arose as of a boy of twelve years of age in terrible pain, and the object bounded off on all fours, uttering meanwhile a plaintive moan or wail, which could proceed from no animal but a human being." The farmer returned home thinking he had shot a human being, though the creature had seemed to run like a beast.

The next day, at first light, the farmer found blood and tracked it into a marsh. He "was startled by the appearance of an animal or being with a distinct human face looking at him from a short distance. As soon as he made a movement, however, the singular creature started off with great swiftness and was soon lost to sight." In the creature's hiding place, the farmer discovered "the marks of human hands and feet, somewhat distorted . . . with enormous claws, but sufficiently displayed to remove all doubts as to the matter."

The farmer fetched the police, who, of course, didn't believe him. However, he seemed so sincere, they decided finally to check it out. They searched the swamp but found nothing. Then, just as they decided to call it a night, a rustling in the grass alerted them to a presence.

On turning, they beheld a sight which startled them. It was without question a human face, but resembled that of a brute so closely as to be almost unrecogniz- able as such. They made a movement as if to approach it, when it darted off, leaping like a wild cat. As it receded, they could obtain a good view of the creature's body, which was covered with hair, but at the same time appeared altogether different from that of any animal in existence. The shape resembled most closely that of a human being in the act of running or leaping on all fours. They attempted pursuit, but the creature was soon lost in the dim shades of the woods.

A tantalizing reference to a similar hairy creature appears in the *History of Wood County, Wisconsin* (1923) in a discussion of the Smoky Hill Mounds. Charles Brinkman, a twenty-year resident of the sixty-acre Smoky Hill area, said that Native Americans would occasionally visit the hill to trap animals, but would not remain after dark for fear of encountering the hairy man or monster that lived there.

In January 1908, lumberjacks from the Kaiser Lumber Company in the town of Winter arose one morning to find the snow trampled by bare feet. The tracks of two bare feet came from the north, circled their shanty several times, and then disappeared to the west. A letter to the editor of the local paper concluded that "the boys were curious to learn who made the tracks and why."

In July 1964, a Delavan man was nearing home on Highway 89 after working the late shift at the Admiral Corporation. Driving on Richmond Road, he received the shock of his life as a "big hairy creature" ran into the glare of his headlights. "I first noticed him on the north side of the road, in a cornfield," the man said in a videotaped interview in 1993. "He jumped a four-and-a-half-foot fence, ran across the road, and jumped the fence on the other side. Estimated height: seven to eight feet. Estimated weight: four-hundred to five-hundred pounds." What threw the man most was that although the creature was

time on November 13 while hunting deer. Earl Boyles recalls that the hunters had stumbled out of the woods after they had "spotted this huge, hairy thing on the far side of a small clearing. It was half-ape, half-man. It was seven or eight feet tall and had long arms. [The hunters] were so amazed they never thought to take a shot at it." One of the hunters, a guy named Dick Telloch, reported that the creature "sort of danced around and then got in behind the bushes." The hunters were all consistent in their descriptions of a barrel-shaped body covered with dark hair some four inches long.

Renowned crypto-zoologists Ivan T. Sanderson and Bernard Heuvelmans trekked to Wisconsin through a blizzard to visit with the men and judged their accounts to be genuine. Sanderson and Heuvelmans even joined the men in a December Yeti hunt, at which time the group found seventeen-inch tracks in the snow. However, rumors soon spread that a burly, bearded prankster masquerading in a coonskin outfit was really the source of the tracks.

covered with dark fur, it ran on two legs, swinging its arms like a human, and then cleared the fence without breaking stride. "Scared the devil right out of me," he said.

There was a sighting of what is known as the Fremont Yeti on October 19, 1968, by three bow-and-arrow hunters in the Deltox Marsh near Fremont. Curiously, that same trio, along with nine other hunters, saw it for the second

Local Notables

Colorful characters and local loonies—
every town, no matter its size, has at
least one person who stands
apart from the crowd, whether by choice or as a
result of undesired notoriety. Some of these
characters are looked upon with fondness and
affection by their neighbors; others are written
off as kooks and are ignored or mocked.

But one man's wacko is another
man's eccentric hero. What would
the world be without its original
thinkers or, more importantly, without
those who can muster original thoughts
and then summon the élan to act upon
them? The people in this chapter are notable
for doing just that in one way or another.

Edward Ben Elson—Loony Lawyer

Attorney Edward Ben Elson was a child of the 1960s. He lived in McFarland on the shore of Lake Waubesa and practiced law in Madison. He was a free spirit with a big heart. He championed the rights of the poor and the downtrodden and specialized in helping the mentally ill, arguing that it was their right to refuse medication. His business card read FAR OUT LAWYER, SPECIALIZING IN LOONY LAW.

He had a number of slogans as well, including "Live and let live" and "Obey only good laws." All were eminently sensible. Then enter Comet Kohoutek.

During the energy crisis of 1973, there were long lines at the gas pumps and escalating prices. In mid-December of that year, Elson began proclaiming, "The Comet Kohoutek will mix with the atmosphere on Christmas, and the earth will drown in a sea of petroleum oil. It's ironic that the world's energy crisis will be solved, but the solution will extract such a terrible price."

Supposedly, he knew all this because a "beautiful, black womanly angel" had come to him and said, "Eddie, because of the goodness in your heart and courage in trying to bring some measure of goodness to the mentally ill, you are the man we picked for this."

Elson's explanation must have been logical to him: "The angel told me that 144,000 people would be picked to be saved before the end of the world, and on December twenty-fourth, the comet would hover over McFarland, an astro-escalator would descend, and we would all climb up and leave before the great petroleum spill." Elson wasn't sure where they would all be going. But, he said, "from the way the angel smiled, it must be someplace especially nice."

Elson maintained that on Monday, December 17, a spaceship had landed on his lawn. A ten-foot-tall visitor emerged and made ten trips to his basement, carrying ten

one-bushel baskets. In the ten baskets were 143,000 little people, each of whom was one inch tall. All were in a state of suspended animation. The tall visitor told Elson it was up to him to pick the remaining thousand people to be saved.

Elson was a little short on cash, and he claimed he sold two of the tiny humans to a Belleville car dealer, who planned to use them as hood ornaments. "I didn't want to," Elson explained, "but I had to raise some money." According to Elson, the alien gave him one thousand tickets for the remaining passengers. Elson gave some of

WILL THE Kohoutek Comet MAKE You THINK ABOUT GOD AND HIS DESTINY FOR YOU AND THE WORLD? YOU CANNOT ESCAPE IT! ARE YOU READY FOR IT?

the tickets away and tried to sell the rest. He claimed that he raised $65,000.

The tickets had Elson's picture on one side. Under his photo were the words "Your Savior, Edward Benelson." Above the picture it said, "Admit one to the Kohoutek Comet, an Intergalactic Spaceship Leaving Earth Dec. 24, 1973."

On the ticket's back was a warning: "Caveat Emptor—Let the Buyer Beware. This ticket is paid for on faith. No refunds allowed whether or not you're carried away. No warranties expressed, implied, or even hinted at."

Written like a true attorney!

Locals were used to Elson's shenanigans and laughed away the story. However, reporters from around the country began calling, some looking for a lovable kook to brighten the holidays amid the dreary economic news, others taking him at his word. After all, he was an attorney.

Of course, Christmas Eve came and went without any aliens, and the Comet Kohoutek failed to stop over McFarland. When asked about it, Elson replied, "Comet? What comet?"

On February 8, 1983, some nine years after these events, Elson committed suicide in his garage by remaining inside his car with the windows closed and the motor running.

We hope that in death Elson found his womanly angel and that he is flying with her through the comet fields of eternity.

Some folks want nothing more out of life than the opportunity to share their talents with an adoring public. Some go on to stardom, but many toil in obscurity waiting for that one big break. Whether these entertainers are being cheered by the masses or ignored, they are fulfilling their destiny. They give of themselves for the enjoyment of their public. So let's lend them an ear and give them all a big hand!

Elvis Aron Presley Is Alive in Phillips, Wisconsin!

Serving up foamy glasses of Bud in a bar called Bloom's Tavern, next to the Heartbreak Hotel in the Price County town of Phillips, you'll find a man with swept-back dark hair and a curl to his lip. A tiny stage hugs the wall opposite the bar, and most evenings, the barkeep can be counted on to leap from behind a beaded curtain, dressed in a white jumpsuit and a rhinestone cape, to croon "Blue Suede Shoes" or "Hound Dog." His name— his actual, legal name—is Elvis Aron Presley, with "Aron" spelled just the way Mama Presley put it on her son's birth certificate. This Elvis is very much alive, and even though he has taken on the King's name, he fervently believes that the original Elvis is still alive someplace.

But this Elvis Presley's ambitions are more political than musical; his goal, he says, is to be mayor of Phillips. He ran for the office in 2000 and almost won, and he has served on the city council as both alderman and president. He says he'll try again for mayor come the next election. He believes that his love of public service befits the true spirit of Elvis Presley; he claims that holding office means more to him than a hundred platinum records ever could.

Unlike the original Elvis Presley, this one started out in life with a different name. He was born Gary Arthur Caron. He grew up in northern Illinois, but it was at Lake Geneva's former Playboy Club that he got his start in the Elvis business. "I was in Illinois with a fifties and sixties band," he says. "We had played at McCormick Place one time and did 'Teddy Bear.' People were screaming, and I wondered what the guys in the band were doing behind me. Then we were at the Playboy Club, and I had learned another song. This time, I'd dazzled it up a little, got some little knickknack things to hang on me, and the same reaction happened from the crowd, but I couldn't catch the boys doing anything."

Of course, the crowd was screaming for Elvis. An agent for a Las Vegas resort caught the act at the Playboy Club and pursued Presley and his band relentlessly until they agreed to fly to Vegas and perform. "They made us an offer you couldn't refuse," says Presley. The agent then costumed him in the "Condor" outfit. "I put it on; it made me feel just like the King," he explains. He continued feeling like the King through many more contracts and tours. At one point, he did three hundred shows in nine months. The most that the real Elvis did was two hundred and sixty-one shows in one year.

Gary Caron didn't change his name until 1996, after years of being Elvis on stage. But people started calling him Elvis all the time, so he decided he might as well change his name legally. However, he stresses that he wasn't motivated by hopes of profit. "My reason was more to uphold his name," he says. "I didn't like the way the cheap news media played on Elvis about the drugs and everything. Elvis had a lot of health problems, and that's why he needed all that medicine, but they said he was just on drugs. What I liked was his way of caring about people, his generosity."

Despite Gary Caron's honorable intentions, Elvis's estate tried to stop Caron from changing his name to Elvis

Presley. They alleged that the name change would be trademark infringement. However, it turned out they had trademarked only "Elvis Aaron Presley," with two *a*'s, a spelling Elvis had taken to using later in his life. There was no trademark for "Elvis Aron Presley," so Gary Arthur Caron became Elvis Aron Presley. "The courthouse was full of publicists," he says. "It was total pandemonium. It started the roller coaster."

The roller coaster finally sped out of control and crashed a couple of years after Caron had changed his name, when he collapsed onstage from exhaustion during a performance in McCormick Place. He decided to quit touring for health reasons. Although he owned several homes by then, he wanted a place where he could kick

back and be closer to his mother. She lived in Fifield, so he bought Bloom's Tavern in nearby Phillips.

The bar is Wisconsin's oldest continuously operating tavern and is on the National Register of Historic Places. Presley hasn't gussied it up, other than adding a stage and a big plastic teddy bear complete with shades. But he tries to uphold the standards of decency he believes the other Elvis would endorse. A sign on the bar wall labeled RULE FOR BLOOM'S reads THE "F" CUSS-WORD IS **NOT** ALLOWED IN THE TAVERN. Customers are warned twice, then asked to leave if they do not abide by this house rule.

Presley's wife, Terese, is a pleasant down-to-earth woman, who helps run the bar and who says that no, she will not be changing her name to Priscilla. "If your

husband jumped off the bridge, would you do it too?" she asks.

Presley and Terese have moved to a farm in the nearby township of Worcester. He bought an old rooming house next to Bloom's and dubbed it the Heartbreak Hotel; he plans to renovate it into rustic accommodations for hunters and fishermen.

His old way of life has no lure for him these days, he says. He's blown off David Letterman to work on fund-raisers for the Make-A-Wish Foundation. "Leno and Oprah Winfrey wanted me too, but [the foundation] meant more," he says. "Now I'm fifty-five years old, and I do onstage what Elvis did in his thirties. I have diabetes and am at risk for a heart attack, but I've accepted that."

Presley's goal is pretty clear: He wants to be Phillips' teddy bear.

Devolution of a Star

At one time in her life, Pauline L'Allemand was the toast of the European opera scene. She was the most famous coloratura soprano in Vienna, Paris, and Berlin and a personal acquaintance of both the emperor of Germany and the tsar of Russia. But the talented diva, who was born in Syracuse, New York, in 1864, had a vision, one that would prove her undoing: She wanted to create an American opera scene that would be Europe's equal in every respect. By the early 1900s, L'Allemand had made a sufficient fortune to finance her own touring production of an opera she had written herself. She may have been a brilliant vocalist, but unfortunately, she was no Mozart. The venture flopped, and L'Allemand was left with only a pittance with which to support herself and her gifted eighteen-year-old son, Edgar, a musician.

She made it to Milwaukee with her company before it disbanded in 1909. She was talked into buying a property near Black River Falls that, according to developer E. J. Vaudreuil, was to be the cornerstone of a utopian community. Edgar, new to the realities of pioneer life, built a house with the same techniques used to assemble stage flats.

To say they lived a meager existence would be sugar-coating the truth. They lived in a drafty shack on grain-feed mush, dressed in the shabby remains of their opera costumes, and rode to town in a sled or light buggy drawn by a steer. They had very little furniture and seldom entertained. Pauline, now toothless, was convinced that she and Edgar were the victims of a conspiracy of unknown persecutors who performed such evil deeds as shooting all the ivory keys off her old organ. She began talking about this vast conspiracy to anyone who would listen.

Eventually, in 1920, Edgar was accused of stealing four bags of cement, but the charges were subsequently dismissed. Nevertheless, Edgar and Pauline were examined by physicians, who pronounced them insane, with the result that they were packed off to Mendota, the state mental hospital in Madison.

They somehow managed to escape to Illinois. Edgar had invented an aluminum violin, and he and his mother probably hoped it would turn their fortunes around. But by 1925, when Edgar was involved in a legal wrangle with a woman to whom he had been briefly married, it became known that he and his mother were living in a "woodchopper's cabin" near Edwardsville. And in 1929, an article surfaced in a Chicago newspaper revealing that Pauline L'Allemand had brought charges against a woman rooming next to her in a boardinghouse. Pauline claimed that the woman, who was a ventriloquist, intentionally harassed her by aiming "odd voices" through the walls.

After mother and son died, they remained virtually forgotten until Michael Lesy's 1973 book *Wisconsin Death Trip* brought their surreal life to the public's attention. In the book, the stark images by nineteenth-century Black River Falls photographer Charles Van Schaick are coupled with news accounts that appeared in the Black River Falls newspaper, the *Badger State Banner,* around the turn of the century. The articles are deadpan accounts of the murder, mayhem, and madness that occurred in Wisconsin during this period, and L'Allemand and her woeful tale match the book's dark themes only too well.

Leaping Leopards and Lost Alligators

Colonel George "Popcorn" Hall

Over the years, many circus personalities have chosen Wisconsin for their winter headquarters, turning towns like Baraboo, Delavan, and Evansville into havens for exotic animals and eccentric people. One of the best-loved circus moguls was Evansville's Colonel George "Popcorn" Hall. Hall deserves the gratitude of every Wisconsinite for introducing the state to the delicacy that became his trademark—popcorn.

Starting circus life as a stowaway on a wagon that passed through his native New Hampshire, young George used to run away with the circus every summer, then return home to New Hampshire for the winter. His first circus job was as a popcorn vendor, and he learned how to make his tubs of popcorn so delectable that people clamored for them. At the age of thirteen, George tried his luck hawking popcorn on the streets of New York City, where he invented the popcorn "brick," a forerunner of the popcorn ball. He was acquainted with Horace Greeley, the famed editor of the *New York Tribune,* who was said to have given young George the nickname Popcorn. In 1861, George's longing for the circus life took him to Delavan, where he worked for the famous Mabie Brothers Circus. Although promoted to barker, he still saw to it that the brothers' circus offered good popcorn to its eager customers. In time, after running various curio museums and road shows, he began traveling with his own small circus troupe.

Evansville, a small town in Rock County, became Hall's winter quarters in the 1880s. The townspeople became used to having crates of wild animals arrive at their train depot to be hauled in wagons to the circus headquarters. Camels, lions, bears, and elephants regularly rode the rails to Evansville, and at one point, Hall brought in the only living gorilla in the United States.

The most memorable of Pop's animals, however, was probably the leopard that escaped in September 1901, terrorizing the people of Evansville for three long days, despite the efforts of an armed posse. The leopard killed some cattle and sheep on its "vacation," then made its way to a farm belonging to an elderly farmer named Hess in nearby Magnolia Township, where it took refuge in a tree. Hess called

the sheriff after he found two of his sheep dead, and a militia of thirty armed men went out to the farm. The six-foot cat, perhaps realizing it was surrounded, attacked the old farmer and mauled him badly. It then leaped on one of the other men, Walter Tullar, who managed to shoot it in the jaw at close range—this despite the fact that the leopard had sunk its teeth into Tullar's arm. The animal was then dispatched by the rest of the posse. The men hauled its bullet-ridden carcass back to Evansville, where it was hung on a lamppost next to a drugstore on Main Street for the townspeople to view. After that, the former star attraction of Pop's circus was made into a rug.

It wasn't the first time that the townspeople had to keep their children indoors for fear of attack by one of Hall's critters. In 1890, an alligator on the lam had Evansville in a panic. Pop had just purchased the huge reptile, and people feared it had made its way to the millpond, a popular swimming hole. However, it was soon

Circus Wagons

"Charlie"

veterinarian who was trying to remove a splinter from his foot and tossed the hapless man quite a distance away. Another time, Charlie freed himself from an Evansville park, where he'd been staked, and set off through town with his keeper hanging determinedly onto his tail. After traversing Evansville several times and uprooting chicken coops and other small structures, Charlie made for the circus headquarters, where he tore through the gate, then chucked a piece of wood through a window. He became harder and harder to control, and finally the Halls decided they had to put him down.

found in a marsh south of town. To capture the alligator, a few brave circus workers crammed a wooden board into its mouth, then secured it around the neck with a chain. The reptile lived to perform again.

Hall kept many circus animals in his Evansville home, including a lion named Dooney. Hall's wife, Lou, was a snake handler, and in the winter, the pair kept Lou's twenty-four-foot python in a box near the stove to keep it warm. One time, while recuperating from a broken hip after an encounter with an angry twelve-foot-tall elephant named Columbus, Hall was paid a visit by the local doctor. When the doctor saw the python's head rise up from behind the stove, he dashed for the door, knocking over a monkey cage and releasing a terrified marmoset. It took an equally terrified animal keeper to put all the creatures back where they belonged.

Freakish animals were another Hall specialty. He bought a three-headed calf from a local farmer and also advertised a two-headed, three-eyed, three-horned cow in his exhibits. Hall also acquired another cranky pachyderm. This one, named Charlie, once wrapped his trunk around a

Pop Hall loved to travel, and he took his circus on several excursions to Mexico and the Caribbean. He was said to have been attacked in Mexico during a minor revolt, and although details of the incident are sparse, he somehow came away from the fray with the title of Colonel.

The Colonel managed to pass his love for circus life down to three generations of descendants, who kept the Hall Circus running under various names for years after his death.

Today, the riotous days of lost alligators, stampeding elephants, and leaping leopards are all but forgotten in Evansville. There are no plaques or memorials, other than a small section of a mural inside the city hall to commemorate the kind and colorful ringmaster who always gave orphans and Civil War veterans free tickets to his shows. Even his grave in Maple Hill Cemetery is curiously free of any circus or popcorn references. The next time the opportunity presents itself, whether you're in a movie theater or at the kitchen microwave, perhaps it would be appropriate to raise a bag of "extra butter, salted," in memory of Colonel George "Popcorn" Hall.

Art for Our Sake

Some folks see things a little bit differently than the rest of the world. Where some people just write off their dreams as the mind's nonsensical nocturnal ramblings, others write down their dreams in fanciful prose. Fortunately for all of us, the following Wisconsinites have chosen to share their unique — if at times skewed — visions, giving us a rare glimpse into their weird worlds through the unusual crafts they create.

Bill Vienneaux and the Sawdust Factory

Bill Vienneaux is a man whose legs are a little shorter than average. Consequently, he designs all his hand-carved chairs to sit closer to the floor than usual, regardless of who buys them. "These chairs are all made for people who aren't very tall, because I'm not very tall," he admits. Putting himself into his art is, quite literally, a habit with Vienneaux. Sitting perched atop one of his wooden rocking dragons, his voluminous gray beard bristling in all directions, he looks exactly like a new species of Elfdom that's emerged from the pages of a Tolkien fantasy. In fact, he calls his workshop the Hobbit House. It's surrounded by a hodgepodge of similar small dwellings, about a dozen in all, which he has cobbled together out of recycled building materials. Every summer these tiny workshops along Highway 13 just south of Washburn are occupied by a variety of artists, and Vienneaux calls his agglomeration the Sawdust Factory.

"I've never read Tolkien," he says, "but Middle Earth, little people, the simpler life — all that interests me." He spends most of his time in the wood-crammed Hobbit House. As we lowered ourselves into the low-slung chairs for a long chat, a mouse skittered away. Classical music played in the background, and a variety of wooden creatures stared at us from every angle of the room — a bucktooth troll, big-headed aliens, even a wanton mermaid.

Vienneaux is more ambitious than the average North-woods carver, most of whom seem to restrict themselves to creating mushrooms, bears, and eagles. Vienneaux will carve these items too, but he also creates voluptuous nude females, furniture accented with gnomelike faces and intricate designs, totem poles, and whatever else strikes his fancy. He isn't picky about his sculpture tools, using everything from chain saws to bottle openers to get the effects he's after. But his finished works show a refined command of form often lacking in the mass-produced wood carvings found at roadside stands. Many of his pieces are done for his own enjoyment, including the massive figures standing around a firepit. He calls them Woodhenge. The day we visited the Sawdust Factory, we also

talked to artist Kathy Johnson, one of the colony's summer artisans. She identifies her own quaint shop with a carved sign that reads KATHERINE'S WORLD. Her pieces have a more delicate style than Vienneaux's, but they blend well into the rustic surroundings.

"Every year different artists come," says Vienneaux. "Some years it's as many as eighteen artists, depending on which ones can get away and come here." The one constant of the place is Vienneaux, a lifelong Washburn resident and a Highway 13 fixture since 1987. And he doesn't appear ready to go any farther down the road than his giant rocking dragons will take him.

The Worst Novel Ever Published in the English Language

It's difficult being a writer. You sit in a room by yourself and bleed your life out onto the page. Worse, you wake up the next day and realize that what you wrote the previous day is utter garbage. You throw it all away and start over. It's enough to make you wonder why you do it.

Writers are often their own worst critics, reading their creations with a scalpel-happy surgeon's eye, then carving away the excess to reach the essential. Ultimately, the day arrives when they launch their beautiful jewels into an uncaring world, hopeful of finding an audience but fearful that they won't.

Imagine, then, being retired University of Wisconsin–Whitewater English professor Robert Burrows when he fielded a phone call from *Washington Post* columnist Gene Weingarten in February 2003. Weingarten offered Burrows, age seventy-nine, a Faustian bargain—the chance to be interviewed and have his book, *Great American Parade*, reviewed in the prestigious *Post*, with the potential of reaching at least two million readers. The only catch, Weingarten said, "is that I am going to say that it is, in my professional judgment, the worst novel ever published in the English language."

After an eternal moment of silence, Burrows offered up a simple "Okay."

Truly, the book is a yawner. Burrows's self-published tome is a satire on the Bush administration's tax and economic policies. "My idea," explains Burrows, "is that the concentration of wealth among a small percentage of Americans is inimical to democracy."

Weingarten mocked Burrows throughout the review, noting that student newspapers at the University of Wisconsin and Wayne State University variously called his novel "simply an awful book," "unskilled," and "an agonizingly slow read." Then he applied the skillful dagger: "I think *Great American Parade* is a wretchedly terrible product that shames the American publishing industry."

But as all writers know, even bad publicity is better than no publicity, so long as your name is spelled correctly. After the review, Burrows became a bit of a cult phenomenon, as Internet chat rooms and online publishers picked up his cause, and the sales of his novel increased. Of course, whether those purchased novels were ever read remains unknown.

Burrows is working on his second novel, an alleged page-turner focusing on President Bush's "plan to exempt stock dividends in perpetuity from taxes." This time, may he find his audience.

Inventors— Bless 'Em

It has long been said that necessity is the mother of invention, and who could argue? Just try to imagine what our daily lives would be like without the modern conveniences that we all now take for granted. Imagine what life would be like without the combination potato masher and milk shaker!

Wily Wizard of Waukesha

In the first half of the twentieth century, Americans went gaga over the steady stream of gadgets coming into their homes. In Waukesha, an ad salesman named Russell E. Oakes took advantage of the mania for household machines—and went on to become a national TV star in the process. Oakes, who was known as the Wily Wizard of Waukesha, filmed dozens of short movies for the *Popular Science* series to showcase a wacky assortment of devices he put together in his basement workshop. People thrilled to his daffy demonstrations of the chewing-gum fan, the combination potato masher and milk shaker, and the tie bib. The fan, a typical Oakes device, attaches to a person's jaw. When that individual chews gum, the resultant motion drives a fan that cools the gum chewer's head.

"There is never a dull moment in the weird Wisconsin laboratory of the Wily Wizard of Waukesha," intoned one film's announcer as Oakes sighed and grinned, winking at the camera as he soaked up electric "sunbeams" in his indoor armchair beach environment. When a two-dimensional bathing beauty popped up on an adjacent television screen, Oakes let out a high-pitched "Whoo-hoo!"—the perfect nutty professor finale.

Oakes was born in Hixton but fell in love with Waukesha when he attended Carroll College there in 1911. After graduation, he worked for a number of different Waukesha firms while creating his goofy machines as a hobby. In 1935, he showed a few of his inventions at a Rotary Club meeting and was so encouraged by the positive response that he began entertaining at local

Oakes' chewing-gum fan

banquets, conventions, and schools. He started filming the *Popular Science* movies in 1939, making the long trip from Wisconsin to Hollywood's Paramount Studios every summer for five years. He also appeared on such national TV shows as *You Asked for It, We the People, Hobby Lobby,* and *The Garry Moore Show.*

Oakes died in 1961 at the age of seventy-one, but his zany inventions live on. Some of the more memorable contraptions include a snore-activated light system for people afraid to go to sleep in the dark, a dripless mechanical doughnut dunker ("a godsend to people afraid of scalding their thumb and forefinger," explained Oakes in a 1954 *Waukesha Freeman* article), and a mechanical third hand, complete with red fingernails, to shoo flies away from picnic food while eating.

His most outrageous invention, doomed to unpopularity with PETA because it required animal labor, was the hydraulic cigarette lighter. This was activated by pouring a glass of water into a tube with a sponge at its end. As the sponge filled with the water, it released a lever that opened a cage containing a rat, exposing the rat to a piece of cheese. To get the cheese, the rat would hit a paddle that released another lever, which in turn popped a balloon. That action released a weight, which caused a flywheel to spin and scrape its sandpaper-covered rim, creating enough of a flame to light a cigarette.

Other Waukesha natives have claimed to be wizards of one sort or another, but Oakes will surely remain the only native son to reach the zenith of wizardry with a hydraulic cigarette lighter powered by a rat.

Gadgeteer Edward F. Rammer and the Flying Saucers

The Flying Saucer Age officially began with a famous sighting by Kenneth Arnold on June 24, 1947. On that day, Arnold, a pilot, was flying near Mount Rainier when he banked his craft and was alarmed by a "tremendously bright flash" in the distance. He witnessed more flashes and then discerned a series of nine objects flying diagonally at tremendous speed. Their movement reminded him of a flat rock skipping across water. After Arnold talked to the media, a reporter transformed these skipping objects into flying saucers, and a craze was born.

Saucer mania reached a fever pitch around the July Fourth holiday that year. Excited observers across the country reported objects in the sky, and Wisconsin was no exception. Speculation about the objects was rampant. While there were many reports in good faith of strange phenomena in an effort to help solve the mystery, an equal number of hoaxers, pranksters, and kooks got in on the action too.

In a story published on July 8, Edward F.

Rammer told the *Milwaukee Journal* that he was the culprit behind the flying saucer phenomenon. He claimed that what people were seeing were bolts of light fired from his cosmic-ray gun. "There is no reason for everyone to get so excited," he said. "I don't think they will hurt anyone."

Rammer was a mason and an amateur inventor. He

had discovered the cosmic-ray principle years earlier, he said, while devising a new method for baking bricks. He wanted instantaneous bricks, not those made by the traditional slow-baked process. "I shot my charge into [the brick], and as I shot, the entire sky seemed to have an electrical storm. Lightning flashed from Green Bay to Fond du Lac, and then it rained. The brick was pulverized."

Clearly, either the aptly named Rammer had created a powerful device, or a coincidental thunderstorm ignited a fanciful delusion. Whichever it was, over the next several years, Rammer embarked on a mission to create a series of weather-control devices. He claimed responsibility for snowfalls, thunderstorms, and extreme weather across Wisconsin and even credited his experiments for the Dust Bowl phenomenon in the 1930s. "I can't actually prove that I caused it, but as soon as I quit [experimenting], it ceased."

In 1941, Rammer got a job in Manitowoc at the shipyards. There he began pondering the destructive possibilities of the cosmic-ray principle and decided that a new condenser in his ray gun might do the trick. He tested his device by firing toward Mexico. From a newspaper account the next day, he concluded his test had been a success. "For the first time in history," he declared, "a volcano was born right under man's eyes. Came right up in the middle of a cornfield. From my calculations, it couldn't have been fifty feet from where my rays struck."

Rammer alleged that further experiments led to earthquakes in the Dutch East Indies and to tidal waves in Japan. He even claimed to have knocked Japanese fighter planes out of the air and probably a few American planes as well. "Well, I couldn't help it," he said. "I probably hit everything in the sky."

In 1947, Rammer warned some friends in Washington State about an upcoming cosmic-ray demonstration and asked them to write to him about the results. Nothing happened. Rammer decided he had aimed too high—his beams had flashed harmlessly into outer space.

"Next time I shot lower," he said, "and then the reports started coming in about flying saucers. I don't really know for sure that those are my cosmic bolts, but it's logical. I imagine they hit something and flatten out—a mountain probably."

With that, Rammer disappeared from the media spotlight. Today, it's difficult to imagine any newspaper giving him any sort of coverage, although the Internet would surely provide him with a good home.

Clearly, however, flying saucers were here to stay. Connie Dunbar, a Pittsburgh man, told divorce court Judge Harry H. Rowand that "there was no mystery about the flying saucers in his home—they were wife propelled." Dunbar was granted his divorce.

Rammer alleged that further experiments led to earthquakes in the Dutch East Indies and to tidal waves in Japan. He even claimed to have knocked Japanese fighter planes out of the air and probably a few American planes as well.

Janesville's Mad Scientist

In a case that still has international terrorism experts talking, a wild-haired Janesville man named Thomas Leahy was found in 1997 to be running his own bioweapons workshop in his basement and garage. His vast collection of pickle jars, petri dishes, and other lab equipment was only discovered after the unstable "scientist" shot his stepson in the face (the boy recovered) and the boy's mother told police about her husband's laboratory.

Leahy's wife had become worried because he had been telling family members he was working on bacteria he planned to send to people in envelopes that also contained razor blades. He had also stated his intention to poison Lake Michigan and boasted that he had created undetectable poisons to kill his "enemies," whom he was naming on an ever-expanding list. Leahy, who suffered from schizophrenia and drug and alcohol abuse, talked openly of his admiration for Hitler. Relatives and friends who knew about the laboratory had already dubbed him the Mad Scientist.

Most probably, however, no one realized just how mad Leahy really was. In his garage, police found enough of the deadly toxin ricin to kill over one hundred people. Police also confiscated a spray bottle containing a mixture of another toxin, pure nicotine, mixed with a solvent that would allow the poison to be absorbed through the skin on contact.

But Leahy didn't stop there. When apprehended, he was hard at work trying to grow his own anthrax cultures.

In December 1997, Leahy received an eight-year prison sentence for shooting his stepson, and the following month, he was sentenced to an additional twelve years and seven months in prison for possessing a "weapon of mass destruction." An appeals court later reduced that sentence to six years because he had never actually used his toxins on anyone.

Thomas Leahy

In his garage, police found enough of the deadly toxin ricin to kill over one hundred people.

The Value of a Good Muffler

John Wesley Carhart, a Racine inventor credited with building the first actual automobile in 1871, was also a preacher and a writer. He gained notoriety when he added a steam engine to a standard horse buggy and it ran. Unfortunately, the engine was so loud that Carhart was accused of killing a nearby horse with the sound. Owing to local outrage over the incident, he ended up having to dismantle his brainchild and get around town with regular horsepower, like everyone else, leaving the auto invention field open for a guy named Ford.

People kill for different reasons. There are crimes of passion and anger, as well as murders for profit. In these cases, the motive is usually crystal clear. But there are also those who commit their heinous crimes for their own impenetrable reasons. The inner demons and twisted mind-sets that drive these psychopaths often baffle the rest of us. Wisconsin has had its share of all kinds of killers. Here, now, is a short parade of some of the most infamous. We call them Wisconsin Badasses.

Poison Widow

One of Wisconsin's most sensational, yet least remembered, murder trials titillated the public in the 1920s, when a petite churchgoing housewife from Whitewater was dubbed the Poison Widow by the newspapers. SORDID, SHOCKING! read the headlines as she and her college-student boyfriend were tried, separately, for killing Myrtle's husband with strychnine. And yet the pair's perfidy would never have been discovered if thirty-six-year-old Myrtle Schaude hadn't also tried to murder her four beautiful children as well.

Myrtle grew up in a conservative, religious farm family outside Palmyra. She was only seventeen when she wed Edward Schaude, a farmer twice her age. The couple had four children and moved to a small farm on the outskirts of Whitewater, where the town's university athletic complex now stands. The university was then the State Normal School, and Myrtle and Edward decided to board students to make extra money. They took in two young men, one of whom was a gangly World War I veteran named Ernst Kufahl.

Kufahl took a shine to the pretty Myrtle. He began flirting with her at every opportunity, and soon they were involved. Edward, meanwhile, came down with a mysterious illness that kept Myrtle busy nursing him. One evening in March 1922, Ernst told his landlady that she would "have some rest tonight." Somehow, between the two of them, they managed to pop a lethal dose of strychnine into Edward's bedside glass of prune juice. He died an agonizing death that very night. The

Myrtle and Edward Schaudes' wedding portrait.

Mrs. Schaude

coroner attributed his demise to stomach flu. No one suspected perfect little Myrtle or thought to check her cupboard for rat poison.

Myrtle sold the farm, bought a bigger house in town, and proceeded to house and feed Normal School students. Kufahl transferred to a different campus, then to a farm in Minnesota, and he and Myrtle continued their courtship in earnest, writing each other almost every day and planning to marry. But Kufahl's letters seemed to indicate that her children wouldn't exactly be welcome, so Myrtle hatched a plan. She claimed it was at Kufahl's insistence, but he was cagey enough not to leave any evidence of complicity in what then transpired.

In September 1923, Myrtle bought four chocolate bonbons and stuffed each one with enough strychnine to kill a horse. She then arranged for her children to take a drive to the country, with her oldest son, Ralph, sixteen, at the wheel, and handed them each a bonbon, instructing them not to eat the candy until they were in the country. Her plan was that the children would all die of strychnine convulsions and Ralph would crash the car, so it would look as if an auto accident had killed them. The carefully laid plan went awry, and while there was a car crash and Ralph swallowed what could have been a lethal dose, all the children survived.

Myrtle made up a story about getting the candy from a Milwaukee door-to-door salesperson, and the police launched a manhunt. By then, however, the local district attorney was suspicious, and he finally succeeded in getting Myrtle to confess. Edward was exhumed and autopsied.

The murder trial began in February 1924. Kufahl was acquitted for lack of evidence. Myrtle wasn't so lucky. She was sent to the prison in Waupun, but conned her way free in a few years. She married again and had a second family in Illinois. They were totally unaware of her past until *Weird Wisconsin* found them and showed them the old newspaper clippings. They were shocked, to say the least, for as Myrtle's step-granddaughter exclaimed, "How well do you ever really know anyone?" Myrtle, dead by then, had cooked for her extended family for many years. They will never know for sure if any of the candies or cookies she had made contained a few "special" ingredients, courtesy of the Poison Widow.

Ed Gein

Ask any non-Wisconsinite to name the first things that come to mind about Wisconsin, and inevitably they are cheese, the Green Bay Packers, and Ed Gein—not necessarily in that order.

It was November 16, 1957, a Saturday and the opening day of deer season in Plainfield (population just over six hundred).

Gein got up early that morning and drove into town. He parked in front of the Worden hardware store and went inside to purchase antifreeze. He had been there the night before, ostensibly checking out the price.

Bernice Worden was working alone. She probably wasn't too pleased to see Gein, as he had taken to hanging around the store. But a customer was a customer, and Gein's family had been customers for years.

Bernice filled Ed's order, and Gein slouched out the door. However, he came back a few moments later, claiming he was considering trading in his Marlin rifle for one on display in the store. Bernice handed him the rifle he had pointed out, and as she gazed out the window, Gein reached into his pocket, took out a .22 shell, loaded the rifle, and shot Bernice in the back of the head. Apparently, he had come to perceive her as a wicked creature deserving of divine punishment and

Ed Gein's farmhouse

thought he was God's agent. He then placed her body into the back of the Worden hardware truck, locked the door, and drove to his farm.

At five p.m., Bernice's son, Frank Worden, who was also the deputy sheriff, went to the store and found his mother missing. He saw a pool of blood on the floor, with a trail leading out the back. He frantically dialed Sheriff Art Schley in the neighboring town of Wautoma and cried, "Murder."

Gein had been a suspect in the disappearance a few years earlier of Mary Hogan, a tavern keeper in nearby Pine Grove, but there was no hard evidence to warrant his arrest. Frank Worden immediately suspected Gein was involved in his mother's disappearance.

The police arrested Gein a short time later at a grocery store. Meanwhile, Captain

Lloyd Schoephoerster of the Green Lake County Sheriff's Department had gone looking for Gein at his farmhouse. In his report, later read at Gein's trial, Schoephoerster described what they found:

> It was eight p.m. We tried the doors. They were locked but the door leading into a woodshed attached

to the house didn't seem to be latched too tight. I put my foot against it and pushed and the door came open. Knowing Gein had no electricity, we took our flashlights and went in. As I tried to open the door going from the woodshed into the house, Sheriff Schley looked around a portion of the woodshed. I heard him cry out, "My God, here she is." I went over to where he was and saw a woman's nude, headless body hanging from the rafters by her ankles. . . .

We then went into the house and found it to be in a terrible state, completely littered from one end of the house to the other with bones, barrels of junk, stacks of clothes, papers, and so forth. . . .

It was so horrible. We found skulls and masks; that is, the skin portion of the head that had been stripped from the skull and preserved and put in plastic bags. . . . We found leg bones and discovered the chair seats were made out of human skin. . . .

There was one upper portion of a woman's torso from the shoulders, cut down both sides to the waist. Gein told Dan Chase that he would put these female parts on himself at night and go out in the yard and parade around in them.

It eventually emerged that Gein had acquired much of his home-decorating materials by robbing graves. The root of his problem was harsh religious indoctrination and an unnatural fixation on his mother, Augusta, who had died twelve years earlier, in 1945.

Though suspected of several more murders, Gein admitted to killing only Mary Hogan and Bernice Worden. Many people felt he was also

responsible for the death of his brother, Henry, in a grass fire in May 1944, but he was never charged. He also confessed to grave robbery.

Following a hearing after his arrest, Gein was sent to the Central State Hospital for the Insane in Waupun. Ten years later, having finally been declared fit to stand trial, he was brought to court to account for his crimes. In declaring him fit, however, the Central State staff meant only that they considered him capable of intelligently working with his lawyer and participating in his own defense; they still considered him insane.

Gein was tried for the murder of Bernice Worden. He was found not guilty by reason of insanity and was once again committed to the Central State Hospital for the Insane. In 1978, Gein was transferred to the Mendota Mental Health Institute in Madison. He died there at age seventy-eight in 1984 of respiratory failure while suffering from cancer. His obituary appeared in newspapers around the world.

Gein's house was scheduled to be sold at auction on March 30, 1958, but a few nights before the sale, a mysterious fire burned the house to the ground. A pine forest was planted at the site where the house once stood. In the gentle breeze that stirs the pine boughs, some still hear the lingering cries of Ed Gein's victims.

Jeffrey Dahmer, the Milwaukee Cannibal

In 1991, however, Ed Gein was totally eclipsed by Jeffrey Dahmer, a new hot nova of depravity unlike anything ever seen before.

No one was prepared for the grisly horrors in room 213 of Milwaukee's Oxford Apartments, although someone should have seen it coming. The year 1991 was the most violent ever in Milwaukee's history, with a total of 168 people murdered. *Newsweek* magazine even dubbed the city "The New Murder Capital." Many of the homicide victims were African Americans. It was a hot summer, with record heat waves and simmering racial tensions. The events surrounding the arrest of Jeffrey Dahmer only exacerbated these volatile conditions.

Two police officers cruising the Marquette University neighborhood on the oppressively hot and humid night of July 22, 1991, spied a short, skinny African American man with a pair of handcuffs dangling from one wrist. Assuming that he had escaped from another police officer, they stopped to question him. His name was Tracy Edwards, and he was thirty-two. To the officers' surprise, he poured out a bizarre tale of the "weird dude" from whom he had just escaped. He told the officers that he had been "with the devil" and that the devil had pulled out a butcher knife from under his bed. The devil said he would cut out Edwards's heart, then eat it. The two policemen could smell alcohol on Edwards's breath. At first, they were inclined to dismiss his tale as a drunk's ramblings, but somehow Edwards convinced them of his sincerity, and the officers decided to check out his story.

Instead of the devil, a polite soft-spoken sandy-haired thirty-one-year-old man answered the door. He smelled faintly of beer, but a more pungent oppressive stench was coming from inside the room, pervading the entire hallway.

Jeffrey Dahmer invited the officers inside. They asked him if the handcuffs were his and if he had the key. Dahmer said the key was in his bedroom. As he turned to fetch it, Edwards piped up about the butcher knife under Dahmer's bed. Officer Rolf Mueller stopped Dahmer and said he would get the key.

After Mueller entered the bedroom, he peered into an open dresser. To his horror, he saw Polaroid photos of several males in various stages of dismemberment, pictures of skulls in the apartment freezer and kitchen cabinets, and a shot of a skeleton hanging from a showerhead.

Mueller shouted to Officer Robert Rauth to cuff Dahmer—they were taking him in. Dahmer struggled with Rauth, but Rauth wrestled him into submission. Edwards then pointed at the refrigerator and told the officers how Dahmer had "freaked" earlier when he had gone to get a beer. Mueller opened the refrigerator door. Inside was a human head.

No one had ever encountered anyone like Jeffrey Dahmer before. All told, he had killed seventeen men—fifteen in Milwaukee, one in West Allis, and one in his native Ohio. Nine years separated the killings of his first and second victims, but by the time of his arrest, Dahmer was averaging one victim a week. His youngest was fourteen; his oldest, thirty-one. All were male, and all but three were African American. When he was arrested, Jeffrey Dahmer was living in a primarily African American neighborhood.

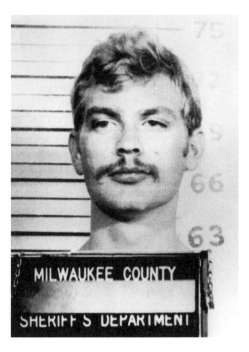

Dahmer's mode of acquiring victims was consistent. He would invite young men to his apartment to share drinks or to watch sex videos or to pose for nude photos, for which he offered them money. Once there, he'd lace their drinks with sedatives. When the drugs kicked in, Dahmer would strangle his victim with a leather strap or his bare hands. He would frequently have sex with the corpse, then record the grisly details with his Polaroid.

Unlike Ed Gein, Dahmer was a true cannibal. He said he ate his victims' flesh because he believed they would come alive again inside him. "I suppose in an odd way it made me feel as if they were even more a part of me," he said.

Probably the most tragic aspect of the horrific murder spree was that Dahmer could have been stopped sooner. On May 27, 1991, his youngest victim, Konerak

Sinthasomphone, had escaped from Dahmer's apartment and run out into the street; he was naked and dazed as a result of drugs. A 911 call summoned police officers and paramedics to the scene. Then Dahmer showed up. He was able to convince the officers that the fourteen-year-old was really a nineteen-year-old lover who'd had too much to drink; the two had quarreled, Dahmer said, and the young man ran outside. The police believed Dahmer and released Konerak into his care, accompanying the two men back to Dahmer's apartment. Everything seemed to be in order. However, had the police checked the bedroom, they would have found the decomposing corpse of a man Dahmer had killed three days earlier. Had they checked the bedroom, Konerak wouldn't have died after they left.

The trial of Jeffrey Dahmer was the most expensive in Milwaukee County history. Alhough he pleaded guilty but insane, he was found guilty and sane. In July 1992, he was sentenced to fifteen consecutive life terms—nine hundred and fifty-seven years—in prison.

Dahmer's stay at the Columbia Correctional Institute in Portage was short. In the early-morning hours of Monday, November 28, 1994, he was beaten to death by fellow inmate Christopher Scarver. "God told me to do it," Scarver said.

What drove Jeffrey Dahmer to commit his crimes may never be understood. He once said, "Maybe I was born too late. Maybe I was an Aztec," referring to the Aztecs' acts of ritual sacrifice and cannibalism. Maybe that's as close to an explanation as we'll ever get.

Personalized Properties

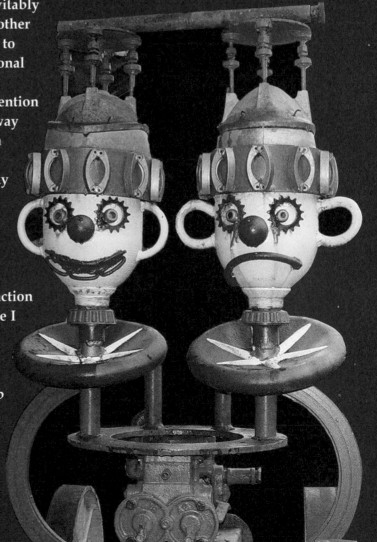

We wish we could say that no Wisconsin lawns have ever been blighted with wooden cutouts of grannies bending over in polka-dot bloomers. Sadly, in the Badger State, as elsewhere, a quick tour of most neighborhoods inevitably reveals yards adorned with concrete deer, plastic geese, and other mass-produced lawn kudzu. So when a bold visionary dares to shirk the mundane and create original art for his or her personal environment, people notice.

Not that they always approve. But sooner or later, the attention the upstart receives because of creative audacity begins to sway the locals. Tourists arrive to snap photos, art critics may even dub the creator an outsider artist, and before long, cultural foundations are swooping in to preserve the sublimely wacky objects for posterity. After all, the creators of unique home enhancements have often made something out of virtually nothing. On the following pages, such throwaway items as plastic soda bottles and rusty machine parts take on new dimensions as elements in works of art.
"Who would have thought anyone could make a tourist attraction from *that*," neighbors say, scratching their heads. "How come I didn't think of it first?" they secretly ask themselves.

But that's just the point: These personalized properties are special because it would never dawn on the average person to string stuffed animals around a wire frame and top off an outrageous construction with a discarded bowling trophy. And while a small percentage of people might actually create a wild and rash monument, those who have the artistic instinct to fashion a cohesive statement rather than just an assemblage of junk are few and far between.

That's why the following places are worth seeing. They were brought to exuberant life by people compelled to follow their inner Picassos rather than the humdrum vision embraced by the rest of the herd. Usually self-taught and eager to use whatever is at hand, these creative visionaries had the guts and aesthetic savvy to turn the ordinary into something wondrous. Their works reveal the angels and demons that romp inside their heads, and the rest of us become privy to their unique visions.

Dr. Evermor's Sculpture Park

A ten-acre creation located five miles south of Baraboo on Highway 12, this dream-in-metal sculpture park blows you away the first time you see it. Is it a tract of sprawling machines from the set of a science-fiction movie or just a vast junkyard fairyland forged by nineteenth-century children raised by robots? Take your pick. One thing's for sure, though: Mutant colors run rampant here—Kool-Aid lime, meltdown red, radiation-glow green, and Popsicle purple. The hues are delightfully appropriate, for this fantastical garden of weird sculptures occupies the site of a former schoolyard.

The main attraction is the startling, grandiose Forevertron, the largest sculpture in the world made of scrap metal. Weighing some four hundred tons (and still growing), this massive creation is one hundred twenty feet wide, sixty feet deep, and fifty feet high. Its purpose: to propel its creator, Dr. Evermor, into outer space and to provide entertainment and viewing stations for the assembled royalty and masses who will gather for that momentous occasion.

Each separate piece of the mega installation serves a particular function. The wrought-iron gazebo is where the royal family will enjoy their tea while they observe Dr. Evermor's blastoff. There's a telescope for the doubting Thomases, so they can determine for themselves if Evermor made good his escape. Then there's the Graviton, a device to "de-water" the burly doctor and thus reduce his weight, which will facilitate his voyage into space. The Jockey Scale is where he'll weigh himself before climbing the spiral stairs to the copper-sheathed glass egg, the flight capsule where he will sit while he is propelled into the heavens by a magnetic lightning-force beam. The Celestial Listening Ears are for attendees to listen to the voices from the heavens. The urn-shaped Overlord Master Control is for controlling the capsule's gyronic flight. And let's not forget the Love Guns, aimed at the butt of anyone not smiling.

The Forevertron is surrounded by various gazebos, where popcorn and other refreshments will be served. And if all of this isn't enough to titillate you, an orchestra comprising more than four dozen metal birds, bugs, and beasts will provide soul-stirring music for a rousing send-off.

But you ask, Who is Dr. Evermor? Born in Madison in 1938 and

whose entire life has been influenced by a childhood incident. As a young boy, the story goes, Dr. Evermor had asked his father, a Presbyterian minister, where lightning came from. His father replied, "From God, my son." From that day forward, the young Evermor "dedicated his life to creating a machine that could harness the energy of lightning and which might eventually propel him into the heavens to meet God."

Thomas Every admits that his Dr. Evermor persona is a "total figment" adopted by a "man under great duress." He

originally known as Thomas O. Every, the good doctor spent most of his life in the scrap-metal recycling business. By the early 1980s, when he gave the business to his son, he had dismantled over 350 factories, power stations, mills, breweries, and other large-scale manufacturing sites in Illinois and Wisconsin.

Sometime around 1983, Thomas O. Every was reborn as Dr. Evermor and began work on the Forevertron. At the time, he was depressed and upset with the world. He believed that the judicial system was a failure and that fundamental fairness had gone by the wayside. He found himself increasingly dismayed by society's rush toward a disposable culture. He became annoyed with phonies and wanted to get away from people. Life, he felt, needed to be simpler, more meaningful.

It was in this frame of mind that he turned to welding as therapy. He also imagined himself as an eccentric professor living in England in the nineteenth century,

admits that though he began his project in a mood of frustration, his outlook changed over time and he has come to view the world with a good bit more humor. Eventually he became driven more by artistic inspiration than by a need to savage a society he hated.

The Forevertron was built in accordance with the mind-set of 1890, when the forces of electricity and magnetism fired the imagination. Each assembled part of the giant machine preserves some rapidly vanishing facet of early technology or machine culture. The materials used include 1882 dynamos created by Thomas Edison, as well as vintage wiring, gears, brass knobs, springs, electrical parts, nameplates, and a variety of curious mechanisms.

Some newer material has also been incorporated. There are pieces of an X-ray machine in the Graviton, a sign from the Mars hamburger chain that has been reborn as the glass space capsule, and old theater speakers from Beloit that have been reverse-engineered into the Celestial

Listening Ears. Most interesting are the decontamination chambers salvaged from the Apollo space mission of the 1970s.

The Forevertron is exactly what state-of-the-art rocket science would look like if it had been created during the Victorian Age. The fact that the Forevertron seems as if it might work, says Evermor, is more important than whether it actually functions. As you stand awestruck before it, this ostentatious device convinces you that it works: The ground seems to quiver in anticipation of imminent liftoff.

"I was an industrial wrecker for a great period of time, and we destroyed a lot of things," says Evermor. "It gets working on your psyche—tearing all this stuff down. I wanted to build something up instead."

Evermor doesn't use blueprints or drawings and has no traditional art training. "No sketches, no models, no nothing. I just go for it," he says. "Touch something—it's for real. Nothing's phony."

Evermor's use of the flotsam and jetsam of discarded culture—pipes, steeples, glass, machine parts, even ratchet-toothed gears—continues to inspire people from around the

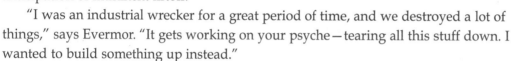

world. Visitors to his sculpture garden walk away with huge grins on their faces, building their own scrap-metal creations in their heads. Indeed, it's easy to find Evermor imitators scattered around the country. And lately, as the buzz has increased, folks have held weddings and even funerals on the grounds of his park.

Although age is slowing down Evermor's steps, he has much more work to do. We're all eagerly awaiting that day when the Forevertron is finally complete and the good doctor de-waters himself, ascends the spiral staircase, waves to the assembled crowd, crosses the bridge to enter the copper-sheathed glass egg, and pulls the lever to actuate the force that will propel him on a high tight beam of electrons out into the cosmos. Long may he ride!

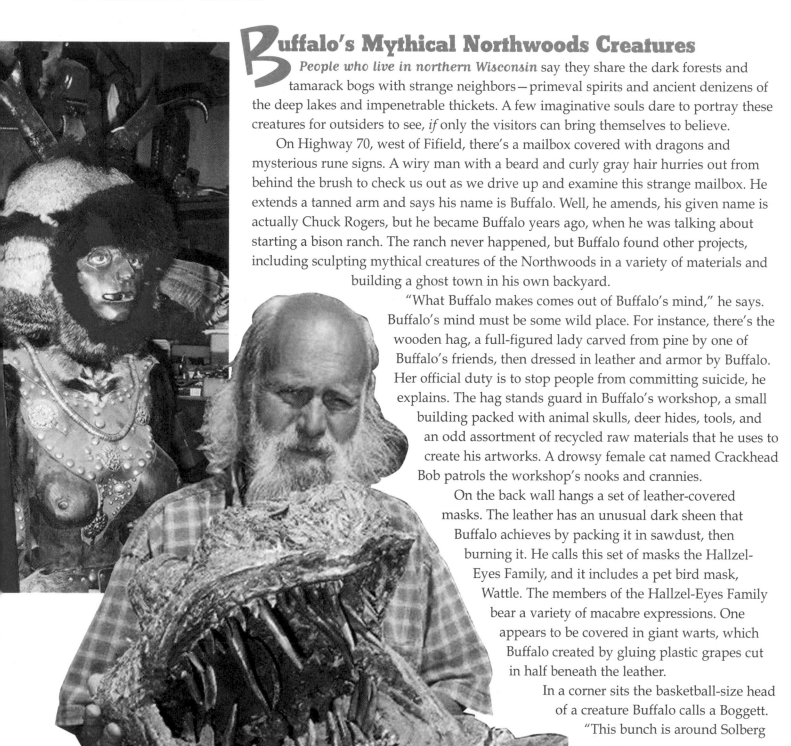

Buffalo's Mythical Northwoods Creatures

People who live in northern Wisconsin say they share the dark forests and tamarack bogs with strange neighbors—primeval spirits and ancient denizens of the deep lakes and impenetrable thickets. A few imaginative souls dare to portray these creatures for outsiders to see, *if* only the visitors can bring themselves to believe.

On Highway 70, west of Fifield, there's a mailbox covered with dragons and mysterious rune signs. A wiry man with a beard and curly gray hair hurries out from behind the brush to check us out as we drive up and examine this strange mailbox. He extends a tanned arm and says his name is Buffalo. Well, he amends, his given name is actually Chuck Rogers, but he became Buffalo years ago, when he was talking about starting a bison ranch. The ranch never happened, but Buffalo found other projects, including sculpting mythical creatures of the Northwoods in a variety of materials and building a ghost town in his own backyard.

"What Buffalo makes comes out of Buffalo's mind," he says. Buffalo's mind must be some wild place. For instance, there's the wooden hag, a full-figured lady carved from pine by one of Buffalo's friends, then dressed in leather and armor by Buffalo. Her official duty is to stop people from committing suicide, he explains. The hag stands guard in Buffalo's workshop, a small building packed with animal skulls, deer hides, tools, and an odd assortment of recycled raw materials that he uses to create his artworks. A drowsy female cat named Crackhead Bob patrols the workshop's nooks and crannies.

On the back wall hangs a set of leather-covered masks. The leather has an unusual dark sheen that Buffalo achieves by packing it in sawdust, then burning it. He calls this set of masks the Hallzel-Eyes Family, and it includes a pet bird mask, Wattle. The members of the Hallzel-Eyes Family bear a variety of macabre expressions. One appears to be covered in giant warts, which Buffalo created by gluing plastic grapes cut in half beneath the leather.

In a corner sits the basketball-size head of a creature Buffalo calls a Boggett. "This bunch is around Solberg

Lake," he says. "They grab people off the nature walk. Once, a Boy Scout stuck a stick in one's eye, and it ate him." Just as fearsome is the Flambeau Sand Slayer. "He lives in the Flambeau River; he has a long body, eel-like, and is cannibalistic but also eats dogs, fish, and people." Buffalo notes that an early Jesuit priest-explorer who mysteriously disappeared from his party was most likely devoured by the Sand Slayer.

Buffalo also displays what looks like a shriveled human head in a decorated box. He says it's the head of the evil dwarf featured in the movie *Black Robe*.

For his own protection, he wears the tattoo of a bear claw on his chest. The bear is his totem animal, he explains. Buffalo is part Jewish, but he now combines Christianity with Native American traditions. From the highway, visitors can see his authentic-looking Plains-style burial platform, heaped high with the bones of bears, buffalo, and wolves that people have given him over the years. "This is where we go to pray," he says.

Not surprisingly, there's nothing run of the mill or predictable about the rest of Buffalo's property. He has long been fascinated by ghost towns, so much so that in his backyard he's busy building his own frontier-style ghost town, with half a dozen small wooden buildings in various stages of construction. There's even a sheriff's office. His four children and a friend are helping. "We plan to just sit around on the porches like people used to," he says. "It's just for our own pleasure. I don't want a bunch of flatlanders running around here."

"What Buffalo makes comes out of Buffalo's mind," he says. Buffalo's mind must be some wild place.

Poland's Backyard UFO Landing Port

"Hi. I'm Bob," says Bob Tohak, genially offering his hand in greeting after we pull up in his driveway outside the minuscule community of Poland. Noticing the giant tower labeled UFO LANDING PORT, WE'RE NOT THE ONLY ONES directly behind him, we can almost imagine him welcoming a contingent of creatures from another planet with the same gesture. But then we spy a tattoo of the cartoon character Marvin the Martian on Bob's forearm, directly above his right hand. A message reads EARTH IS FULL. GO HOME.

If that's how Bob really feels, we want to know why he is making it easy for alien invaders to land here. Bob grins, ruffling his sandy-blond hair as he scratches his head. "Well, one of my inspirations was the people in the town. I've been here twenty-eight years, and I first had an excavation business, and they wanted me to move it to the other end of town."

Always an independent sort, Bob decided to stay right where he was and build whatever he pleased on his property. Eventually the excavation business gave way to a steel-fabrication company, which now constructs bridges and other structures. Then in 1992, Bob decided to take his feelings a step farther. "If I'm not going to work with the white, yellow, and red man, I might as well work with the green man," he says, waving toward the impressive tower behind him. "If you look at it from the top," he continues, "it looks like a flying spacecraft." His design was inspired

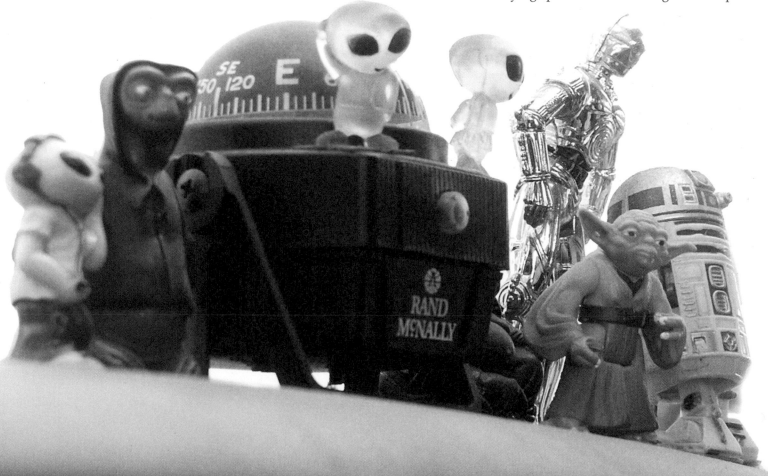

by a landing pod in one of the *Star Wars* films, he explains. "I was watching that movie and just thought it would be cool to make one. It's all scrap stuff left over from our jobs."

Inside the tower is a spiral staircase, which opens onto the top of the landing port with a hatch Bob had bought as salvage from the coast-guard cutter U.S.S. *Coral Sea*. The whole tower lights up at night, although Bob says he has to be careful, because he uses a flashing blue light, which is normally used by airports. He wouldn't want any ordinary earth craft to mistake his port for a runway. It's meant for UFOs only!

Bob also has his very own alien—a gray rubber space mannequin that was used as a prop in a movie about an alien operation. It was given to him by a friend he had met in Roswell, who had just finished filming and didn't need the mannequin anymore. "I used to drive around with it in my truck," says Bob, "but I was afraid someone would take it." He keeps his alien in a safe place in his house now.

As for the landing port, Bob is still tinkering with it. The sign has become weatherworn over the years, and he's in the process of completing a new one, which will also deliver a jab at government secrecy about those little humanoids and their flying machines. The sign will read IF THE GOVERNMENT HAS NO KNOWLEDGE OF ALIENS, WHY DOES TITLE 14, SECTION 1211 OF THE CODE OF FEDERAL REGULATIONS, IMPLEMENTED ON JULY 16, 1969, MAKE IT ILLEGAL FOR U.S. CITIZENS TO HAVE ANY CONTACT WITH EXTRATERRESTRIALS OR THEIR VEHICLES?

Good question, Bob!

Elkhorn's Smiley-Face House

Carolyn and Michael McCann just like smiley faces—that's the Elkhorn couple's explanation for turning their front yard into a giant shrine for the grinning 1970s icon. But the McCanns probably would never have turned smiles into yard art had it not been for Carolyn's desire to give an ex-boss a birthday present.

Carolyn's boss collected smiley faces, so she asked her husband to create a few large ones out of plywood. Michael, a chef, whipped up several on his table saw, and the couple liked them so much that they decided to make some for themselves. The McCanns are avid Packers fans, and their first effort was a green-and-yellow "Go Pack" tableau. This was followed by a red-and-green Christmas smiley-face display. Then there were red-white-and-blue smileys for a patriotic summer theme and, of course, orange-and-black ones for Halloween. The smileys light up at night. "They look awesome then," says Carolyn.

The smileys are mounted on specially built frames that stand on either side of the couple's garage on North Church Street. "The posts are cemented right into the ground," explains Carolyn. "Whoever buys this place from us someday is probably going to be mad at us." In the meantime, most passersby are enthusiastic. They stop and take pictures. And of course, they inevitably grin back at the smileys.

Giant Fuzzy Dice of Walworth County

They're furry, they're way oversized, and they'll have you seeing spots. But don't be alarmed. After all, what's not to love about giant fuzzy dice? Bob and Carole Phillips, who sew and stuff dice by the cartload in their rural Burlington home, find them not only lovable but lucrative. To their surprise, they have become the nation's largest—and possibly only—makers of giant fuzzy dice.

Bob, a former operator of the Country Estates Sanitary District, cuts the faux fur with a pair of rotary scissors and punches out the dots with a specially made die. He then attaches the dots to the fabric with a hot glue gun. Finally, Carole sews the squares together on a machine that was once used to create bunny costumes for the former Playboy Club in Lake Geneva.

The giant dice, which are used mostly for skating games, are sturdy enough to take a beating. "They say a roller rink will wear out one in a year," Bob says.

So how did two nice people from Wisconsin get into the mega-dice racket? Actually, dice were not the Phillipses' first fuzzy product. Their foray into the furry universe started unexpectedly when Bob's sister and brother-in-law, who were part owners of a roller rink in Burlington, told him that they couldn't find anyone who was still making pompons for skates. Bob was laid off from a trucking job at the time and figured he could pop out a few pompons to help the rink. He and Carole devised an assembly-line method that would later prove workable for giant dice as well.

At one point, they tried making stuffed animals to sell at craft fairs but then decided they could never compete with Toys 'R' Us. Looking around, they learned that roller rinks feature games where skaters use colored paddles to whack giant dice around the rink. Someone had to make those big dice, and the Phillipses decided it might as well be them. They stopped making the pompons several years ago to concentrate on the dice.

The neighbors like having the dice factory next door because it brings the UPS truck out every day. "Last year, I came home from work one day near Christmas," says Bob, "and there were thirty-two neighbors lined up in the living room, waiting to fill out forms and send stuff."

Extraordinary Fence of Daniel Erbstoesser

Daniel Erbstoesser always liked to dabble in cement, says his son, Steve. So when the Sheboygan policeman retired from the force, he decided to spruce up his Whitcomb Avenue yard with something more permanent than the old wooden fence. Actually, he'd already started on the project back in the 1950s, when he had affixed concrete tree trunks to the ends of the fence. So now it made sense to make the whole thing out of cement. Mixing his concrete in a wheelbarrow, Erbstoesser did not complete the sculptured panels on the fence until 1976: a chimney on a shed inside the yard, two shrines to the Virgin Mary, and various columns and panels scattered around his property. A wall next to the garage features the startled-looking face of a Nazi soldier, his mouth frozen in an eternal gasp.

Another disturbing image, reminiscent of the figure in Edvard Munch's famous painting *The Scream,* stares at passersby from the front fence. Other subjects include frolicking Keystone Kops (in honor of Erbstoesser's career on the police force), a Viking boat, and Russian Cossacks.

As often happens with outdoor art, the panels are beginning to crumble, and the Erbstoessers may consider seeking help to preserve them. For now, though, the cement artwork may be enjoyed from the sidewalk by all who pass by. Just consider it a panoramic view of the inside of a Wisconsin policeman's head.

Oconto's California Raisin House

We heard it through the grapevine: Some people just can't get over those smooth-stepping 1980s Claymation raisin guys who used to sing Motown ditties in TV commercials and Christmas specials. Why else would this house on Park Avenue near downtown Oconto be painted raisin-purple and topped with a California raisin guy cutout? No one was home at the time of *Weird Wisconsin*'s visit, but the decor pretty much speaks for itself.

James Tellen Woodland Sculpture Garden

Black River, just south of Sheboygan, is home to one of Wisconsin's most remarkable personalized properties—the James Tellen Woodland Sculpture Garden. Leafy and sun-dappled, the garden feels like a place created for magical spirits. Maybe that's why visitors are not surprised when they realize that the realistic-looking fence of fallen logs and twisted tree trunks was created by art rather than nature. The concrete limbs twine like old undergrowth as they support a bear clambering after its cubs, as well as a somber Native American chief peering uneasily at the road, as if to guard the nearby woman and child from intruders. Beyond the fence, other figures beckon.

For most of his life, James Tellen worked as a decorative painter at one of Sheboygan's famed furniture factories, honing his artistic skills as he adorned furniture with intricate designs. He carved wood as a hobby and also attended industrial art classes. The inspiration for his woodland

fantasy came in 1942, when he was hospitalized during an illness. He was sixty-two, and he suddenly found himself with the time to study the cast concrete statues in a churchyard across the street. Something clicked, and as soon as he regained his health, he began making the concrete statuary that now adorns the woods surrounding his family's rustic summer cottage. By the time he died in 1957, Tellen had created over thirty compelling sculptures, including that of Abraham Lincoln and the Virgin of Fatima. Always striving for realism, he was a stickler for correct proportion. But he also had a sense of humor: A concrete tree topped by two sly gnomes invites people to look within to view the person they love. Inside is a mirror!

Tellen's forest garden, on Evergreen Drive, has been preserved by the Kohler Foundation. It can be viewed from the road at any time, but to arrange a tour, you need to contact the John Michael Kohler Arts Center.

Wisconsin Grotto Culture

You can't tell by looking at the smooth southeastern prairies that Wisconsin is a rock-rich state. But try driving west into Coulee Country, where roads are cut through stone, and you'll immediately see the rocky richness. Or drive north and observe the piles of boulders the early settlers had pried out of the fields, then dumped in piles that still mark the boundaries of farms today.

It seems that whatever people wanted to do in the Badger State, rocks were always in the way. But over the years, a few visionaries began to view them as more than mere impediments to agriculture and travel. For these determined souls, the rocks and pebbles in their yards represented both an inexhaustible resource and a versatile means of expression. They used them to transform the landscape.

Large-scale sculptures made from rocks and cement by self-taught artists abound in Wisconsin. Give people with a few philosophical thoughts in their heads enough rocks and a little time, add a good dollop of cement, and what you get, evidently, is the rock grotto culture that dots the western and northern parts of the state.

Besides rocks, most grotto artists also work with old bottles, stained glass, seashells, and shards of broken pottery. Some have been fueled by religious conviction, and their creations qualify as true shrines, while others seem to have been impelled by nothing more than an urge to create something big, beautiful, and lasting. What they all have in common, however, besides their humble materials, is a sense of playfulness. A visitor to one of these rock grottoes can almost hear the trowels full of wet cement slapping the wood and chicken-wire bases, see the boxes and barrels full of rocks and glass shards, and feel the artist's deliberation over which shape and which color to press next into the gray matrix. But don't be fooled — making these heavenly creations involved a tremendous amount of work. Naturally, not all of them have survived. For those marvels that still remain, what's left is to admire them. And those who are so inclined may stuff a buck or two into the contribution boxes to make sure that all these sculptures of horses and castles, steamships and pioneer people, continue to stay put in all their exuberant weirdness. We owe that much to those who shared their visions.

Wisconsin Concrete Park

Fred Smith, tagged by some newspapers as the Picasso of the Pines, created his amazing Wisconsin Concrete Park—with over two hundred life-size figures— in the Price County town of Phillips after his retirement from the lumber trade in 1948. By that time, he had already built a stone-covered drinking establishment called the Rock Garden Tavern on Highway 13. When the Cleveland Indians won the World Series the year he retired, he made a rock-and-mortar barbecue on his tavern lawn as a tribute. He was sixty-three, and once he started, he couldn't seem to stop. Even though his joints were gnarled with arthritis,

he began crafting giant animals and people out of concrete, stone, and glass.

Nobody paid much attention when the first few animals went up, except to poke fun at them, but Fred Smith was undeterred. After seeing the movie *Ben-Hur,* he was inspired to build his own full-size chariot and horses. Naturally, being a former lumberjack, he also felt impelled to create a Paul Bunyan figure. Bunyan appears to stand on a globe and is the tallest statue in the park. Historical figures like Abraham and Mary Todd Lincoln, Kit Carson, Sacajawea, and Sun Yat-sen all ended up on

the lawn of Smith's tavern. The animal kingdom is well represented too, and Smith's unique menagerie includes deer, moose, horses, cats, wolfhounds, owls, and, of course, the American eagle.

Although many local people didn't much care for Smith's ever-expanding yard decoration, increasing numbers of tourists would stop and have their pictures taken next to the intriguing concrete sculptures. Word began to spread, and soon the town of Phillips found itself with a new tourist attraction in addition to its abundant lakes.

Smith just kept on building, including a huge re-creation of the Budweiser Clydesdales. That was to be his final effort. Before he could start the next project waiting on the back burner of his fertile imagination, the old lumberjack was felled by a stroke, and he died in February 1976.

The tavern was sold, and most of the statues were moved to the grounds of his house, where they were purchased and restored by the Kohler Foundation. Another nonprofit group now maintains the collection, and people come from all over the world to stare into the enigmatic faces of Smith's creations.

A few even say that the statues have taken on a life of their own. Author Dennis Boyer, in his book *Northern Frights,* reports that some Phillips residents claim the statues come alive at night. "We've got ghosts by the dozens moving into concrete statues," says one of Boyer's unnamed informants. "There are times at night when the concrete forms start to move. Some sort of dance. Others rocket straight up in the air and don't come down for hours."

The informant doesn't say who the invading ghosts might be. However, if anyone is really making those statues dance, most locals figure it's probably Fred and a few good lumberjack buddies.

Dickeyville Grotto

Wisconsin's outsider art is at its weird and wonderful best in the Dickeyville Grotto, which was begun in 1919 by Father Mathias H. Wernerus to spruce up the cemetery of the Holy Ghost Church in Dickeyville. He started building a not-so-remarkable soldiers' memorial, but by 1924, he had caught grotto fever and started covering the surfaces of cemetery urns with flowers made from broken china and glass. His parishioners chipped in with zeal, helping him bridge the gap between cemetery and rectory with fantastically constructed shrines and grotto areas, all encrusted with

a bewildering array of glass, crockery, seashells, and stones. The altar of the Grotto for the Blessed Mother holds a pipestone cross, which, according to legend, was made by the first Native American convert of the missionary-explorer Jacques Marquette. Many of the pieces of glass and crockery were donated by parishioners, so that the entire grotto, although intended as a devotional area, is also a sort of historical record of the Catholic households of the Dickeyville area.

One of Father Wernerus's main assistants was his cousin Mary Wernerus. She was also his housekeeper, and the priest called her his "flower girl." Her death in 1930 left him too desolate to continue his work, and he died the following year.

At one time, as many as 10,000 people would visit the Dickeyville Grotto on a summer Sunday, and it is still a well-maintained and popular tourist and religious attraction. Doubtless, it has inspired many a spiritual seeker, but Father Wernerus also has to be congratulated posthumously for his sheer bodacious artistry. He certainly spiffed up that cemetery.

Wegner Peace Monument

It's amazing what can be accomplished with a little teamwork.

Immigrants Paul and Matilda Wegner and their five children had a farm north of Sparta, just south of the hamlet of Cataract in western Monroe County. The Wegners were introduced to the joys of concrete when they built two silos for grain storage. Decades later, in 1929, they made a fateful trip to Dickeyville to see the famous grotto, and, as they say, light bulbs went on. Starting with a fanciful fence, the couple moved on to fill their yard with cement statues encrusted with glittering shards of glass and crockery. Many of their efforts were patriotic or religious in nature, and the small but usable Glass Church was one of their crowning achievements. Since they used mostly colored glass to accent their cement, they called their yard the Glass Works. It later came to be known as the Peace Monument because of the sign they built facing Route 71 that reads FOR PEACE ON EARTH.

Their two most personal creations were their replica of the *Bremen*, the ship that had brought them to the United States in 1886, and the giant glass version of their fiftieth wedding anniversary cake. The most intimate of all their sculptures, however, are the glass-and-concrete headstones that mark their final resting-places in a little cemetery adjacent to their farm. Each one spells out REST IN PEACE. Paul and Matilda certainly got their message across—and in a permanent way. Visitors can give peace a chance most days during daylight hours.

Nick's Grandview

Nick Engelbert did indeed have a grand view from his farmhouse off Highway 39 just west of Hollandale. A good view is not unusual in rural Wisconsin, and his house was surrounded by a gorgeous landscape of rolling hills and bucolic farmland. Still, in 1937, Nick began to feel the need to enhance his surroundings. With the kids gone, what else was there to do? He started by building an elaborate front porch with a series of concrete-covered arches that he bedecked with bits of china, glass, buttons, pebbles, seashells, and beads. He may have gotten the idea, some art historians say, after visiting the Dickeyville Grotto.

Wherever his original inspiration came from, Engelbert enthusiastically embraced the art of concrete embellishment and made it his own. His wife, Katherine, helped him design the stonework that would ultimately cover the entire exterior of the farmhouse. He also separated the yard from nearby hills and fields with a delicate arched fence punctuated by encrusted flower urns. He then created the first of the some forty figures that eventually graced his yard.

Engelbert sometimes called his creations "scenes from my life," and his life certainly had been full. Born in 1881 in what was then the Austro-Hungarian Empire, he worked as a machinist before joining the Austrian army. He later traveled throughout Europe on a bicycle and then explored the world as a nautical engineer. He came to the United States in 1912 and married Katherine Thoni, a Swiss immigrant. The couple settled in Hollandale, where they established the Grandview Dairy.

Out of Engelbert's eclectic life and vivid imagination and into his yard sprang all sorts of statues, including sculptures of King Neptune and a cavorting mermaid, Snow White and her dwarfs, a glass-covered peacock with a glorious tail, an American flag, and a double-headed Austrian eagle. He worked on the sculptures for fifteen years, and it didn't matter to him that he wasn't located on a major highway so that droves of passersby could admire his handiwork—he was too busy fulfilling his own dreams. It's hard to know, however, what nightmare had inspired the tree full of scampering monkeys, with a drunken man holding a bottle seated at its base. (A plaque says the monkeys represent Engelbert's family, and the drunken man, a transient who visited the farm, but don't let that stop your own interpretation.)

An organ-grinder with his monkey is possibly one of the most compelling of Engelbert's artworks. The statue that stands at Grandview today is a reproduction; the original is at the John Michael Kohler Arts Center in Sheboygan. In 1991, the Kohler Foundation rescued Grandview from dire deterioration, buying it and restoring the house and grounds. No one had lived there after Engelbert's death in 1962, and the sculpture park was nearly swallowed up by the surrounding wild Wisconsin countryside. The Kohler Arts Center also displays some of the two hundred paintings Engelbert created after he turned seventy and could no longer sculpt. The Pecatonica Educational Charitable Foundation now owns and operates Grandview—or at least it thinks it does. As is obvious to anyone who takes a moment to feel it, the spirit of Nick Engelbert is still palpably in charge here.

A plaque says the
monkeys represent
Engelbert's family,
and the drunken
man, a transient
who visited the
farm, but don't let
that stop your own
interpretation.

Prairie Moon Sculpture Gardens

Herman Rusch was in his seventies when he retired after forty years as a farmer. It was 1952, and to amuse himself and "kill old-age boredom," he began gathering a huge collection of rocks, photos, old tools, and various oddities. He decided that his treasure trove needed a home or, more precisely, a museum, where he could display it. And so he rented, then purchased the Prairie Moon Dance Pavilion, located between Fountain City and Cochrane, and began the process of transforming it into his personal museum. By the late 1950s, the former dance hall was crammed to the rafters with curiosities, including a washing machine powered by a goat on a treadmill, and Rusch was in need of another outlet for his creative bent. He took a good look at the grounds surrounding the museum, decided they looked a little empty, and began constructing concrete sculptures embellished with wildly colored mosaics.

Like many Wisconsinites, Rusch fell under the irresistible spell of dementia concretia. He visited a weird templelike Asian palace in Davenport, Iowa, called A Little Bit o' Heaven and was inspired to build his own Hindu temple topped with cone-shaped spires. He constructed a loopy fence out of steel wagon-wheel rims, then used additional steel rims to create a freestanding pyramid of arches. He made towers of tinted concrete and sculptures of dinosaurs and cacti. And to show who put the whole thing together, he fashioned a bust of himself, which he set atop a pebble-covered speaker's platform. His garden soon became a veritable fantasyland.

Finally, at the ripe old age of ninety-four, Rusch decided he wanted to devote more time to fishing and fiddling, and he auctioned off the museum and his collection of oddities. He died in 1985, shortly after turning one hundred.

Again we have the beneficent Kohler Foundation to thank for the preservation of Prairie Moon. The pavilion turned museum had literally gone to the dogs after Rusch sold it, having been used as a kennel, and his sculptures had begun to disintegrate. In 1992, the Kohler folks purchased the former museum and the colorful artworks, spiffed them up, and donated the site to the local township. The fanciful figures remain as an antidote to boredom at any age.

World's Most Beautiful Barbershop

"An unabashed artist" is how Palmyra historian Mary Tutton describes Rudolph "Rud" Smith, a German immigrant who settled in the town of Palmyra in 1896, when he married a local farm girl. Rud set up a barbershop in a Greek Revival building on Main Street and moved in his family upstairs. But the townspeople soon began to suspect that this was no ordinary house of hair. Rud installed three chairs, and in between waxing customers' mustaches and trimming around their ears, he would sneak outside and dash down the sidewalk entrance to his basement. There Rud maintained a different place, one where he stuffed wild birds and created intricate, inlaid designs on wooden furniture.

Eventually the bird mounts, furniture, and other odd items, such as cattle horns, unusual lamps, and assorted cages for live birds, began making their way upstairs to the barbershop. The shop's tin ceiling tiles were painted in a checkerboard of colors, and the place was heated with an ornate Garland stove. Once his shop had reached the bric-a-brac saturation point, Rud hung a sign above his door that read WORLD'S MOST BEAUTIFUL BARBERSHOP. There was barely enough room left in which to cut hair.

In good weather, Rud hung his birdcages outside the shop next to the barbershop pole. Mary Tutton tells the story of one local man who walked by the barbershop with a fishing rod, only to hear Rud's parrot screech, "Goin' fishin', goin' fishin'." When the man ignored him, the parrot shrieked, "Betya don't catch any, betya don't catch any!"

Rud died in 1931, but his beautiful stove, restored to its original splendor, can still be seen today at the Carlin House Museum in downtown Palmyra.

Beastly Lair in Williams Bay

Most of the fifty-plus admitted witnesses of the wolfish creature called the Beast of Bray Road will tell you they still think about what they saw, some on a daily basis. But only one witness has gone so far with his obsession as to create a personal werewolf environment based on his experience with the Beast.

Williams Bay store owner and artist Marv Kirschnik had his encounter of the fur kind in 1981 while driving near Bray Road in Walworth County on a pleasant September afternoon. Something caught his attention outside the window of his van, and he turned his head to see "a thing" standing next to a fallen tree. Kirschnik pulled over for a better look and peered out the passenger-side window, eyes agog. He was looking at what appeared to be a tall wolf or dog standing on two legs, and it was staring straight back at him! The improbable beast was covered with dark brown fur and didn't appear the slightest bit worried that Kirschnik was looking at him. Kirschnik lost the stare-down after what he estimated was a full minute. "I finally got scared and left because I didn't know what the heck it was. It watched me drive away."

Kirschnik went straight home to his drawing board and made a pencil sketch of what he'd seen; he still has the yellowed drawing. And then he started making other wolfish artifacts. Today, visitors to his bead-and-jewelry shop, called Mrs. Beadz (after his mother), will find themselves walking into a werewolf wonderland.

Kirschnik's favorite creation is the giant fuzzy werewolf marionette he calls Willie B. His other fabrications include wooden werewolf dioramas with moving parts, such as the Elvis *Blue Hawaii* werewolf; a working werewolf guitar; hand-cast white werewolf garden stones; and tiny pewter werewolf charms. For dressy occasions, Kirschnik has made himself a pair of faux fur werewolf pants, complete with tail. He says that it's all just his way of working through the shock of the sighting, which still haunts him even though it happened over twenty years ago. Making werewolf items, he's discovered, is a safer way to get the Beast out of his system than telling people about the encounter. "When I first saw it, I didn't tell anyone for two weeks, and then I told my wife, and she laughed at me," explains Kirschnik. Figuring other people would also respond with derision, he clammed up on the subject and quietly took to his workshop. But in Kirschnik's case, every werewolf item is worth a thousand snarls.

Jurustic Park

Marsh dragons. A whirlysaurus. The dreaded Siamese twin dragon. The prodigiously propagating rusty positron female bird, which always nods her head—yes, a courting male's dream. The octanoggin bird—proving eight heads are better than one. Creatures of nightmare? No, more like creatures of whimsy.

Located just outside Marshfield on County Road E, Jurustic Park is amateur paleontologist Clyde Wynia's valiant effort to raise supposedly extinct creatures from the McMillan Marsh muck they had inhabited hundreds of millions of years ago. Composed of ferrous metal, these strange creatures are possessed of a ferocious charm. If they still prowled the marsh, they'd certainly make you smile even as they grabbed you for dinner.

A retired attorney, Wynia has created an outdoor sculpture gallery of the gargantuan monsters that stalk his imagination. Here, prehistoric birds hang from trees, and

guardian creatures pull sentry duty on the moat's bridge at the property's entrance. Rusted to a deep orange color, the behemoths stand poised in dark contrast to the brilliant sunlight that slants through the surrounding foliage. Wynia's genius is evidenced by the mysterious atmosphere his looming giants manage to evoke. It feels like you are standing anywhere but in present-day Wisconsin.

The nearby Wynia home is a jarring reality check, as is the tiny cottage set amid the clusters of freakish oddities. This

Composed of ferrous metal, these strange creatures are possessed of a ferocious charm. If they still prowled the marsh, they'd certainly make you smile even as they grabbed you for dinner.

enchanted little Hobbit House is the domain of Clyde's wife, Nancy. An artist herself, she creates and sells glass-bead, flower, and other sculpture creations, and dolls of all sizes. But there's no doubt about it—her husband's cavorting saurians own the landscape. Luckily for Wynia's fans, Jurustic Park is no mere museum; it's a working monster garden where many of the creations are for sale.

Collected Exhibitionism

First, it must be said that Wisconsin boasts one of the finest networks of public museums in the country. Nobody beats a Cheesehead when it comes to showing off large rocks and fossils, Native American artifacts, or even fine art. What many outsiders and even a few insiders don't realize, though, is that the Badger State boasts a number of private, delightfully eccentric—if not downright wacky—museums. It seems that Wisconsinites love museums so much, they often just plunge ahead and create their own private ones for whatever purposes suit them. Some exhibition spaces aren't technically museums, and many exhibits would likely give a professional curator a case of the vapors. But if a fellow has amassed a few thousand ancient pebbles that look like human body parts and, sometimes, Barbra Streisand, what else is there to do but display them?

Many of the museums featured here were established by individuals who simply felt an urge to diverge. Sometimes, there was a commercial tie-in, but most were avid collectors motivated by nothing more than a desire to share their obsession with the world.

And who knows that these folks aren't simply ahead of their time in recognizing the value of their own collections? It may be that these eccentric collectors and entrepreneurs will be recognized someday as guardians of our culture and honored for their tendencies to acquire unusual things. In centuries to come, the human race may well have Wisconsin to thank for preserving its knowledge of squirrels, yo-yos, and plastic penguins.

Concretion Museum

NOTHING LIKE IT IN NEW YORK! Now, there's a sign guaranteed to bring in curious Wisconsinites. At least that's what retired philosophy professor Byron Buckeridge is counting on. He has painted the message in tall letters on the side of his grandson's pole barn, on Highway 14 one mile west of Arena, in the hope that people will come to see his "funny" rocks from Lake Superior. Actually, these rocks are more than just funny. Scientists call them concretions, and the Bad River Chippewa call them spirit or grandfather stones. Buckeridge calls them art.

The oddly globular mounds and calcified puddles of clay and sand are found almost exclusively along the southwestern shore of Lake Superior, where the ninety-year-old Buckeridge used to own land. There are other types of concretions elsewhere in the world—for example, in northern England—and possibly even in other parts of the solar system, with some geologists claiming to have found a version on Mars. But the Lake Superior concretions that Buckeridge began collecting over thirty years ago with his late wife, Dorothy, are shaped like nothing else found in nature. The organic odd-looking rocks are formed, it's theorized, from deposits shaped by water currents over time. They have a creamy fossil center and a hard cementlike outer coating and are estimated by geologists to be between ten thousand and twenty thousand years old.

The Bad River Chippewa believe that concretions were specially created by God, each with a tiny soul. Since 1995, they have declared that concretions are sacred and belong to their tribe on the Bad River Reservation. That's where the lion's share of the formations are found, says Buckeridge, so he has curtailed his collecting. But he has already accumulated over fifty thousand of the rocks, including some that measure several inches in diameter. He also owns a multitude of inch-size specimens. He sells some of these as good-luck charms for $1 each; others he fashions into mobiles, balancing them with a pair of dice. Each mobile comes with a handwritten Albert Einstein quote: "God does not play dice with the universe."

The pride of Buckeridge's collection is a complex three-foot-tall concretion that he has named "Flute Player." Most of the other rocks are for sale, with prices ranging from $15 to $250. He displays them on pedestals outdoors and in an upstairs room that also serves as the office of his grandson's construction business. One featured grouping here is the "Shakespeare Collection," which includes Antony and Cleopatra, Julius Caesar lying in a puddle of blood, and even Juliet on a high tower of driftwood, with a wistful Romeo below.

"Eyes for You"

Buckeridge has named one of his favorites "Miss America," because it looks like a female bosom. Another looks like a stack of melted scoops of ice cream that Buckeridge has dubbed "Mermaid." There's even one that looks like a well-rounded potbelly, which simply had to be called "Buddha."

Granted, it takes some imagination to see all of these things in the water-worn little rocks. But to Buckeridge, the resemblances are as plain as the nose on the "Richard Nixon" concretion's face. (That one, with its companion piece, "Mao," can be seen at the Nixon Library in Yorba Linda, California.)

But are they art? It's true that they weren't sculpted by human hands. But if Picasso could make art by calling a bicycle seat and handlebars *Bull's Head,* can't Byron Buckeridge claim art is a piece of sandy clay he calls "Barbra Streisand"?

Buckeridge hopes that some larger, more established museum will see it that way and accept his collection for permanent display. Until then, people will just have to travel to Arena to find out what nature's version of King Lear looks like.

House on the Rock

Words quail, fail, and just generally come up short when it comes to describing this place. The House on the Rock, with its stupefying, immense, and diverse displays, is the super-king granddaddy of all roadside attractions. It must be seen to get even a fair idea of what it contains. The "house" is in reality a conglomeration built atop a sixty-foot rock chimney in the countryside on Highway 23 about nine miles south of Spring. For starters, the long, leafy driveway and the parking lot are delineated by humongous sculptured urns covered with dragons and lizards, serving notice that this is mad-genius territory.

This amazing palace of pulchritude, unique in the entire world, began as a fourteen-room house-studio built by Madison resident and workaholic artist Alex Jordan. Jordan built the first stages in the 1940s by scaling Deer Shelter Rock with baskets of mortar and stone on his back. As soon as he finished his low-slung bachelor pad with its spectacular view of the Wyoming Valley, he began adding huge rooms to the place. For the next seventeen years he averaged one room a year in order to house the incredible collections he was acquiring. These included antique weapons, room-size automated orchestras and music machines of all kinds, Tiffany-like stained glass, glass paperweights, dolls and dollhouses, and musical instruments, including organs. Jordan's acquisitions included the world's largest carousel, located in a room whose ceiling is hung with wooden horses and female mannequins outfitted with wings and breast-baring togas. And that's only a fraction of what is now ensconced on the two-hundred-acre grounds. You'll even find a butterfly exhibit and a collection containing a million-piece miniature circus collection, complete with a life-size automated circus band and

The fourteen-room house (above) *is situated atop Deer Shelter Rock. The Infinity Room* (left) *projects 218 feet out over the Wyoming Valley.*

orchestra. And everywhere you look, there are mannequins in outlandish costumes.

One of the weirdest and eeriest sections of the Rock House is the cantilevered Infinity Room, a long tapering white hall with a glass bottom that allows visitors to look straight down 156 feet to the forest floor below. The room extends 218 feet from the main building, and its glass walls contain more than three thousand windows.

At the House on the Rock, size matters indeed. The main point of many displays seems to be sheer enormity. Notable in this respect is the Heritage of the Sea exhibit, which depicts a battle between a huge octopus and whalers against a two-hundred-foot "sea creature." The room also contains model ships, a scrimshaw collection, a *Titanic* display, and a music machine playing the Beatles' song "Octopus's Garden."

And for car buffs, there's a transportation building crammed with all manner of autos, including one covered in ceramic tiles. Getting tired just reading about it? Well, Jordan also threw in buildings full of Gothic armor, model

The largest carousel *ever built has hundreds of handcrafted animals but not one horse.*

airplanes, and replicas of England's crown jewels. Nothing, it seems, was too unassociated with Wisconsin to be included.

Jordan died in 1989, a year after selling his creation to collector and associate Art Donaldson. When he was alive, Jordan had delighted in walking with tour groups, incognito, just to gauge people's reactions. A few have whispered that his ghost still walks the winding halls. Donaldson has continued Jordan's tradition of adding new exhibits of epic proportions, so there's always something for Jordan's spirit to come back and inspect.

Rock in the House

If the House on the Rock is over the top, then the Rock in the House is rock bottom—literally. Named as a deliberate riff on its famous oversized cousin, the Rock in the House happened when life handed a Fountain City couple a boulder and they decided to make stone soup.

Maxine Anderson was standing in the kitchen of her house on the Mississippi River on Highway 35 one fine day in April 1995 when the world fell in. Or at least a good-sized piece of it did. A massive chunk of stone weighing fifty-five tons bounced 550 feet down the cliff behind Maxine and Dwight Anderson's backyard, crashed through the roof of their house, and landed smack in the middle of the couple's bed. The boulder rocked forward a few feet against the bedroom wall, then settled back and has not moved one inch since. Smashed fragments of the bed frame and tattered, dirt-encrusted remnants of the bedroom carpet can still be seen around the giant stone's edges. Strangely, although the rock reduced the bedroom to smithereens and left a large crack in the kitchen ceiling, much of the rest of the house remained unscathed. The bathroom, a few feet from the smashed interior bedroom wall, is still intact and usable, and the living room still boasts its great river view and comfy sofa. But the bedroom was just a little too open to the elements to sleep in, not to mention crowded, so Maxine and Dwight sold the house to their friends Fran and John Burt.

The Burts discovered that moving a rock that size would entail expenses as massive as the rock itself, so

they decided to operate the place as the anti–House on the Rock instead. Admission is $1, collected on the honor system in a metal box fastened to the porch. There are also souvenir rocks of various sizes for sale on the porch's shelves. But they are *not* chips off the actual old block, says Fran Burt, just local pebbles.

Visitors can walk around the patio area to view the rock from its entrance point and then wander inside to inspect the damage (and surprising lack of same) inside.

And if one casts an apprehensive eye up the cliff, it doesn't appear that another boulder ejection is imminent. However, it should be remembered that the Andersons had had no warning either. Gravity and geological pressures will have the final say at a time and place of their own choosing, and this surely must make the neighbors nervous.

Bjorn's Fine Clothing Store and Museum

We almost missed it. We didn't have a clue that it lurked in all its glorious largesse right there on Sixth Avenue. But while tooling around downtown Kenosha in search of haunted theaters, a glint of golden strangeness caught our eye. Our heads swiveled in tandem, and there it was—emblazoned on the stuccoed front with the word MUSEUM and a row of gilded plastic penguins on its roof. The building's façade also featured an Egyptian sarcophagus embedded next to the words PATENT PENDING, and masks of Uncle Sam, U.S. presidents, and other gems of kitsch were attached in a random manner.

Wacky as this sounds, all this was not adequate preparation for what awaited us inside. Think Redd Foxx clutching his chest in mock heart-attack mode and gasping, "I think this is the big one." Mike Bjorn's Fine Clothing Store and Museum is the antimall, the un–Wal-Mart. It's a pop-culture paradise, one in which all possible surfaces are plastered with Bjorn's personal montage of the absurd.

Suspended from the antique tin ceiling is a skeleton riding a bicycle. Along the walls are rows of galloping hobbyhorses that Bjorn has collected over the years and, like the roof penguins, sprayed with gold paint. (It's a big help to have friends in the junkyard business, explained Bjorn.) There are blow-up plastic aliens, mounted waterfowl, mammoth carnival-quality silver chains with "diamond" pendants as big as your fist, stacks of classic horror movie stills, and Pee Wee Herman dolls. It's a wonder Mike Bjorn can still find room for clothing racks.

He does, though, and successfully. In the stairway corner, he proudly points to his "men's clothing store wall of shame," which is smothered with dozens of newspaper articles on ex-competitors who have failed to market their merchandise as imaginatively as he does.

A big part of Bjorn's business comes from weddings and proms. Accordingly, the store's basement is a tuxedo cornucopia. Every funky color that any wedding planner has ever dreamed up after a few too many sneaky tikis can be found down here, along with the required white patent-leather shoes and matching belts. All the fitting rooms have themes, Princess Di's being the most popular.

Bjorn himself is a gregarious presence behind the counter. Some days he's nattily turned out in a shirt and one of his four thousand (actual count) ties, but on summer days you may find him in one of his genuine made-in-Hawaii Hawaiian shirts. Having recently "cleaned out" a hat company, he now gives away free straw hats with every Hawaiian-shirt purchase. But Bjorn is always seeking to improve his "museum" attractions as well as his inventory. When *Weird Wisconsin* visited, he had just bought a seven-foot submarine to hang from the ceiling. He had found it in a Delavan antiques shop. "To most other people it looked like junk," he explained, "but I saw it and said hey, we can have some fun with that."

His next idea is to build a model of the Wright brothers' plane and mount it on the roof of his store to commemorate the hundredth anniversary of their flight. "I never wanted to live in a world of blah-Mart," says Bjorn. "If the day ever comes when you can't walk into a place like this, as a human race we're finished."

Spinning Top Museum

The world-famous Spinning Top Museum in Burlington is the result of the vision and formidable collections of a woman named Judith Schulz, who is sometimes known as the Yo-Yo Mama. It all started many years ago, when Schulz, an educator and inventor, bought three spinning tops on impulse. She now owns thousands, not counting her gyroscopes and yo-yos. Always seen in her trademark long skirt and wide-brimmed hat, she has become an expert top spinner. Every museum visit includes a live demonstration. However, although Schulz shows visitors how to pull the magic strings that set the

tops in motion, the best part is that everyone gets to spin them. Of course, the antique tops and yo-yos are for looking only, but the variety makes them fascinating eye candy. They range in size from miniature (the size of a thumbnail) to big old push-down metal versions with glass tops and tiny carousels inside. There's also a museum within the museum—the Logic Puzzles Museum (also hands-on) and a gift shop—with a wide assortment of wooden puzzles and toys that are hard to find anywhere else. The museum's hours vary, so you can't just drop in. Phone ahead to reserve your two-hour visit. It's worth the extra trouble. The museum is on Milwaukee Avenue, in one of Burlington's historic downtown buildings.

Sam Sanfillippo's Squirrel and Chipmunk Museum

Here's a question few people have probably ever lost any sleep over: If albino squirrels could drive, what would their vehicle of choice be? A Madison man by the name of Sam Sanfillippo has made it his business to provide the answer to this curious question. It's a Barbie dream car painted hot fuchsia to match the platinum-furred critters' tiny pink eyes. Sanfillippo has preserved both the squirrels and the rodent-size cars to prove it.

They are on display in a series of weirdly compelling dioramas he has created and built in the basement of the Cress Funeral Home, of which he was owner and funeral director until his recent retirement. Beyond a reception room still decorated in full 1970s glory, including antler lamps, Sanfillippo has arranged numerous highly imaginative *tableaux vivants* composed of mounted costumed roadkill set in miniature habitats.

Although Sanfillippo is not a taxidermist, he is a decorated World War II veteran who started collecting fishing and hunting trophies as a boy. Some of these adorn the walls of several basement rooms. But it's the recycled roadkill that gets the most attention.

It was a buddy of Sanfillippo's, the late Wisconsin governor Warren Knowles, who helped him get started with the roadkill menagerie by asking game wardens to peel the least flattened specimens off the roads, pack them in dry ice, and ship them to the funeral home. Sanfillippo then let his imagination run riot to create the unusual scenes.

Chipmunks are featured in a large grouping called the "Woodland Fair." In one scene, "Louie's Bar and Grill," a smoking chipmunk takes a puff while perched on a barstool made out of a beer-bottle cap. A few inches away, four blithe chippies ride a merry-go-round as they clutch balloons and cotton candy. There's even the unforgettable "Topless Girlie Show," featuring topless chipmunk hoochie-koochie dancers in wispy grass skirts. If chipmunks have a heaven, they couldn't do much better than this.

Equally impressive is the larger-scale bar and poker-game scene using gray squirrels. The squirrels lounge on handmade chairs exactly their size, holding and folding teensy decks of cards. As a gesture of cross-species goodwill, one chipmunk is sitting next to a squirrel. There's also a suave piano-playing squirrel, pawing a really baby baby grand in front of a smoked-glass mirror. The selection of booze in tiny glass bottles, which would do any bar proud, obviously keeps all the squirrelly customers happy as they hunch on their red barstools and contemplate the irony of a miniature moose head on the wall.

The white squirrels hail from an albino squirrel club in Maryville, Missouri. Sanfillippo contacted the club asking for bodies, and the members complied. Most of the albinos carry out a transportation theme in Sanfillippo's universe: Besides the dream-car drivers, two of them peel out on a fire chief's tricycle (designed, probably, for a small child to ride—few Wisconsin firemen ride tricycles) and one gallops on a plastic horse, while others ride a Jeep and a dune buggy.

It's an expensive hobby, costing Sanfillippo $300 for each small animal he has mounted, but he says he feels that in a way, he's bringing these animals back to life. And there is some poetic justice too in the fact that many of the road-killed critters in his displays now exist eternally captured in tiny versions of the vehicles that had dispatched them.

The Cress Funeral Home, at 6021 University Avenue, Madison, Wisconsin, is free and open to the public when funerals are not scheduled.

Bong Heritage Center and Museum

Just to make things clear from the get-go, the Bong Heritage Center at 305 Harbor View Parkway in Superior is not a giant collection of head-shop implements. It's a memorial to the Wisconsin man who was arguably the best pilot the United States ever had—World War II ace Richard I. Bong. One of our favorite things about the Richard I. Bong World War II Heritage Center (to give its full name) is the incongruity of seeing the re-creation of a South Pacific island, complete with palm trees, sandbags, and a Quonset hut, against the backdrop of icy Lake Superior. The island is part of the museum's centerpiece, the recently restored P-38 Lightning that Bong had flown to such heroic effect. He had named it Marge, in honor of his wife. The Lightning has been painstakingly brought back to life, complete with the picture of Marge that Bong had affixed to its exterior, along with the symbols of all the enemy planes he had shot down.

Rudy Rotter's Museum of Sculpture

The brick warehouse on Buffalo Street in downtown Manitowoc may look plain and unimposing, but what Rudy Rotter put inside the two-and-a-half-story building over the course of forty-plus years is anything but. With some seventeen thousand pieces of artwork, all by one self-taught dentist, this has to be one of the biggest one-man art shows anywhere. And Rotter, who died in 2001 at the age of eighty-eight, didn't even begin making art until he was forty-three.

Just window peeping can give you a sneak preview of what's inside. There's a giant cardboard wheel, but if you look closely, you'll see that the spokes are really naked people. Other pieces include a portrait of Jesus done in Magic Marker and a wooden sculpture of a woman with a young child and infant in front of her, with the infant standing on the child's head.

The museum is mostly devoted to sculpture, but there are also paintings, drawings, and strange assemblages on display. And for admirers of Rotter's outsider art there's the welcome news that many of the pieces are for sale, with prices starting at $5. Hours can be sporadic, but stop by anyway. As Rotter liked to say, "That's the fun of experiments."

Millard Dinosaur Store

The windows of the Millard Dinosaur & Taxidermy Store, in the small Walworth County community of Millard, are crowded with examples of owner Jim Boyd's taxidermy prowess—a buck so bleached from sunlight that people think it's an albino, a magnificent tom turkey with tail feathers in full fan, and assorted antlered heads. What most people don't realize, however, is that Jim Boyd is southern Wisconsin's version of Indiana Jones and that the back of the store is a virtual museum crammed with animal remains of a different, and much older, type. Boyd is a dinosaur hunter, and he's been digging on a private ranch in Montana for the past seven years. Pieces of leg bones belonging to a creature whose hip socket stood about nine feet off the ground lie spread out on his worktable like an ossified jigsaw puzzle. Up front, he sells bits of bone from an *Edmontosaurus,* a type of duck-billed vegetarian dinosaur estimated to be about sixty-five million years old. You can buy your own small piece of "Ed" for as little as a buck. A hand-lettered sign over the bones reads YES, YOU MAY TOUCH.

Jim says he has loved "old stuff" since he was a kid. "And this is the hottest stuff going in the world these days—the dinosaurs," he adds. He made his first discovery by accident in Montana while hunting, and he was soon turning up finds like a sixty-five-million-year-old turtle shell, a rare piece of fossilized dinosaur hide, and, of course, the *Edmontosaurus*.

As his eye became more trained, Boyd even discerned that his ranch-owner friends in Montana were using a few dinosaur bones in their rock gardens, unaware of what the bones really were. But you can tell bones from rock, he says, because the bones have tiny holes running through them where the veins and marrow used to be. It also helps that he is well versed in animal anatomy through his taxidermy work. Like the game birds of today, for instance, the *Edmontosaurus* had three toes, the longest one in the middle. Knowing that and how a bird's leg fits together has helped Jim achieve breakthroughs, such as figuring out that a pile of seemingly unrelated pieces he had were in fact all part of a duck-billed dinosaur's leg.

Boyd recently found a front claw of a *Tyrannosaurus rex*, only the fifth one ever discovered, but his most recent discovery is the one he calls pay dirt. It's a rare species of dinosaur, sixty-six million years old, called *Thescelosaurus*. "We found the best, most complete skull of this animal in the world," says Boyd. He named it Bert. "We think we have everything from the hips up," he adds. The partial skeleton is on display at the University of Wisconsin–Madison Geology Museum.

If Boyd had his way, life would be nothing but one long dino dig. But he still spends most of his time preserving the outer coverings of modern animals. He charges $425 for a shoulder mount of a white-tailed deer, $450 for a turkey, or a bargain $80 for a mounted hoof. The dinosaur pieces are much cheaper, and you don't have to shoot them first.

National Fresh Water Fishing Hall of Fame

The National Fresh Water Fishing Hall of Fame in Hayward includes four interconnected museums. But the main attraction, and one of the great icons of Wisconsin's north, is the Shrine to Anglers, a colossal walk-through structure hand-sculpted in the likeness of a leaping muskie. Made of fiberglass, concrete, and steel, the giant fish is half a city block long and four and a half stories high. It is one of those things that must be seen to be believed. Even if you've seen the photo, it's still startling to see that huge fish head loom out of the treetops for the first time. Visitors can walk through the muskie, and up to twenty people can stand on its big lower jaw, which doubles as an observation deck. The adjacent museums house amazing collections that include five thousand lures, countless new and antique rods and reels, a slew of boat motors, and, of course, more mounted fish than you could shake a pencil bobber at.

Houdini Historical Center at the Outagamie Museum

Don't miss A.K.A. Houdini, the exhibit that has outraged many professional magicians because it shows exactly how the slippery Harry Houdini, who hailed from Appleton, managed to perform some of his trickiest escapes. It even features a box that visitors can climb into and duplicate his famed "Metamorphosis" illusion. The exhibit also discloses many fascinating secrets about Houdini, such as where he hid his picks and keys when he performed naked, which he did so that people wouldn't think he was hiding any tools. But of course, nobody checked inside his mound of well-coiffed hair or looked between his toes or peeked in, um, other places where the sun don't shine. The exhibit is on permanent display at the Houdini Historical Center, housed in Appleton's Outagamie Museum, at 330 East College Avenue. If you've always had a yen to buy toy shackles and big marbles that look like eyeballs, the museum's gift shop is the place to go.

On display *at the museum are many of the tools Harry Houdini used to break out of a crate (right) or "fix" a handcuff for easy release (above right). Above: Houdini prepares to jump handcuffed into Boston Harbor.*

Elmer's Auto & Toy Museum

Located on Elmers Road in Fountain City
and run by Elmer Duellman and his wife,
Bernardine, this museum is a must for car and
toy aficionados. On view are over six hundred
pedal-powered cars and one hundred pedal tractors,
as well as hundreds of antique and classic autos and
trucks. Elmer also has collected thousands of antique
toys and dolls that manage to entertain and delight
without requiring batteries!

SPIRIT OF St. LOUIS

WEIGHT 52½ lbs. LENGTH 54¼ in. GIRTH 27½ in.
CAUGHT JUNE 24, 1950 IN LAKE COURT OREILLES
OUT OF MOCCASIN LODGE, BY HARRY FULKERSON
HAYWARD, WIS. LICENSED GUIDE of MOCCASIN LODGE

Moccasin Bar and Wildlife Museum

Although thought of as a single institution, this is actually two separate places. The Moccasin Bar, at the corner of Highways 27 and 63 in downtown Hayward, has some fun things to look at, with its glass-encased dioramas of mounted woodland animals playing cards and otherwise mimicking human behavior. There's everything from a bobcat dressed as a sheriff to a skunk fight manager weeping over a kayoed Rocky Balboa raccoon. There's even a pipe-puffing bear cub (the original Smokey Bear?). Local legend has it that the animal dioramas grow increasingly realistic in direct proportion to the amount of beer consumed while viewing them.

The Wildlife Museum is attached to another bar, at 15708 County Road B. If you've ever wondered what a passenger pigeon looked like, this is the place to head. If you haven't wondered that, well, you can still see some other fun animals and drink your favorite beverage.

Honey of a Museum

Quick, what's the difference between a Polish beehive and a Slovakian beehive? If you don't know the answer, you can find out at the Honey of a Museum. It's on Highway 67 about two miles north of Ashippun, which is a Native American word that, depending on which tribe you talk to, means either "raccoon" or "decayed lungs." Neither, of course, has anything to do with the honey museum.

Most of the time, your host and tour guide will be Walter Diehnelt, whose family honey heritage goes back to a German beekeeper who came to America in 1852. Diehnelt has scoured the world for beekeeping lore and artifacts. You'll see the fanciful Slovakian hive decorated with a man's face next to the museum entrance, while a Polish-style example carved from a tree trunk by Diehnelt himself guards the driveway.

Diehnelt's family owns a large operation called Honey Acres, and admittedly, part of the museum's *raison d'être* is to sell honey in the gift shop. But the displays themselves are highly informative, with exhibits that illustrate the history of beekeeping and the various beekeeping techniques from around the world. For example, there's an ingenious high-rise hive from Yugoslavia that looks like a chest of drawers. It has a different scene painted on each drawer to help the bees remember which "apartment" is theirs. But the highlight is probably the bee tree, with a glassed-in hive for a close-up look at just what it is that bees do all day when they're hidden away from prying human eyes. It's the honeybee version of a live TV reality show — with much better plotting!

Museum of Medical Progress

This is one of several museums situated in the former military fort on South Beaumont Road in Prairie du Chien. The road is named after Dr. William Beaumont, often called the father of American physiology. The famous attractions of the museum are the two transparent female mannequins. The innards of one of the "twins" light up organ by organ, while her sister shamelessly reveals her skeleton. The nonskeletal twin provides an eerie commentary that describes what's going on in both their bodies. If that's not creepy enough for you, glance over at a nearby mannequin lying helpless in an iron lung.

Dioramas in another section of the museum, originally from the Chicago World's Fair, show gruesome early medical practices, like amputations and operations without anesthesia. The buildings that now house the museum exhibits were part of Fort Crawford until 1856. The fort's former military hospital, which has been restored, is where Dr. Beaumont performed his famous live experiments on Alexis St. Martin, "the man with a hole in his stomach." Dr. Beaumont would tie a piece of sausage on a string and drop it into St. Martin's open belly, then pull it out at intervals and record the effectiveness of St. Martin's gastric juices. And for those who desire additional evidence of our forefathers' sufferings, there is also a dentist's office from the early 1900s, with all of its diabolical instruments on display.

Dr. William Beaumont *experimenting with digestive juice by tapping a fistula in the stomach of Alexis St. Martin.*

Roads Less Traveled

The movie *Nightmare on Elm Street* embodied the concept of the spooky lane; it's no accident that the film was named for the location of the nightmare and not the murderer. Every community has its version of Elm Street. It's the haunted road that prompts the driver to grip the wheel more tightly. It's the route where your friends dare you to stop the car and get out to face your fear. It's the lane where young lovers find their amorous activities interrupted by something unspeakable. It's the track lined with cemeteries, crumbling buildings, and dark forests encroaching on both sides. In short, it's the road that gives us the heebie-jeebies.

Many tales about such roads reflect the archetypal imagery of nightmares—ghosts, ferocious beasts, witches, vampires, even the devil himself. Maybe there is actually nothing intrinsically scary about these roads. Maybe they merely serve as conduits to our own innermost demons. If this is the case, then a trip down one of these legendary byways may be a journey of profound self-discovery.

Of course, people who enjoy exploring hellish roadways may do so purely to scare themselves and their friends out of their wits. Who hasn't, as a teenager, piled into an overcrowded car around midnight and set off to explore a haunted route? Night riders on these jaunts inevitably get so caught up in the retelling of scary legends and the anticipation of experiencing something awesomely terrifying that by the time they arrive at their destination, their eyes may play tricks on them. A stray dog might become a hellhound, and an innocent jogger might mutate into a ghostly apparition.

Whether these roads are actually epicenters of the hypermystical world or merely hot spots for nocturnal joyriders is a matter for debate. Perhaps they're a little of each. In any case, the abundance of weird and hallucinatory folk tales surrounding Wisconsin's roads less traveled makes them especially intriguing.

Old Man Weary

Located about a mile south of Evansville, Weary Road is a narrow paved track lined on both sides by woods and cornfields. Like many haunted highways, overhanging trees create dark tunnels in places, which only add to the road's spooky ambience. As far as we can determine, the legends here are fairly recent, reminiscent of a certain contemporary horror movie icon. Although no one has reported any too-real nightmares, Old Man Weary's story bears more than a passing resemblance to that of Mr. Freddy Krueger. Some advice: When passing this way, if you value your sanity, avoid glancing in the rearview mirror.

Rumors Abound

Witnesses report seeing a phantom train, imps in the trees, strange lights, and a green glow toward the end of the road that is said to be the ghost of Old Man Weary. The story is that he favored entertaining local children, and their parents accused him of being a pedophile. Although this was never proved, the parents got together and burned his house down. It is said that not only was he innocent, but several children were present when the parents set fire to the house, and they perished in the resulting blaze, along with Weary. The house no longer exists, but out of tradition, visitors park by the space in the trees where Weary's driveway supposedly was. They report having seen phantom cars, and a phantom motorcycle has followed some visitors to a right-hand turn before disappearing.
—*Anonymous*

Lights Out on Weary Road Bridge

There is a bridge along Weary Road where, if you turn off your car and lights, it will not restart when you turn the key. There are also tales of a young man who died car-surfing on the road.—*Anonymous*

Chased and Scratched on Weary Road

I was first introduced to Weary Road about six years ago. I haven't been back since. Weary Road is a deserted road that has some seriously strange things going on. The first time I was there was at eleven p.m. with five other people. We began to "walk the road," and as we got about one quarter of the way down, I got the strangest feeling that we were not alone. This fear grew in me to the point of hysteria, and I wanted to leave. The group thought that this might be a good idea, so we turned around. All of a sudden, there was this huge ruckus in the trees, and something unseen flashed past right in front of us. We screamed in fear, then ran—but it was following us. When we got back to the cars, I looked down at my arms, which were now burning, and I noticed that I had five fingerlike scratches down both arms! This alarmed me, since I don't remember getting scratched. Then there was the distinct smell of kerosene in the air. We hightailed it out.

This place scares the hell out of me, and the thing is that there is a true story behind the haunting of Weary Road. It is funny how mad people get from the town when you bring it up. The fact that a boy was killed on that road a few years back adds to the mystery.—*Jokin94*

Three Trips to Weary Road Does the Trick

Weary Road has been an urban legend among teenagers for a while now. The first time I heard about Weary Road, I was about sixteen or seventeen years old. As the story goes, there was a cruel man who supposedly owned almost all the land in this small town. The townsfolk called him Old Man Weary. He lived on Weary Road. He had the typical big house, with servants and family. The townsfolk hated him with a passion, as well as his family, from what I hear. There are two versions as to how he died. One is that everyone got together, tied him to his bed, and set the estate on fire. The other version is that he himself had murdered his family and then set the estate on fire with himself in the house. Either way, he died in a fire.

Well, what happens on Weary Road is strange. You have to visit it three times before you see anything. I know from personal experience. Strange coincidences happen the first two times, like, for example, you might see a flash of light to the side of the road the first time you visit, and the second time, you may hear something on your car. That is just the beginning.

What happened to me was that a friend of mine and myself heard the story and decided we wanted to see it for ourselves. The first time we went, we were driving along the road, when out of the blue, a giant white owl came flying out of the bushes. We just blew it off as an eerie coincidence and didn't think anything more of it. The second time we went, the car radio became staticky, and we thought we heard a group of people bustling around and talking at the same time. Of course, we thought it was just the radio. The third time made me a believer. We were driving on the road, and we decided to park and get out. We got out and walked around the car

and thought we heard something in the field. We decided to leave because it was getting way too creepy. As I was getting in the car, I looked in the rearview mirror and saw a man standing behind us. But he was standing a long way back. I said to my friend, "Oh my God, turn around. There's someone behind the car!"

She turned around, as I did, but we didn't see anyone. So of course she thought I was full of it. I thought I was losing my mind. I then turned around to start the car, but I looked in the mirror again, just in case. And just like before—only closer—was the man! I said, "There he is again." She turned around; she saw nothing. I said, "Look in the mirror."

She did, and he was directly behind our car. We could see his face and what he looked like. One thing for certain—his face looked as though he was extremely upset that we were even on the road. Needless to say, I drove out of there. As we left, we both saw him on the side of the road. He was smirking at us.

I've heard about other people having experiences out there. We went to Evansville, and no one would talk about it. We went to the library to look up past fires, and there was no information that we could find. We even asked the "old" folks, and they said they couldn't talk about it, because "bad things happen when you talk about him."

I find all this too eerie. We couldn't find anything about Weary Road, and no one will talk about it.—*SP & TH, aka LadyxLeox*

Witnesses report feeling an eerie presence here. They describe hearing inhuman screams and seeing short, robed shapes in the woods.

Paradise Road Is Anything But

Paradise Road, located just east of Jefferson off Highway 18, is another winding paved country road that meanders through rolling farmland, scrub brush, and scattered pockets of woods. Even if you don't know where the haunted spot is, you'll have no trouble finding it. After rolling down a slight incline, the woods grow close to the road on either side. The canopy looms over the roadway. The road becomes darker, cooler, and more mysterious-looking. For those who can't feel the spooky vibes, the spray-painted warnings on trees on both sides are dead giveaways. If you're looking for Wisconsin's version of the Blair Witch, chances are you'd find her here. Couples test their bravery along Paradise Road.

Hot dates. Big scares. It's a story as old as time.

Inhuman Screams, Decapitated Raccoons

Witnesses report feeling an eerie presence here. They describe hearing inhuman screams and seeing short, robed shapes in the woods. Some have even seen a raccoon, decapitated, with blood glistening in the headlights, but no blood on the road and no head anywhere in sight. Our advice is to STAY OUT OF THE WOODS ON THE LEFT-HAND SIDE.
—Anonymous

During the day,
the road appears
somewhat normal except for
the "odd" feeling you get when
you are there. You can almost always
hear noises that are not everyday sounds—
footsteps, or what we think are footsteps—
and you can catch shadows moving around.

Someone, or Something, Is Out There

Me, my girlfriend, and three friends decided to check out Paradise Road. We drove out and took photos and some video with a night-vision camcorder. During the day, the road appears somewhat normal except for the "odd" feeling you get when you are there. You can almost always hear noises that are not everyday sounds—footsteps, or what we think are footsteps—and you can catch shadows moving around. I do not have an explanation for any of it, but I can tell you it's the same thing all the time, and we have been there several times. I do believe someone or something is there and, for whatever reason, would like to interact or tell you of its presence, if you know what I mean. I guess after you have been there, you might be able to get some more insight into the whole thing that will make more sense.

Besides this, I did find out something else about Paradise Road. Turns out a guy I work with says his mom knows something about its history. She said that some time ago, some kids died there. She didn't say how, but I'm gonna see if she knows. She was an EMT for the area and said that the area is cursed. It's had some bad accidents, and the unearthly screams that are reported can be heard around one to three a.m.—*Kurt*

Sound of Midnight Chain Saws

We went to Paradise Road in Jefferson. By the time we got there, it was dark. We drove for a while till we got to the "haunted stretch," but we didn't make it over the hill, because no one lives over the hill, yet we were hearing chain-saw noises. Seriously, who is chain-sawing at eleven thirty at night? I had the car stopped—completely shut off. All of a sudden, we heard a loud thud from the back, like I ran over something. We were totally freaked, so we hightailed ourselves out of there.—*Kaylan*

Bad Vibes on Paradise

Paradise Road is on Highway 18. If you have any supernatural feeling at all, you will feel so creepy going down that road. I was down there with a group of people, and all I wanted to do was leave.—*Jessica*

Three Witchy Sisters on Paradise

It's a road where three witch sisters got hung about a hundred years ago. When you go into the forest at night or when it's dark, you hear things following you, like footsteps, and you can hear screaming, and supposedly when you drive by and look back, you'll see somebody hanging in a tree. You see things in the woods too, like ghosts, white and glowing. Me and my friends Erica, Trent, and David went there. Trent and David locked me and Erica out of the car, so we ran, and on our way up the street, we heard footsteps, and when our friends finally picked us up, they said they almost got hit by a truck. Trent said he went there before, and his car died right in the middle of the road, in between the forests, but it started after fifteen minutes. If you plan a trip there, don't go alone.—*Lisa*

Sauk County's Vampire Valley

Cemeteries and vampires—it's a match made in hell. Every town, no matter what its size, has a place where teens like to gather. These spots are often outside the town, away from prying adult eyes. Cemeteries, abandoned houses, rural parks, or narrow country roads that wind through dark woods make perfect gathering places for teenagers.

Cemetery Road east of Ironton is one such road. About a mile past the cemetery, deep in a secluded valley, stands the old John Maucka farmstead. After Maucka died, there was no one to care for his land and buildings; the fields ran wild, and the buildings eventually collapsed.

Around 1965, a group of high school girls thought it would be cool and daring to spend Halloween tramping through the fallen buildings in search of ghosts and other beasties that go bump in the night. Since there are no secrets in high school, a group of boys learned of the girls' plans and devised a practical joke.

The girls, hearts thumping mightily, tiptoed into the decaying farmhouse. The moon was a no-show that night, and dim flashlights were the girls' sole security. Inside, they found a coffin—with a baby in it. Screams, panic. Scared out of their minds, the girls ran to a neighbor's house, where several warm-bodied boys were waiting to offer comfort.

It would have been a shame not to take advantage of a good thing. As the story spread, Maucka Valley became Vampire Valley. Boys began taking girls there for Initiation Night. Could they face the terror of vampires? The boys would force the girls from their cars; then one of the fellows, wearing a cape, would jump out from the bushes, strike a classic vampire pose, and send the girls crying back to their boyfriends' welcoming arms.

Witch in the Woods of Witch Road

On Callan Road outside Rosendale, there is a broken-down abandoned house where a woman reputed to be an evil witch once lived. The events that took place long ago at this house continue to define the road, and these days, Callan Road is known to many as Witch Road.

The witch lived in this house during the 1940s, practicing her dark arts in the desolate wooded area surrounding the place. The effects of her black magic have been profound and are still experienced by people driving on Witch Road today. The cursed sections of the road are said to be significantly colder than other parts. Drivers are often stunned by lights that speed down the road toward their cars and by bright white lights that emanate from deep within the surrounding forest. It's also said that the witch had left her image along the road to haunt all those who would travel it after her death. A tree on the right side of the road has grown into a shape that resembles an old witch to a remarkable degree. Strangest of all are the reports of a young girl who peeks from behind trees as people pass by on Callan Road. It is unclear exactly who this girl is or why she's tormenting motorists on this lonely street.

Legends of Caryville

The Caryville area has been a source of numerous local legends, attracting the curious from all corners of the state and beyond. There are stories about a priest who hanged himself in the belfry of Caryville Church. On certain nights, people can supposedly see a spectral body hanging from a noose in the bell tower. Church members, however, dismiss the stories and assert that nobody ever committed suicide in the church.

According to some stories, a prom queen was killed while driving drunk on Caryville Road when her car swerved off a bridge and into a stream. Now people claim to be chased by phantom cars on this road. It is alleged that you can still see the headlights of the girl's car shining beneath the surface of the black waters under the bridge.

Across from Caryville, in the Chippewa River, is a remote island. At one time, there was a lumber town on the island, and legend has it that there was also a sanatorium built by a doctor who owned several vicious dogs. According to the stories, the dogs have since returned from the dead as hellhounds—black dogs with glowing red eyes that wait at night for their unwary victims. Historians have confirmed that there was a town called Meridean on the island, but there was never a sanatorium there.

People claim to have seen ghostly children playing in the cornfield next to the old Caryville Cemetery. At night, they say, you can hear the hellhounds growling and see their glowing red eyes. Many people report having encountered Blackie, a shadowy demon that has also been sighted at the Caryville schoolhouse and the Meridean boat landing.

Although many of the stories surrounding Caryville are probably just fiction, ongoing reports by people claiming paranormal encounters there continue to fuel the imagination of the curious, thus keeping the legends alive.—*Terry Fisk*

Shooing the Devil

Wisconsinites are a motley crew. It's been said this state received the most varied mix of immigrants in the nation in the nineteenth and early twentieth centuries, with settlers pouring in from every corner of Europe. Some ethnic groups were more tenacious than others in bringing their Old World heritage to a new life in America, and one of the most resourceful was the Polish Catholic enclave of central Wisconsin. To this day, near the small village of Polonia, just off Highway 66 a few miles east of Stevens Point, evidence of ancestral beliefs can be seen in the unique wooden crosses and shrines at country crossroads and farm borders. They were called *kapliczki* in Polish, from the word meaning "chapel."

We drove around the Polonian countryside one summer afternoon, hunting for *kapliczki* at every intersection. According to Polish folk belief, crossroads were optimal places for evil spirits to gather in hopes of attacking passersby. To guard against such deviltry, believers would erect a shrine where evil spirits were likely to lurk. It could be a tall cross, often with a statue at the base, or it could be a hollow column of red brick topped by a metal roof, usually with religious images or relics inside. Another function of the *kapliczki* was to ward off lost souls who might be wandering the countryside looking for living people to haunt.

One of the best-known red brick shrines is at the intersection of Highways I and Z. Inside, we noted statues of the Blessed Virgin, St. Joseph, and the Sacred Heart. A good example of the tall cross-type shrine is at Highway I and Hillcrest Road. The Virgin Mary rests at its base, with an image of Jesus high on the cross above.

The shrines were also places to pray outside church, and they served both as everyday reminders of the faith and as special memorials to saints and departed loved ones. Any *kapliczki* that you encounter should be considered sacred places and treated accordingly. Three bullet holes we discovered in the window glass of one red brick shrine showed that not everyone has been respectful.

Any *kapliczki* that you encounter should be considered sacred places and treated accordingly. Three bullet holes we discovered in the window glass of one red brick shrine showed that not everyone has been respectful.

Grant Park's Seven Bridges

There is supposedly a ghost in Grant Park, in the area called Seven Bridges. The park is on the south side of Milwaukee, leading to the beach. I went there a couple of days ago, and it's a very spooky place. You enter through a bridge under a sign reading ENTER THIS WYLD WOOD. A woman told me that a group of her friends have seen the ghost lady twice.—*Bill*

It is rumored that if you go to Seven Bridges and walk the paths between the times of nine-thirty p.m. and midnight on nights when the moon is full, you will see colored lights dancing around in the woods. If you go farther into the woods, you will hear what sounds like laughter and screams. If you are really quiet, you can hear footsteps in the woods coming towards you, and those footsteps will be accompanied by heavy breathing. If you wait for those footsteps to reach you, a very uneasy feeling will creep over you—an evil feeling.

It's said that adults and children have been killed here and that their murderers have afterwards committed suicide in the park. It's also rumored that if you stand on one of the bridges, a mist or an apparition will appear right in front of you. The apparition is most likely one of the murder victims.—*Anonymous*

Yes, I am a resident of Milwaukee, and I have heard rumors about the woods of Seven Bridges in Grant Park. The rumor goes that you can hear screams and see lights and sometimes hear footsteps and feel heavy breathing. So tonight (October 9, 2004), my two friends and I went to test the rumor . . . and we indeed did hear screams and saw weird lights in the woods. It was especially weird because nobody was around. The park was empty.—*Joe M.*

The park is really spooky at night. I've been there but haven't seen anything. There is reportedly a ghost woman who walks the paths after dark looking for her two sons who drowned.—*Bill K.*

Seven Bridges is definitely creepy. I used to walk through there on many a date and whatnot during the day, and it's easy enough to get lost then. Nighttime is rough. I was there last night, but I didn't see anything. Of course, we didn't have much time to explore, because we stupidly parked in plain view and the cops came. No tickets or anything. We were just shoved on our way. At the very least, Seven Bridges is a fun place to wander at night. Bring a big flashlight and maybe a knife. I'm not horribly trusting of people around there.—*Jay*

I've been at the Seven Bridges area at night a few times, and one of the creepiest areas I noticed was the deck at the beginning of the trail. If you go on a clear night close to the full moon, you don't really need a flashlight. In the wilder days of my misspent youth, we used to party in the woods there, along with every other teenager in the area. Never saw a ghost, but witnessed some interesting goings-on. Another interesting place off Lake Shore is the Seminary Woods in St. Francis. We felt strong energy there and saw childlike cult scribbles on a couple of headstones.—*Mark64RagTop*

Haunted Bridges of Stevens Point

Every city ought to have one, but Stevens Point can proudly boast of at least three haunted bridges.

The Red Bridge, on Casimir Road in the quiet backwater of the Wisconsin River, is popular with fishermen. Apparently, few suspect that this bland crossing, more glorified culvert than proper bridge, is host to a womanly wraith. Most of the fishing enthusiasts, though, are safely in bed by the time she deigns to make her appearance. At midnight, legend goes, you have to park your car on the bridge and turn off your lights. Only then will her tortured form flit into view.

The Black Bridge, a railroad crossing, spans the Wisconsin just down from the roiling spume at the gates of

the hydroelectric dam. Legend has it that unfortunates working in the surrounding factories occasionally tumble into the dark waters here. Worse, perhaps, are the rumors of people dying in industrial accidents and of management quickly disposing of the corpora delicti in the turbulent waters before OSHA could arrive to investigate. The lifeless bodies are said to slap up against the pilings in the churning river and become trapped, releasing their spirits to take shelter on the high ground above. Haunted forms are said to cavort across the narrow bridge.

East of town, on Highway 66 near Jordan Park, is Stevens Point's most infamous haunted spot: Bloody Bride Bridge, which spans the Plover River. According to legend, a bride died on this bridge on her wedding day. Accounts vary. Some say her car veered off the bridge into the Plover; others report that she died in a head-on collision; still others say that she was run over while walking across the bridge for help following car trouble. Regardless, her death was messy and tragic.

A law-enforcement officer had the first encounter with her ghost. While he was driving across the bridge one day, the bedraggled bride suddenly appeared in front of his squad car. He slammed on the brake, but it was too late. When he got out to investigate, her body had vanished. Shaken, he returned to his car, only to find her in his backseat! As he pulled away to take his bloody passenger to the hospital, she vanished again.

Some witnesses have encountered her tattered form along the route. Others have encountered her on the bridge as they sat in their cars, viewing the river or reading a map, and happened to glance in their rearview mirror to see her blood-spattered eyes meeting theirs. You can pass this way during the day for a good look, but the Bloody Bride is only on the prowl after dark, especially in the wee hours before dawn.

Felines and Phantom Joggers in Boltonville

Boltonville's Jay Road is also known as Seven Bridges Road. Those who know the road's nickname undoubtedly also know the many tales of tragedy that are associated with this route.

The first tale of haunting along Seven Bridges Road involves a lonely old woman who used to live here with no one but her many cats to keep her company. A group of local kids took to taunting the woman at night. Soon, they went overboard and began killing the poor felines. This caused a war of sorts between the kids and the woman. Things escalated to the point that they were out of control, and what started as mischief ended with the woman's house burning down. Heartbroken and angry at the kids who had ruined her life, the woman chose to stay in the house while it burned, and she perished in the fire. It's said that her ghost now haunts those who come down the road looking for trouble. And the many stray cats that live along the road are said to be the descendants of those who survived the fire.

The cat lady is not the only woman who haunts Seven Bridges Road. Along one particularly treacherous stretch a young female jogger was struck and killed by an out-of-control car. Her body was never recovered from the swamp along the road. Years later, people still report encounters with the tormented jogger's ghost. They see a young woman in a jogging suit suddenly emerge from a mist in front of their car, inevitably too late to avoid her. After getting hit, the woman either disappears entirely or momentarily appears within the person's car to further torment them.–*Erika M.*

Highway 12's Disappearing Man

Modern times being what they are, it is recommended that drivers don't stop to pick up hitchhikers. It is simply too dangerous to welcome strangers into one's car. Still, there are many motorists who view themselves as Good Samaritans and give hapless wanderers rides from time to time. Those who stop to pick up hitchhikers on Highway 12 in Baraboo are often met with a shock that's well beyond the dangers most people could ever imagine.

Over the years, hundreds of people have reported seeing a man with a dark beard and green jacket hitchhiking along Highway 12. Most often, people pass him by, not thinking twice about what they have seen. A mile farther down the road, the same man appears again. Most people note this odd occurrence and continue on. But some, intrigued by the man's ability to reposition himself, stop and offer him a ride after the second encounter. These people are further shocked to discover that the mysterious man disappears before he makes it to their car!

Picking up hitchhikers is always risky, but this is even truer when dealing with the disappearing man of Highway 12.

Halfway Tree of Halfway Tree Road

For as long as anyone can remember, a craggy old bur oak has stood just south of Broadhead on Halfway Tree Road, thrusting stubborn branches toward the sky. It looks like the kind of tree that should have its own legend, and it does. This ancient oak is supposed to mark the exact center of the distance between Lake Michigan and the Mississippi River, as measured by local tribes before European settlers came to Wisconsin. Local legend has it that an early farmer was told by Indians never to cut the tree down, and it has been preserved ever since.

According to the Wisconsin commissioner of public lands in a story for the *Milwaukee Journal Sentinel,* the tree is about twelve miles off-course. However, nobody is about to change its name or rip down the historical marker. After all, the Halfway Tree is really, really close to the center point. So until somebody plants a tree at the exact center, Old Bur keeps the title.

Apparition of Hilbert Road

The pain of a parent who has to bury a child is unmatched in this world. On Hilbert Road outside the town of the same name, people often encounter a man at the spot where his daughter was killed. This is not simply sad. It is downright scary, for the man is a ghost, and his daughter was killed a century ago.

When traveling on Hilbert Road between midnight and five a.m., people often come upon a solitary man leaning against a tree and holding a lantern. He asks those who stop if they have seen his daughter, who had never come home. It is at this point that people usually notice a number of highly irregular things about the man. First of all, he has only half a face. Second, he is known to disappear, especially when people shine lights at him to get a better look.

It is believed that this man's daughter was killed on Hilbert Road around the turn of the twentieth century. Unable to accept his daughter's death, he took to wandering the road in hopes of finding her. After his death, his spirit continues to do the same.

Ghost Road

There is a road outside Galesville, between Holmen and Galesville. The name of the road is McKeeth Drive, but it is also known as Ghost Road. The story is that a Galesville man died on this narrow one-lane road when he lost control of his car and crashed into a tree. The autopsy showed no sign of drugs or alcohol in his system, so they ruled it "Auto-Suicide." His family does not believe it. They say that tracks near his car showed that he had been chased by someone, but the police did not look into it. Legend has it that if you go out there you can sometimes see his image walking across the road or the image of a car being chased by another car, with the first car crashing into the woods.

I have been to this road twice. The first time I did not experience anything unusual. The second time, I was with several friends. They were all in the bed of my pickup truck, except two who were up front. I saw a white object fly across my hood and windshield. One of my friends sitting up front said he saw it also. Then we turned around about ten minutes later and went back that same way. We saw the silhouette of a man on the side of the road. After that, I left 'cause I was scared witless. My friends in the front saw it also, but our friends in back said all they saw that was weird or unexplainable were brightly glowing white dots all over the place. That is my story. And if you are wondering, we were sober when we went on this road. *–Trevor*

Running-Board Ghost of Ashland Road

Bayfield County's Ashland Road is an old highway with a rich history. The Excelsior Plant and the Kenfield-Lamoreaux Box Factory were located in Slab Town, which was Washburn's lower west end, near Thompson's Creek. Most of the folks who lived there worked in the local sawmills and made their homes from slab wood—hence the name Slab Town. The majority were French Canucks, including a few of my relatives.

If I told you that down in that area, in January 1926, there was a ghost who actually stood in the road, waved his arms, and stopped traffic, then jumped on the running boards of cars, took a ride, and disappeared into thin air between eleven and midnight, you'd think I was ready for the funny farm. But here's what appeared on the front page of the *Washburn Times* on January 21, 1926.

In January 1926, there was a ghost who actually stood in the road, waved his arms, and stopped traffic.

Washburn in the past had been able to boast of many things such as a fine harbor, difficult climate, contented people and many other things, but it is only recently that it has been able to boast of having a real-live ghost, one who frequents that section of Ashland Road between the Box Factory and the Long Trestle Crossing.

It seems to delight in stopping automobiles by standing in the road and swinging its arms, then jumping on the running boards and taking a ride.

Roy Lodle of Lodle's Shoe Shop was given the scare of his life one night last week when he made a trip to Washburn in his car. He was stopped in the road by the ghost, who climbed onto his running board and took a ride, again disappearing into the brush alongside the road. Picking up a companion here in Washburn, Lodle started back for Ashland and was stopped again.

Others from Ashland who have seen the ghost are Earl Smith of the N. P. Freight House, Kohn Kolberg of B&M garage, and a number of traveling salesmen. The William Tell Bow and Arrow Club of Ashland, hearing the rumor, took it upon themselves to investigate and, armed with bows and arrows, proceeded to the region of the sightings. And as they neared the spot, the ghost dashed into the road, and as he did so, the arrows flew thick and fast, and the spirit dashed down the road.

Many Washburn people have been patrolling the Ashland Road as of late, but none have reported seeing the ghost. It is said that it makes appearance between the hours of eleven and twelve o'clock midnight.—*Tony Woiak*

Ghosts of Elk Lake Dam

In 1998, I received a frantic phone call. The shaky voice on the other end stated, "I will tell you how to get there, but I will never go back to that place." The man was referring to the Elk Lake Dam, a well-hidden dam in the scenic valley between Eau Claire and Menomonie. Surrounded by giant green trees and a treasure of a lake, the area is known for its beauty and tranquillity, though the dam itself is dilapidated and long past its prime.

The caller continued. He told me of relaxing at the dam with a friend when he noticed what appeared to be a glowing woman floating in the air behind them. He asked his friend if he knew that there was a ghost standing behind them. "Yes," he answered. After garnering the collective courage to turn to look at the ghostly woman, the two men were relieved to find that she had vanished. They quickly fled the area, with the solemn vow to never return to Elk Lake Dam.

Word of the ghostly sighting spread, and within several months, numerous witnesses came forward with their own paranormal experiences at the dam. One local man reported seeing the ghost of a young mystery woman underneath the bridge as he was night fishing. Other locals encountered a young woman as they drove over the rusting, dimly lit bridge, only to watch her vanish right before their eyes. Over the next year, several other people came forward with similar tales of their bewilderment and confusion as they too tried to explain how a woman could disappear without a trace.

Digging through the local paper, I found an unsolved murder from 1974. The report stated that on February 15, 1974, Mary K. Schlais's bloody body was found in a ditch approximately a half mile from the dam. Police believe Mary was hitchhiking and was picked up by someone in the Minneapolis, Minnesota, area. She was to leave for

Word of the ghostly sighting spread, and within several months, numerous witnesses came forward with their own paranormal experiences at the dam.

Chicago to attend graduate school at around ten thirty a.m. on Friday, February 15. She never made it.

A local man driving home saw a man dumping something on the side of the road, then kicking snow over it. The witness called the police, but when they arrived, the suspect was gone. The witness reported that the man was driving a gold or orange compact auto, and he provided a sketch of the suspect.

After uncovering this new evidence, the press published a story about the murder and the ghost connection. New reports began coming to me that were more bizarre than the previous ones. One witness reported that he was traveling alone through the area at night when he encountered a woman standing on the side of the road near Elk Lake Dam. As he got closer, she disappeared. Another man, while standing on the bridge directly above the dam, felt as though something or someone had taken over his body, and he had an unnerving vision of someone throwing a bag down into the water. He also felt an incredible urge to jump from the bridge. The man then snapped out of his "trance" and hastily fled the area.

Many other people flocked to the dam to see if they too could encounter the ghost of Mary Schlais. Several captured strange mists and lights on film. Most reported having strange sensations while walking over the bridge. Some reported electrical anomalies, such as flickering streetlamps, and one young man reported seeing a dark, almost transparent shadow figure running extremely fast along the shoreline before disappearing.

Fellow paranormal researcher Terry Fisk and I subsequently uncovered the story of Virginia Hendricks, who died in 1995. Virginia lived near the dam and claimed that during the fall of 1994,

Mary Schlais would visit her at her home on a regular basis. Virginia described Mary as wearing a pink angora sweater and white capri pants. She was pretty, in her early twenties, had shoulder-length blond hair, and identified herself simply as Mary. Virginia believed that Mary was an apparition, because she would appear at the same time every morning and afternoon walking through Virginia's garden and tapping on her window. Virginia would take food out to her. Mary always wore the same clothes, always showed up at the same time each day, and nobody but Virginia could see her.

Today, Mary's murder is considered a cold case. No suspect has been arrested, and there are several details that cannot be released to the public due to the open status of this case. But the next time you are traveling through the area, keep your eyes open, because you might be the next person to see Mary, the mysterious ghost of Elk Lake Dam. –*Chad Lewis*

Rolling Backward on Shullsburg's Gravity Hill

They're sprinkled around the country—hills that seem to defy gravity by allowing cars placed in neutral to roll either up or down despite the driver's sense that his car should by rights be going the opposite way. Such a hill is Wisconsin's Gravity Hill in Lafayette County, just outside Shullsburg, and it is a masterpiece of nature's tomfoolery.

It took *Weird Wisconsin* a while to find it on the late August day we went in search of antigravity thrills, because some nimrod had stolen the RENNICK ROAD sign that tells you you're almost there. Still, experiencing Gravity Hill was a kick, even though we figured it would prove to be an optical delusion.

Most directions tell you to look for the water tower in Shullsburg and head past it on County Highway U. About a mile or so outside the town will be a sign on your left that should say RENNICK ROAD (if the sign has been restored). One travel writer has claimed that Highway U "plunges down a good-sized hill," but it's actually a very mild descent. Near the "bottom," before the road starts back up into a second hill, is a rusty fence to your right. That fence is where you put your car into neutral, then sit and get the eerie ride backward, back "up" the hill. It feels as if there's a chain on your rear bumper pulled by some spectral wrecking truck.

The thing to do, which of course *Weird Wisconsin* did, was to pull out a trusty bubble level at that point to see whether the hill really is slanting upward. According to our level the road behind us was actually slanting downhill. It's just a trick of the landscape that makes it seem like an upward incline.

Many gravity hills come with legends, such as that of a ghost that pushes your car the wrong way so you will leave, but we were not able to find any specters around Shullsburg. There, the joy of the free ride backward seems to be enough to ensure the enigma's popularity. After all, you can roll back as many times as you like, barring traffic concerns, and it won't cost you a cent. Who says there's no such thing as a free ride?

Wisconsin's eminent folklorist Robert Gard once wrote, "Wisconsin has more ghosts per mile than any state in the nation." After surveying the spook scene, we have to conclude that he was absolutely correct. You can hardly swing a dead cat without hitting a ghost somewhere in the Badger State.

In addition to Gard, the state owes a huge debt of gratitude to several other pioneers who gathered stories of nightwalkers, moon-flitters and other wispy death survivors. Charles E. Brown collected dozens of late-nineteenth-century and early-twentieth-century stories, not only from the new European upstarts that took over the land, but from the people they displaced— the various Native American tribes.

Badger State Ghosts

In *Haunted Wisconsin*, by Beth Scott and Michael Norman, ghosts were taken out of dusty old archives and put into our living rooms where they belong. And Dennis Boyer has coaxed some amazing stories from saloon habitués, labor activists, and just plain Wisconsinites of all persuasions.

Paranormal researchers and organizations are keenly interested in investigating claims of hauntings and ghosts everywhere, from homes to businesses to abandoned buildings and cemeteries. Groups such as the Wisconsin Paranormal Research Center, the Wausau Paranormal Research Society, Wisconsin Ghost Investigations, and the Southern Wisconsin Paranormal Research Group and researchers such as Chad Lewis and Terry Fisk have all been active in scouring the state for haunted activity. These groups, if they've proven anything, have shown that Wisconsin is even more crowded with nonliving souls than even Robert Gard could have imagined.

What follows is a selected survey, rather than an exhaustive assay of ghosts, featuring some lesser-known and surprising ones. To document all ghosts and haunted spots would require a book far longer than this. Talk to any group of people, and chances are, more than half of the group will have a story to share.

Ghosts of Black Point

Sparkling Lake Geneva, known for the millionaires' mansions that line its shores, hosts thousands of boaters and swimmers every summer, who never suspect the tragedies submerged for centuries beneath its cool waters. But divers know that Geneva's spring-fed bottom is dotted with the wrecks of steamers and sailboats. It's a deep lake, and a sudden squall can punch a small boat into the drink in mere seconds on nights when the old native water spirits quarrel and spit great sheets of rain back and forth. But according to local legends, the storms bring newer water spirits—gentler ghosts.

The locals know just when and where these spirits will appear. If you have a stout heart and if you can find a safe shelter on the southern shore on a night when howling torrents lash the poplars, wait until the thunder is at its most furious. Then look up at the Victorian four-story tower on the manse called Black Point. Built by Chicago brewer Conrad Seipp in 1888 on a promontory named for its black oak trees, the elaborate mansion has remained virtually unchanged from its nineteenth-century glory days. Keep watching. If you're lucky, a shaft of lightning may illuminate several white figures watching the storm with you from atop the tower. One of them, it is said, wears the robe of a Catholic priest.

There is one particular story of a drowned priest's ghost that comes from lifelong Linn Township resident Bonnie Cornue. Growing up on a farm on the southern shore, she heard the tale recounted by relatives and neighbors around countless campfires. As she tells it, one Sunday the priest and several nuns were making their way across the lake in a small boat, after visiting friends on the northern shore, when suddenly a softly overcast sky turned lethal. A hurricanelike storm came out of nowhere, and all those aboard the small craft drowned.

One of the nuns was never found, and as a result, according to the story, the priest and the other nuns can still be seen casting agonized glances at the lake, searching for her body so they can all be together once more.

Turns out, Bonnie's story is about as close to the truth as ghost legends ever get. Apparently, there really was a priest who had drowned—it was on July 7, 1895, when the steamer *Dispatch* tried desperately to ride out a surprise storm. The captain, a young man named John Preston, was attempting to make it back to the landing at Kaye's Park, next to Black Point, when the tragedy occurred. The doomed clergyman was Father James Hogan, a beloved priest at St. Joseph's Catholic Church in Harvard, Illinois.

The passenger list did not include any nuns, however. Father Hogan had made this a family outing, bringing his unmarried sister, Mary; his brother, Dr. John Hogan, who worked for the insane asylum in Elgin, Illinois; John's wife, Kittie; and the couple's two-year-old child. This was the entire Hogan clan. The family's only other living relatives were some second cousins in New York.

The Hogans, who had been visiting friends on the north side of the lake, decided to head for the Williams Bay train station at about four p.m. Captain Preston, familiar with the capricious nature of water travel, scanned the gathering clouds and warned the priest that it might be wise to wait. But the Hogans were anxious to get back to Harvard and insisted that Preston try.

When the rain began pelting the steamer's roof, Captain Preston headed for the nearest port, which happened to be Kaye's Park. But as the storm intensified, he realized the danger of the situation and began blowing the ship's whistle for help. A small crowd gathered onshore, but the storm was now so fierce that no one dared put another boat in the water. All the onlookers could do was watch as the *Dispatch* pitched hard.

Suddenly, Mary Hogan flew overboard into the waves, her summer dress billowing behind her. A huge plume of water soon followed, and the craft lurched and plunged to the bottom, taking its human cargo with it. The last glimpse onlookers had of the Hogans was a flash of white from the baby's frock as Kittie pressed her child close to her breast. In moments, all had disappeared into the dark inhospitable depths of Lake Geneva.

Around sundown that night, when the rain subsided, Mary's body floated into Kaye's Park, the sleeves of her dress acting as water wings. Ever the lady, she was still clutching her kid gloves in one hand and had the strings of her purse wound tightly over her arm.

It took nearly a week for a Chicago diver to recover the remaining bodies. The boat was found first and then the body of Father

Hogan, who was lying in repose under the bow. Dr. Hogan was discovered next, on the other side of the boat, his hands held up as if in prayer. Then they found John Preston, and soon, the baby. Finally, a few days later, Kittie Hogan turned up about half a mile from the boat, far from the currents that had ripped her child from her grasp.

Father Hogan's funeral was a major event. The local paper reported that seventy-five priests attended and that everyone remarked on how natural and lifelike Father Hogan's face was despite the days his body had been in the lake.

It's impossible to know what the family's last thoughts were, but one can imagine their eyes fixed anxiously on what would have been the most visible landmark and symbol of hope—the Black Point tower. Perhaps the Hogans' spirits were able to rendezvous there after the storm, finding it a perfect vantage point from which to watch the dragging operations for Kittie's body.

If you are out at the lake on a stormy day and still watching as the rain begins to soften, squint hard at the misty forms huddled under the pointed cupola. The last thing you will see will be a small flutter of white from the baby's dress as the spirits drift off to wherever it is they wait between storms on Lake Geneva. The Hogans may have no living descendants, but at least they are separated no more.

House for Sale—Exorcism Tools Included

It's not unusual to move into a place and find left-overs from former tenants: a rusty appliance, a forgotten headless doll, a yellowed letter wedged under a cabinet. But what David and Mary Pagliaroni discovered after they moved into their dream home near Honey Lake, Wisconsin, belongs in a completely different realm.

"This house had a lot of closets," declared Mary. And in every one, she found a crucifix, a bottle of holy water, and a rosary. These items had all been placed on the top shelf, where they would not be noticed on casual inspection. Mary didn't find them until after she and her family had moved in and she got up on a stepstool to clean the shelves. Awed, the Pagliaronis were also a little troubled. They knew that the former owners were deceased and that the house had been occupied by their children for a short time. But why would this lovely home require articles of spiritual sanctification?

David and Mary found out as soon as they started redecorating. It began as an eerie feeling of always being watched by some nearby presence. Once, for example, Mary glimpsed a white, foggy form out of the corner of her eye. And then the hellish noises began.

The house was in the country, and one day, when Mary was there alone, she heard the bam-bam-bam of a hammer pounding in the basement. She ran down to check, but no one was there. Another day, David was sitting at the kitchen table when he heard the bam-bam-bam of the vigorous carpenter. He went looking for Mary and found her painting quietly in another room. Again, there was no one in the basement. David and Mary's son would often hear the steady clanging beneath his bedroom when he tried to sleep at night. Spookily, he found that when he yelled for it to stop, the sound ceased. The noise source, then, had to be something capable of understanding human language. And obeying. No misbehaving furnace does that. On top of everything, a dark mood of oppression began to hang over the household, leaving the family in a mystifying state of despair. They began to seek answers.

Upon investigation, the Pagliaronis discovered that the workaholic former owner had died on the property while landscaping the parklike yard. The man's wife, said by neighbors to be on the cranky side, died not long afterward. At last, David and Mary understood: The former owners had decided to stay on in their house.

The noises and oppressiveness continued for eight years, until the Pagliaronis reached their limit. They sold the house and moved to another county. They don't know if the ghosts still haunt their former house, but they did hear that the people who had bought it from them lasted only a few years. Probably wisely, the Pagliaronis have not asked why.

Haunted Kmart

There were no loudspeaker voices announcing phantoms in aisle 6. But employees at the Kmart store on Highway 36 in Burlington were frightened enough to call police to come and check the store for lurking poltergeists. This headline-provoking situation occurred in late March 2000, when the *Milwaukee Journal Sentinel,* the *Journal Times* in Racine, and Walworth County's *The Week* reported the same weird happenings: Late-shift employees at the Burlington Kmart were claiming that phones had started ringing for no reason, toys fell off shelves and rolled down the aisles, and a clean sandwich grill suddenly began wafting the aroma of sizzling hot dogs in the middle of the night.

The police brought in dogs to search the store, but no ghosts or intruders were found. No mechanical problems with the phones were discovered either. A store manager said that to his knowledge, no one had ever died in the store, and he didn't remember any other spooky incidents. But those who witnessed the phenomena remained convinced they'd had an encounter with some blue-light specials from the beyond.

A Grave and a Ghost in a Soap-Store Basement

Christiane Strommen was forty-three when she died in May 1878, probably somewhere near the town of Sparta. Her grief-stricken husband commissioned a beautiful white marble headstone and had it inscribed in Norwegian: HERE LIES THE DUST OF CHRISTIANE, WIFE OF OLE O. STROMMEN. Little did he know that over a century later, his wife's tombstone, if not necessarily her dust, would be cemented into the basement wall of a soapmaker's store called Natural Scentsations and that the store's owners would feel they had more than a nodding acquaintance with the long-dead Christiane!

"It's always mischievous, nothing evil," says Natural Scentsations owner Jean Kempfer. "I'm not afraid, because nothing evil has happened. Just weird stuff." Try weird, audible, visible, and tactile.

Jean and her husband, Dave, bought the former auto livery building in downtown Sparta in 2002, thinking that the brick edifice on historic Water Street, next to the bridge over the La Crosse River, would be a perfect place to make and sell their line of natural soaps. In the past decade, Sparta, which bills itself as the Bicycling Capital of the World, has become a tourist magnet because of its scenic bike path and the mile-long stone tunnel that wends its way to neighboring Elroy.

The Kempfers were completely unaware that anything might be amiss until they started remodeling the old building. "I didn't know the tombstone was here," said Jean. "The basement was spooky, with no lights."

The couple subsequently learned

that their store's site was originally the location of a mill that had been in operation in the nineteenth and early twentieth centuries, until the wooden structure burned to the ground in the early 1920s. The brick building that stands today was built in 1925 to house "newfangled" horseless carriages, and it was at that time that Christiane's headstone somehow became cemented into the stone basement wall. No one knows if this was because her grave was discovered by workmen and left in place or if the headstone was simply commandeered as a surplus item to provide reinforcement for the wall. Using old headstones in such a way was not unheard of, says Monroe County historian Jarrod Roll. It's also interesting to note that there are no extant records indicating that the Strommens ever lived in or near Sparta, leading Roll to conjecture that perhaps they were passing through town when Christiane died. Her husband may have ordered a headstone from the local monument maker and never paid for it, which would explain why the stone appears unweathered despite its age. But no one really knows, since the soil behind the tombstone wall has not been excavated.

Although the Kempfers were astonished when they discovered that their new place of business might also be a cemetery, they weren't about to remove the headstone. So when they drywalled the basement to provide a cleaner environment for manufacturing their soap, they carefully framed the graceful monument and left it in place. Then odd things began to happen. It started with the Kempfers' employee

Kristine Peterson, who, coincidentally, bears the English version of the name Christiane. When the Kempfers hired her she was forty-three, the same age Christiane had been at the time of her death. As Kristine worked in the basement mixing and pouring vats of soap, she began feeling she was not alone. Soon she would not only get the eerie feeling that someone was watching her, but several times she actually felt someone's finger gently stroking her earlobe! The first time it happened, she thought Jean or Dave had sneaked up behind her, but when she whirled around to check, no one was there.

Kristine wasn't too disturbed, though, saying, "I would always just say, 'Hi Christiane.'" But one day, when Kristine was downstairs alone, a plastic hamper began

As she worked in the basement mixing and pouring vats of soap, Kristine began feeling she was not alone.

"jumping by itself," until finally the lid flew off and landed across the room. It seemed Christiane was beginning to make her presence known in a more aggressive way.

Then Dave began seeing a milky-white form in the hallway leading from the basement stairs to the store. "He'd see it in his peripheral vision," said Jean. And late one day, after Jean walked upstairs from the basement, she suddenly heard a woman's voice singing below. "There weren't any words. It was more like chanting," Jean said. She listened for about five minutes. "Then I got kind of spooked. It was the dead of winter, so I just went home."

That day, Jean had also heard noises in the basement wall that sounded something like pounding pipes, but she was perplexed, since she knew there were no pipes in that wall. The next night, she and Dave were watching a movie when she heard on the soundtrack the exact same sound she'd heard in her basement. In an eerie coincidence, the sound in the movie was made by water rushing through pipes in a mill, exactly as it would have sounded in the old wooden mill that had once stood on the property in Christiane's lifetime.

The most spectacular ghostly manifestation occurred on March 16, the day of the store's grand opening. The previous day, Joe Cook, a local high school teacher interested in the paranormal, had asked to tour the building after hearing about the ghostly goings-on. Cook, who later published a book called *The Haunting of Sparta,* asked to see the building's attic, because the louvers of the three attic windows kept opening by themselves. When he managed to get through the small trapdoor in the back room's ceiling, he saw an antique oak kitchen chair near the window, covered in dust and positioned so that someone could sit and look out over the street.

Cook asked Kempfer if she would like the chair brought downstairs to display in her store. She was delighted with the idea, and the chair was carefully pulled down through the opening and cleaned. Later that day, Cook and several friends elected to stay overnight in the store's basement. They reported hearing a variety of odd, unexplained noises, including one very distinct set of three sharp knocks. The group cleared out by eight the next morning, everyone feeling slightly unsettled.

That same morning, Kempfer prepared a small feast for the opening-day party. She set out bowls of punch and a variety of sandwiches, cookies, and other munchables on two sturdy eight-foot-long tables. The store had begun to fill with people and Kempfer went to fetch something from the back room.

Suddenly she heard a tremendous crash, so she hurried back to investigate. To her shock, the entire contents of a small refreshment table lay in a broken, messy heap on the floor next to the large table. The guests stared, unable to believe what they had just witnessed. Sharon Folcey, director of the Sparta Chamber of Commerce, was one of them. "I'm not one of those people that believes in such things," she said in a phone interview with *Weird Wisconsin.* "But I was standing on one side with some folks, and on the other side were the Little Miss and Junior Miss Sparta. It did not fall like a normal thing would fall; it was like in slow motion. . . . At first, I assumed the kids had pushed it, but then I realized it fell toward them, and they were too far away from it. They were standing there looking at it like everyone else."

It didn't take the Kempfers long to finger their suspect. "I said later, 'Oh-oh, I guess Christiane wants her chair back,'" explained Jean. The chair was eventually restored to the attic, and the intensity of the spectral disturbances decreased.

Christiane's presence is still occasionally seen and heard, but nothing as mischievous as before. Jean commented, "Our store smells like oils and incense, the things people burn at séances. Maybe Christiane likes that."

Ghosts from All Over the State

Boscobel

Ghosts aplenty are said to haunt the old Boscobel Hotel. Celebrity shades John F. Kennedy and his wife, Jackie, may haunt room 19, which the former first lady used as a place to "freshen up" during a campaign stop in March 1960. Or maybe the ghosts of John Nicholson and Samuel Hill haunt the room. These two traveling salesmen met here in September 1898. They later formed the Gideon Society, dedicated to placing Bibles in hotel rooms around the world. Or maybe the spirit is Adam Bobel, who built the hotel in 1865. Columnist Ralph Goldsmith once penned this ode to Bobel, the only bit of Wisconsin doggerel we know of dedicated to a ghost: "The ghost of Adam Bobel came a knockin' at the door. 'Come in, come' I says to him. 'But don't track up the floor. It's newly washed this afternoon.' And then I shook with fright, for Adam stood before me, with the door still fastened tight."

Campbellsport

The Amber Hotel, a popular supper club and bar at 139 West Main, is home to the ghost of Ed "Mush" Bauer, a former owner. A true larger-than-life legend, Bauer once tipped the scales at a not-so-spectral eight hundred pounds and was renowned as one of the world's physically largest hotel-and-tavern owners. At the time of his death in January 1957 at the age of fifty, Bauer had slimmed down considerably, to a mere four hundred pounds. Mush loved the Amber and can still be heard clumping around the building. "There are so many rooms upstairs, and we hear different noises," says Lois Zingsheim, who with her husband, Dale, currently owns the hotel. "We say it's him walking around up there. He gets lonely when we are gone."

Edgerton

The Fuchs family met Pete Oppengaard face-to-face only once, in unusual circumstances on a chilly November morning in 1987. Shirley Fuchs woke from a restless sleep to find Pete standing at the foot of her bed. He was dressed in something blue that extended over his head. Pete had died twenty-four years earlier, in 1963, so perhaps it was a shroud. Shirley had known Pete as a child—she had often visited his home to share sugar doughnuts with the old guy. Now, as an adult, she was living in his former home, and despite Pete's face being covered by the blue shroud, she knew right off who it was. Shirley's son, Alex, saw him too. This was the sole occasion any of the Fuchs family saw Pete in person, though he continued to reside in the house for several more years. The night he chose to reveal himself was the very night his widow, Hilda, died in a Stoughton nursing home. Pete was a playful soul, and when he did manifest himself, it was always in a lighthearted manner—taking small objects, turning lights on and off, moving furniture, and leaving dirty wineglasses on the table, presumably his.

Elm Grove

The two-story farmhouse at 1920 Highland Drive has at least three long-term resident ghosts. They're spooky but friendly. An older female ghost with her hair pulled back sometimes walks down a hallway. She wears a striped floor-length dress gathered at the waist. Sometimes a little girl is seen peering into cupboards and a ghostly dog is heard padding, his toenails clicking across an uncarpeted floor. Demo, the son of the man who owns the house, had the most unnerving encounter of all. "I thought I heard my dad in the other room snoring," Demo said. "It bothered me, and I had to shut the door. I went in the other room and looked on the couch, where I thought he was lying, and he wasn't there. Needless to say, the hair went up on my head. I flew out the back door as fast as I could. It was a good excuse not to do my homework."

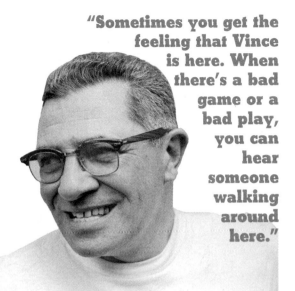

"Sometimes you get the feeling that Vince is here. When there's a bad game or a bad play, you can hear someone walking around here."

Green Bay

For many Green Bay Packers fans, Vince Lombardi was like God—he could do it all. And like God, Vince is all around us even though he can't be seen. Marie Lombardi, Vince's widow, used to "visit with" her dead husband at his exhibit in the Packer Hall of Fame. According to Lombardi's biographer David Maraniss, "She certainly talked to him or believed she talked to him after he died. I got recordings of a speech she was going to give at the Pro Football Hall of Fame. She was practicing it, and she stopped and started, and you could hear her address Vince like he was there."

Mark Kanz of the Packer Hall of Fame agrees. "Once in a while, it looks like something is a little out of place or awry, and it seems like the ghost is a good place to lay the blame." Then there's the local businessman who gave up a fifty-yard-line seat for the 1996 NFC Championship—the first played in three decades—"so Vince's ghost would have a good seat."

John Gehring, a Green Bay psychiatrist, purchased Lombardi's home in 1969, when the coach went to the Washington Redskins. Lombardi used to watch films of games in his basement and had his home office there. Gehring says, "Sometimes you get the feeling that Vince is here. When there's a bad game or a bad play, you can hear someone walking around here."

Fans around the country were startled to see a familiar-looking figure staring back at the TV camera, wearing the trademark hat and brown coat and standing atop a pile of snow as he watched the victory parade in 1997, following the Packers' trouncing of the New England Patriots 35–21 in Super Bowl XXXI. Turns out it was a man who had attended the same church Lombardi had once attended. However, many fans weren't convinced. They believe it was Vince himself.

Still not convinced? Keep an eye on the sports pages or your ears open to football commentary for the number of times Vince Lombardi's ghost is invoked. You'll be surprised. If Wisconsin has a most famous ghost, known the world over, it's that of Vince Lombardi. Asked about replacing a legend, former head Packer coach Lindy Infante said, "There is a ghost of Lombardi here, but it's a friendly ghost."

Hartland

Ghost Harvey's claim to fame is that he contributed to a soundtrack recorded at Hartland's Millevolte Recording Studio in 2000. Owner Vinny Millevolte dubbed the ghost Harvey, naming him after the invisible rabbit from the famous play and movie. Millevolte said that during a recording session, a heartbeat-like sound showed up on one of the tracks, though no one present played that beat. Harvey wasn't the only ghost alone in haunting the building, which backs up against the hill below the cemetery. "Late at night, you can sometimes hear doors creaking, someone coming up the stairs, or something in the kitchen," says Millevolte. "I always have to look."

Madison

In 1989, four university women sharing a house on North Brearley Street experienced lights flashing on and off, appliances coming to life for no reason, and loud music blaring from the switched-off stereo. Joy, who was home alone with the doors locked, was napping one afternoon until blaring music jolted her awake. Every light was on in the living room, and the dining-room chandelier was lit. All the kitchen cupboards were open, the front door was unlocked, and the screen door was ajar, as if the ghost had made a hurried exit. Sarah, whose bed was directly underneath the chandelier, suffered horrible dreams on a nightly basis, and an old hag dressed in white would sit on her chest. Sarah couldn't breathe, couldn't move, couldn't scream. Sometimes the old hag stared down at her from a perch in the chandelier. Amy couldn't stand the feeling of being stared at by an unseen presence while in the claw-foot tub and refused to bathe there. The fourth roommate had nightmares about what was behind the door leading to the attic. Later the women learned that their landlord's mother, who had lived in the house for eighty years, had died in it.

Milwaukee

Hands down, Aunt Pussy has the best name of any ghost we know. Though long gone, she still holds a tight grip on the Brumder Mansion at 3046 West Wisconsin Avenue, as she haunts the Gold Suite. The Victorian mansion is now a bed-and-breakfast, and the Gold Suite was formerly Aunt Pussy's room. An austere, fussy German immigrant when she was alive, Aunt Pussy remains so in death, frequently expressing disapproval for owner Carol Hirschi's ornate decorating. Aunt Pussy is known to rearrange window shades according to her half-shuttered, half-open preference, and she frequently fusses with table settings. Most of all, she doesn't like dogs, especially when they're on the bed. A creepy

feeling awoke Carol one night, and she got the distinct impression that Aunt Pussy was really ticked off that one of Carol's dogs was sleeping with her on the bed.

    The list of Aunt Pussy's alleged ghostly activities continues. A visiting Native American medicine man complained of many chatty spirits in the Gold Suite, and one psychic went "completely off her nut" after spending a night there. At one point, the suite's mirror moved across the room, landing in the bathtub without breaking. Then Carol found fresh droplets of blood in the bathroom, though she was the only person home. And for years, the doorbell refused to work for guests, and the programmable tune would always change from the one Carol had chosen. Eventually Carol let Aunt Pussy pick the tune, and so long as "Take Me Out to the Ball Game" or "Happy Birthday" is selected, she's as happy as any austere German woman can be.

She got the distinct impression that Aunt Pussy was really ticked off that one of Carol's dogs was sleeping with her on the bed.

Pipe

Club Harbor, built in 1846 as a stagecoach hotel and later used as a bed-and-breakfast, began showing its ghostly side after Chris Bray purchased the building in 1999 and began renovations. At first, Bray noticed little things, such as lights being turned on after hours. "Somebody wanted to party," he says. "Some people have stayed here that don't really recall what the checkout time is." A rotund Asian man with a Fu Manchu mustache who had once worked at Club Harbor as a cook manifested before Bray's eyes in a medicine-cabinet mirror. Then there's the mischievous young dark-haired girl with pigtails who runs through the hallways slamming doors. Remember, if you go looking for ghosts, consider taking some time for the ghosts to get used to you. "It's like deer hunting," cautions Bray. "You have to sit still and be like that for a long time before you hear something."

Rochester

The first tavern in western Racine County was the Union House, now Chances restaurant in Rochester, built in 1843. Co-owner Deb Schuerman says, "We've had the cash register do crazy things when it's not even plugged in. And one time, I was on the second floor taking inventory when I heard this beautiful music that sounded like piano music. We don't even have a piano! It was almost like a harpsichord." There's also a young Civil War soldier and a woman in a green dress who are often seen in the building.

Sawyer County

Professional fishing guide and longtime firefighter Al Denninger says, "I intended to keep quiet about it. I didn't want to sound like people who have lunch with Elvis or just talked to God." But people all up and down the Chippewa Flowage were talking about the Polaroid photo Denninger had snapped while fishing the "Big Chip" in October 1991. The picture shows an amorphous humanlike shape shrouded in white and suspended in front of the tree line. According to Denninger, his client was the first to spot the apparition. "All of a sudden he looked at me, his mouth wide open and his face white as a ghost, and said, 'Al, wha-wha-what's that?' I looked up and saw it coming down through the trees on the island just across the channel."

The two fishermen said the white-robed ghost remained in position for about a minute and a half before drifting to the left and away through the trees. "All this time, it never changed shape. And it had been raining for five straight days, so smoke was not a possibility. Besides, I know what smoke looks like." Denninger sent the photo to Polaroid for analysis. "When they gave it back, they said, 'Whatever that thing is, it's not a doctored negative or trick.' Anyway, you can't tamper with Polaroids—there is no negative." Denninger later discovered that for years, locals had been referring to the area of his photo as Ghost Island, based on a number of other strange encounters there.

West Bend

The RESTAT Building at 724 Elm Street was built in 1897 and today houses the RESTAT prescription benefit management company. It previously housed the West Bend High School, and in later incarnations was home to the elementary school, the library, and even the city's recreation center. In an all-too-frequent scenario that's become a ghostly cliché, this building is haunted by a janitor. This janitor committed suicide in the school's basement, and from all accounts, he wasn't—and isn't—all that nice. According to Jackie Maynard, a former instructor at the recreation center, "The ghost tended to mess with females; not too many men ran into him. It was definitely a male spirit. He was never menacing, but there was a distinctive presence, cold spots where you could feel the hair on your arms stand up. In the morning, things would be moved on people's desks."

Ghosts of Wausau

Grand Theater

Reports of the ghost of a former stage manager have circulated at the Grand Theater for years. Larry, as he's called, has been seen in various areas of the theater. Not surprisingly, he is most fond of the stage, where he often observes rehearsals from the wings or the lighting rack. The Wausau Paranormal Research Society has documented a number of other phenomena at the Grand, including a ghostly voice saying, "Don't come back over here"; a video of a ball of light moving across a room; and a photograph of a mysterious luminous blob wrapped around a balcony railing.

Rogers Theater

Now abandoned, this theater has been the site of numerous paranormal incidents. The apparition of a gaunt gentleman has been seen in the basement auditorium, electrical disturbances have been reported throughout the building, and several staff members have had the feeling of being watched. In one spine-tingling incident, an employee was pushed out the theater doors by unseen hands. When the theater closed down, workmen removing seats in the basement auditorium heard a strange thumping. Looking up from their work, they were horrified to see every seat in the theater rocking violently back and forth.

Wausau Club

Legend has it that during the early days of the Wausau Club a woman named Martha was staying in one of the guest rooms in the north wing. Despondent over a failing love affair, she committed suicide. Since that day, she has haunted the stately building. She is fond of turning on lights, causing light fixtures to swing back and forth, and creating cold spots. Her apparition has been seen on the grand staircase and in the doorway to the room where she died. During recent renovations, workers complained of tools and other equipment being moved.

University of Wisconsin–Marathon County Campus

Two ghosts haunt this small two-year liberal arts college: Annie, the shade of a former janitor, and the Blue Cowboy, so named because of the hat he wears. Annie worked at UWMC for a number of years in the 1970s, and since her death, staff members have reported hearing her distinctive chicken-cackle laughter coming from various parts of the building. Phantom footsteps have also been heard in the halls, as has the sound of moving furniture in empty classrooms. In a recent incident, Annie opened all the cupboard doors in the library workroom.

The Blue Cowboy haunts Marathon Hall, a coed dormitory. He has been described as a hazy blue manlike form wearing a hat. He appears in the closet of a third-floor room, then moves down the hall. Sounds of furniture being moved in the room have been reported on weekends when the residents are not there.

Fischer House

Located in Rothschild, the Fischer home was the scene of poltergeist activity during the 1970s, when the family reported the sound of ringing bells, various electrical malfunctions, spontaneous fires, and strange shadows moving in the hallway. The family dog was so creeped out, it refused to go into the lower level of the home. Finally, after a flying razor attacked Mrs. Fischer while she was in the bath, the family decided it was time to move. The cause of all this activity? It is rumored that the house was built on a Native American burial ground.

Wausau Club, site of Martha's ghost.

Old Hospital North

After Wausau's Old Hospital North was abandoned in the 1980s, there were stories aplenty about eerie happenings in the derelict East Hill structure looming over the city. For starters, a group of thirteen cultists were arrested in the hospital's former morgue on a Halloween night in the late 1980s. People also reported strange sounds coming from the abandoned building and seeing shadows moving past the windows. The haunting has continued even though the newest section of the hospital has been renovated and converted into housing for the elderly and is now part of Forest Park Village, Wausau's finest retirement community. Apparitions still appear, often in the elevator; cold spots are encountered; and uneasy feelings have been reported by residents and staff.

Marathon County Historical Museum

Located in the old Yawkey Mansion at 410 McIndoe Street, this museum is reputed to be haunted by its former owner, lumberman Cyrus C. Yawkey. The smell of his pipe tobacco has been reported on the first-floor staircase landing, and a book of poetry is said to be moved from one exhibit to another by unseen hands. A staff member in the basement heard Mr. Yawkey's name being called. Alone in the mansion at the time, the frightened staffer tried to exit via the basement door but found the door held shut. In another incident, a group of employees on break in the kitchen heard and saw a soda-bottle cap move across a table before falling to the floor.

Marathon County Historical Society Library

The old Woodson Mansion is now the home of the Marathon County Historical Society library and museum. Staff members have reported the sound of a telephone ringing in a room that has no phone. Phantom footsteps have been heard marching along the upstairs hallway, then descending the main staircase. Strange odors have been reported in an upstairs room, and the door alarm often sounds when it hasn't been activated.

Wausau Municipal Airport

The story goes that one of the airport's hangars is haunted by a former manager, one Archie Towle, who died in a plane crash there in 1945. Towle's ghost now roams the hangar he had frequented in life. Witnesses have heard ghostly footsteps that sound like "wing tips walking across a hardwood floor." The airport has recently undergone renovations, and the current manager claims that Archie has been more active since then. In one instance, an employee, working late in a second-floor office, heard a pounding coming from inside a closet. He knocked back on the wall and told Archie to keep it down. The pounding then moved from the closet to the outer wall and made its way around the entire building.

Shepherd & Schaller Sporting Goods

Eddie is the name given by employees to the spirit that haunts this building. Staff members have reported that the door alarm will sound by itself. Personal belongings, like keys and pens, often disappear, only to be found again in parts of the building where the employee hasn't been. One employee was on the third floor when a small piece of plaster flew across the room, striking his shoulder. A dog brought to the building reacted to an unseen presence. In another incident, an employee in the basement put his can of soda on the floor while doing inventory. He left the room for a minute, then came back to find the can had a perfect circle of soda surrounding it. No leak in the can could be found.

—Todd Roll, *Wausau Paranormal Research Society*

Cemetery Safari

Every *tombstone* tells a story, and every graveyard tells a tale. The sagas often vary, depending on the raconteur. After all, cemeteries confront us with our deepest fears and innermost desires, our longings and our vanished dreams. Whether we see them as peaceful havens or places full of dread, they highlight what culture finds relevant about the past, as well as our own personal feelings of mortality. Clearly, although cemeteries are home to the dead, they are very much about the living. The departed speak to us from beyond the grave, and their words are written in stone. Sometimes their messages are woeful and full of warning, but other times they are lighthearted and inspiring.

There are fascinating cemeteries throughout Wisconsin, and a walk through any one of them provides a dialogue of sorts with the interred souls. The way people are immortalized offers a revelatory look at how they had spent their time here on earth — or would have liked to. Some had lived in grand style and continue thus in their eternal resting-places. Others, who had lived quietly without fanfare, have earned posthumous accolades because of the memorials erected in their honor. Still others, whose lives were bleak or ended tragically, received recognition only after exiting this world.

Here are a few of our favorite graveyard legends. They are stories of blood and violence, stories of uncommon burials and simple human accomplishments, stories that leave us hushed and awed.

Sad Story of the Dollhouse Grave

In 1907, a little girl named Bertha was born in Wisconsin's Northwoods. Something must have happened to her parents, because at the age of five, she was living with her half-sister Hulda and Hulda's husband, Dan, on a primitive farm in a wilderness area. Bertha was a pretty child, with hair that fell to her shoulders in long sausage curls. Dressed in a dainty frock, a matching ribbon in her hair, and in high-button shoes, she posed for a photograph, smiling happily with her little black dog at her side. Around her neck she wore a gold locket with the inscription DARLING—perhaps a gift from her mother.

Bertha owned a lovely bisque doll with long blond hair and a white dress, but she was allowed to play with it only on rare occasions due to her young age and the fragility of the doll.

One summer day in 1912, Hulda and another sister, Anne, went into the woods to pick berries. They left little Bertha at home, perhaps to spare her from mosquito bites and scratches from berry bushes, and they cautioned her to be good and stay there. However, when Hulda and Anne returned, Bertha was nowhere to be found. They immediately launched a search, and eventually it was a neighbor who found Bertha drowned in a pond. Her life had ended tragically at the age of five.

Bertha's grieving sisters and brother-in-law laid her to rest in a nearby cemetery. Next to her grave they erected a small dollhouse with a glass front. Inside, they placed Bertha's bisque doll and a tiny doll-size dresser with little items on one side and a funeral wreath on the other. Hulda then placed Bertha's gold locket around the doll's neck and, in front of the doll, a recent photograph of Bertha.

Since 1912, Bertha's bisque doll has sat by her grave, a lonely memorial to a little girl who would never grow up. The first dollhouse deteriorated, and in time it was taken down and a more weatherproof version was put up. Bertha's doll was cleaned and the locket polished so it shines brightly once again. The doll still sits there, keeping watch through all seasons, her smile never dimming. On a moonlit night, it is not hard to imagine a little girl with long curls, playing happily with her doll among the shadows of the lonely cemetery. At least this writer likes to think so.—*Elaine A. Roberts*

Juda's Nine Angels

It's easy to find gravestones with pictures representing something loved by the deceased etched into them. It's less usual to find a memorial that's a full-size sculpture of a favorite object. But just outside Brodhead in Green County is a replica of a piano carved from a solid block of red granite. It was created in memory of a young girl named Nelva Jean Smith, who had loved music. Nelva was only seventeen years old at the time she died in 1967 with eight of her high school classmates from the small town of Juda (population, four hundred). The nine girls were killed on their senior class trip to New Orleans when an airplane on a training flight smashed into the Hilton Inn where the thirty-two seniors who had made the trip were staying.

A few of the students were outside, and some of those inside managed to escape the nightmare scene. But the Delta DC-8 had crashed directly into a room that housed a number of the girls. Some of them were trapped in the resultant fire, some were thrown by the impact, and some were found in the bathroom under the running water of the shower, where they had gathered for relief from the flames. Ironically, according to one of Nelva Jean Smith's relatives, the group had originally planned to stay at a different hotel but had switched to the Hilton because it had a swimming pool.

The twenty-three class members who survived were, understandably, deeply shaken. They returned home on a bus, but the dead girls were transported from Louisiana to Wisconsin in white hearses. Memorial contributions came pouring in from all over the country, and fifteen hundred people, almost four times Juda's population, attended the memorial service held in the high school gym. The town put the memorial funds to good use, constructing a park with a "Nine Angels" memorial stone and planting nine pine trees in honor of the girls. Juda periodically holds Angels in the Outfield baseball tournaments in the park.

The nine "angels" were Nelva Smith, Sandra Goecks, Nancy Siegenthaler, Linda Moe, Marilyn Rassmussen, Linda Hartwig, Joyce Kaderly, Sheila Babler, and Doreen Williams.

Little Lord Fauntleroy

Waukesha, located just west of the bustling city of Milwaukee, was a quiet little town in the 1920s. It was quite a shock to its citizens, then, when on March 8, 1921, a very well-dressed little boy was fished out of an old quarry, drowned. He was about five years old. Adding to the horror was the fact that he'd been hit on the head with a blunt instrument.

The police were mystified, so the local citizens tried to help. Someone put up a $1,000 reward for information regarding the boy's identity. A Waukesha funeral home displayed his body for viewing for a few days in the hopes someone would claim the body, but no one showed up. Then a Milwaukee funeral home laid him out for viewing; still no one came forward with information about him. Because of his expensive clothing and shoes, he was dubbed Little Lord Fauntleroy. Police finally concluded that he had been kidnapped from a well-to-do family in another town, killed when he became too difficult to deal with, and dumped in Waukesha, where no one would recognize him.

A sympathetic woman named Minnie Conrad didn't want to see the little boy go to a pauper's grave, so she passed the hat and soon collected enough to buy a modest headstone for him. He was buried in Waukesha's Prairie Home Cemetery on March 15. Minnie watched over his grave as if he were a member of her own family, bringing flowers and keeping the burial plot tidy. Eventually, in 1941, she was buried in the same cemetery, not far from the mystery boy.

According to those who lived at the time near the cemetery, a heavily veiled woman—someone other than Minnie—would sometimes be seen placing a bouquet on the little grave. The woman always managed to get away before anyone could catch up with her to ask who she was. She had to be, it was speculated, someone who knew Little Lord Fauntleroy's true identity. Otherwise, why the secrecy? Unfortunately, if she had indeed known the boy, the veiled woman has by now taken the secret to her own grave, and his true story will most likely forever remain a mystery of the Prairie Home Cemetery.

A Woman of Three Centuries

In centuries past, rarely did a person possess the extraordinary luck to reach a major milestone in life, such as living to be eighty, ninety, or even one hundred years old. But such was the case of Mary Glovchaski. She not only reached the ripe old age of one hundred, but exceeded the century mark. In fact, she lived to be a startling one hundred twelve years, four months, and ten days! But her remarkable story does not end here.

Mary Glovchaski was born in the Polish section of Bromberg, Germany, on February 25, 1798. At the time of her birth, the first president of our country, George Washington, was still living, and our second president, John Adams, was in office. Only sixteen states existed in the Union at the time, the dust had not yet settled from the French Revolution, and the electric battery had just been invented.

In 1828, when she turned thirty, Mary married. She had nine children, kept house, and raised her family. Amazingly, in 1881, at the age of eighty-three, Mary decided to immigrate to the United States in order to spend what she assumed would be her few remaining years with her children and grandchildren, who had already moved to America.

Mary settled in Parcherville, Wisconsin, a village to the north of Wausau. During her twenty-nine years there, she was renowned for her remarkable intelligence and her lively and active interest in current events. In all that time, she was in excellent health, walked unaided, and never wore glasses.

In July 1910, Mary went to stay with a granddaughter who lived in Wausau. It was a particularly hot summer, and once there, Mary became ill from the oppressive heat, drawing her last breath on July 5. When she left this

earth, our twenty-seventh president, William Taft, was in office, and air conditioning, hydroplanes, submarines, helicopters, and automobiles were all newfangled inventions.

Mary Glovchaski outlived all but three of her nine children. She also left twenty grandchildren, twenty-five great-grandchildren, and five great-great-grandchildren, for an astounding total of fifty-three living descendants.

If you ever visit Wausau, Mary's grave is located in the St. Michael's section of the Pine Grove Cemetery on Grand Avenue.

—Shawn P. Blaschka, Wausau Paranormal Research Society

Cleopatra of the South

Civil War feelings still run surprisingly deep in certain parts of the country, and things smacking of old Dixie usually aren't too well received in Yankee territory. So what is a rebel spy's fenced-in grave adorned with the Confederate flag doing in a cemetery in Wisconsin Dells? The resting-place of Belle Boyd dates back to the turn of the century, when Wisconsin Dells was known as Kilbourn.

Growing up as a spirited tomboy in the Shenandoah Valley of western Virginia, Belle was only seventeen when she shot a Yankee soldier who had pushed her mother during a mild altercation in their house. Nothing happened to Belle after the incident, though she did manage to become friends with some of the Northern occupiers and soon began picking up scraps of information that she passed on to her Confederate connections.

Tall and graceful, Belle was not classically beautiful, but she was considered attractive. She was an unabashed flirt; in fact,

newspapers would later call her the Cleopatra of the South. Often bolder than the soldiers themselves, Belle was known for riding through the night and into the live fire of battlegrounds to deliver important messages. She was arrested, jailed, and traded back to the South several times. Finally, suffering from typhoid, she was sent to England to regain her health. She eventually fell in love with a Yankee ensign, and they married and lived a short while in England, where he died at a young age. Belle was a widow at the age of twenty-one. While in England, she wrote her memoirs and married two more times. She died in Kilbourn, Wisconsin, in 1900, during a speaking tour of the United States. She was buried in the Kilbourn cemetery, to lie for eternity among the Yankees she had once spurned. Her tombstone was erected by a sympathetic Southerner, who had it engraved BELLE BOYD, CONFEDERATE SPY.

Double Strong

The giant glacial boulder that sits partway up a hill in Lake Geneva's Oak Hill Cemetery bears a word with a double meaning. It says simply, STRONG, which both represents the name of the general from whose lakeshore estate more than three miles away the monster rock was dragged and describes the eight horses it took to pull the craggy monument to his gravesite.

Family Trees

It's so nice when families can agree on a theme for their gravestones. The Atkins clan of Oconto chose a rustic log motif for their plot at Brookside Cemetery. There's one large tree stump in the center and a group of smaller stumps surrounding it, each with a unique carved design honoring a different family member. Since the timber industry was big in Oconto in the 1800s, when most of the headstones were erected, we guess that the Atkins family had something to do with the industry and wished to memorialize their lumber connection. Also, cut-off tree stumps sometimes symbolize lives cut down in their prime, and several family members fit that profile.

Shagging Fly Balls in Eternity

Jutting forlornly from a small knoll just behind left field of Veterans baseball park in the village of North Prairie is a white marble shaft, meeting the sky with nothing to blunt its stark form but the occasional fly ball. A replica of a railroad car is carved on its base, and a few feet away run the tracks that have been the community's mainstay. It's obvious that the ten-foot pillar honors someone who was important to the railroad, but why would anyone be buried here, far from the town's cemeteries, with no other graves in sight?

The name etched in the marble is that of George E. Price, an employee of the Milwaukee & Mississippi Railroad. He died on March 23, 1859, following an accident that, according to the inscription, occurred in Milton, Wisconsin, on March 7, 1859. According to old newspaper stories, he was the conductor on a train from Janesville to Milwaukee that crashed into a railroad car full of lumber that had been left sitting on the track near Milton Junction. Price landed on his skull in one of the lumber cars, and died two weeks later.

A five-car train adorned with funeral decorations brought dignitaries and friends from Milwaukee to Janesville, where his funeral was held. Price was then given the most unusual honor of being buried on railroad property. It seems that one day, as the train was passing through North Prairie, he had pointed out the spot where he is now interred and said that that was where he wanted to be buried.

People often say to be careful what you wish for.

A tour of Wisconsin cemeteries would not be complete without considering the graves of those who were here long before the white settlers. *Weird Wisconsin* must emphasize that we do not consider any indigenous burial customs "weird" in the same offbeat sense that we consider many other things mentioned in this book to be weird. But there are certain graves and places that intrigued us because of their unusual circumstances or that simply entranced us, such as Indian Bill Cemetery. We respect all Native American burial places in the same way we honor all hallowed grounds—even the occasional animal cemetery. A grave's a grave. But here are a few Native American burial sites we found notable on our safari of the dead. We came away from each location with a sense of awe for the lives so interestingly commemorated.

A Concrete Wigwam for a Princess

Stories about relations between Native Americans and European settlers tend to dwell on the skirmishes. But sometimes things went better than that. Take the story of the descendant of a Ho-Chunk queen, Ho-po-ko-etaw, or "Glory of the Morning." She married a French fur trader named Descarie, a name that mutated to Decorah by the time their grandson Chief Spoon Decorah was born. Decorah lived near Galesville and had a nearby peak named after him, got along famously with his neighbors, and was called a "friend of the white man." His son Winneshiek, for whom another bluff was named, had a well-regarded daughter named Marinuka. When she died at the ripe old age of eighty-two in 1884 near Arctic Springs, on the Galesville lake that now bears her name, the Ho-Chunk tribe and the local townspeople joined forces to honor her with a large funeral procession.

In keeping with the custom of her tribe, the princess was buried at midnight, after drums had pounded for several hours. Her grave was subsequently relocated twice to nearby spots; during the most recent move, her remains were placed in a metal container. The tin box was set onto eight inches of concrete, and the entire tomb was filled with cement so that the remains would not be moved again. The inscription gives her genealogy and adds: SHE WAS BURIED HERE AT THE REQUEST OF HER TRIBE. AT MIDNIGHT, WITH INDIAN RITES, HER HEAD TOWARD THE RISING SUN. G. E. FREEMAN AND OTHERS WITNESSED THE BURIAL.

To further honor the princess, a concrete wigwam was erected next to the tombstone. Both the headstone and the wigwam hunker close to a park shelter near the Arctic Springs Supper Club on County Road T, and they can be easily visited by anyone wishing to pay their respects to the princess.

Indian Bill Cemetery

Powers Bluff, the highest point in Wood County, was home to the Ho-Chunk and Ojibwa tribes until 1933. It was an area rich in nature's bounty—game, wild rice, cranberries, maple syrup, and basket reeds. It was a slow drive through steep, narrow roads, but eventually *Weird Wisconsin* arrived at the bottom of Powers Bluff in front of Indian Bill Cemetery, a small burial ground surrounded by a fence.

The graves themselves are covered by spirit houses— small wooden structures with shingled roofs. The houses are in varying states of decay, but that's as it's meant to be, since they are intended to serve as spirit shelters until they fall apart, at which point they are no longer needed by the person whose grave they cover.

As we stood before this sacred space, with the sun slanting through surrounding pines onto the sheltered graves, we experienced an almost palpable sense of sanctity. The spirit houses slump and slouch as they serve out their final days. Eventually they will be one with the earth, and the spirits will have departed. Perhaps once that happens, this little village of the dead might be considered the world's smallest ghost town.

Indian Baby Grave

Very close to the lapping waters of Petenwell Lake, surrounded by a wrought-iron fence, lies a single tiny grave marked INDIAN BABY 1854. The stone marker is a copy of the original wooden one, which was destroyed by vandals hoping to find valuable artifacts in the grave.

The baby's story came from a pioneer woman named Emily Winters St. Clair, who had buried her infant daughter in Petenwell Lake as she and her family crossed the lake en route from Pennsylvania to Wisconsin. As they reached the shore and continued on, they heard grief-stricken sounds coming from a Native American campsite near the lake. There they found a young woman whose baby son had just died, and they stayed to attend the infant's burial on the lakeshore. The St. Clair family settled nearby, and Emily watched over the little grave for the rest of her life as a reminder of her own lost child. Area residents later took up the watch, adding the fence and plantings. To this day, visitors often leave flowers. Most of them never realize they are actually honoring two dead babies: the little Indian boy and Emily's baby girl.

Lords of the Rings

Wisconsin was not yet a state when two brothers named Mabie brought their circus to Walworth County in 1847. The brothers had such a good time hunting prairie chickens near Lake Delavan that they bought some land and made Delavan their winter headquarters. Other circuses decided that Delavan was the place to be, and as many as twenty-six nomadic circus troupes made their headquarters there during the town's heyday in the 1870s.

The circuses changed the town. Local manu-

facturers turned their hands to cranking out circus wagons, elephants could be spied grazing in local fields, and residents grew used to sharing their town with a variety of performers, including clowns, foreign acrobats, and "differently endowed" humans. Many of the circus people bought houses in Delavan and considered it their true home, among them famous equestrians and Circus Hall of Famers George and Rose Holland. In fact, it's rumored that secret communities of retired circus performers who had once earned their living by exhibiting their special body features still exist around Delavan Lake. But the town's most riotous circus days had petered out well before the twentieth century.

Today, the main reminders of Delavan's big-top glory are the giant elephant and giraffe statues downtown. But a trip to Spring Grove Cemetery at the north end of 7th Street can bring back memories of Delavan's circus people. Their graves, about seventy in all, are identified by oval metal markers next to the headstones.

A cluster of Mabie graves surrounds a large white column emblazoned with the family name. George and Rose Holland can be found inside the cemetery's gigantic granite-and-limestone mausoleum built in 1911, which contains 240 crypts. The mausoleum is locked, but the key can be obtained from the local police department.

Some claim to have seen circus ghosts rollicking inside the cemetery at night. That may be plausible, since not all of the graveyard's circus inhabitants died peacefully or of old age. Circus manager Joseph McMahon, reportedly well known by the Delavan police, was shot by an officer because a gesture he had made to grab a handkerchief looked a little too much like he was going for the officer's gun. And hot-air balloonist Dr. Upp (R. A. Palmer) bit the sawdust a few months after smashing into downtown Delavan's brick hotel when one of his guidelines became snagged. Throw in a few deceased roustabouts, and you have a small troupe of restless spirits—perhaps enough to keep at least one circus playing in the ether of Delavan for a long time to come.

Does Cow Heaven Beat Hog Heaven?

What fun would heaven be for a dairy farmer if there were no cows there? One might argue that most dairy farmers, after a lifetime of milking chores, would not want to be tied down to those chores in the next life. But surely in heaven cows don't need to be milked. So you can't blame the dairyman in Monroe County's Southridge Lutheran Cemetery for wanting to go to his eternal rest with old bossy at the helm. The cow headstone is, after all, the quintessential Dairy State monument.

Wisconsin Horse Burials

People often bury dogs, cats, and guinea pigs in their backyards. Given their size, horses are more problematic. But in Wisconsin, there are monuments that attest to the bond between people and their mounts.

Horses do sleep standing up, so perhaps it's only natural for them to meet their eternal rest that way too. That's how a beloved racehorse named State Rights was buried by the side of his owner, Chauncey L. Roberts, in 1889 on the Old Military Road, about five miles east of Portage.

Roberts was a staunch advocate of the states' rights doctrine, which held that individual states possessed rights that made them almost like sovereign nations. So when his Hamiltonian bay stallion was born in 1861, he named him after that doctrine. The horse proved more successful than the political doctrine, which was arguably trashed after the Union defeated the secessionist states in the Civil War.

State Rights, the stallion, could run a mile in two minutes and twenty seconds, and Roberts was still entering him in races at county fairs when the horse was the ripe old age of twenty-eight, by which time most racehorses have long been put out to pasture. When the stallion fell dead on the track in Racine in 1889, his heartbroken owner had a grave dug that was large enough for the horse to be buried upright. The Columbia County Highway Department later preserved the grave area in a tiny triangular park, and local 4-H groups have since tended the headstone, which reads STATE RIGHTS DIED JULY 9, 1889, AGED 28 YEARS. Roberts probably intended that as a political statement as well.

Another tribute to well-loved horses is found near Fond du Lac where a farmer nicknamed Uncle Joe Kinsman lost four horses to the grim animal reaper between 1849 and 1869. He buried all four near one another and put up a marker that reads HERE LIES TOM AND BILL, THEY DONE THEIR DUTY WITH A WILL. ALSO DOLL & KATE, AS TRUE AND FAITHFUL AS THEIR MATES.

The marker wasn't built to withstand Wisconsin winters, however, and the Wisconsin Humane Society eventually replaced it with a more permanent one. The new marker is located on the Lake Winnebago side of Highway 45 North (the east side of the road), five or six houses north of the intersection of Lincoln Road and Highway 45.

Chickening Out at St. Peter Cemetery

Todd Roll of Wausau alerted *Weird Wisconsin* to a fabulous but brief encounter a gentleman had in St. Peter Cemetery in Stevens Point sometime in the mid-1990s. St. Peter is a wonderful little quiet spot along the Wisconsin River, just down a bit from the infamous haunted Red Bridge. That gent reported that while driving past the cemetery grounds one evening, he glanced over his shoulder toward the river and witnessed an eight-foot-tall white headless chicken roaming the deserted graveyard.

Upon later investigation, Roll found no tracks or signs, except for a single white tail feather near the river, possibly from a chicken.

Most of the people interred in St. Peter are Poles and Czechs, and their graves impart an Old World look to the tiny burial ground. Of all the cemeteries we've visited, St. Peter reminds us most of the one in George A. Romero's film *Night of the Living Dead*.

Weird Wisconsin has also investigated the headless chicken. Like Roll, we've failed to find any evidence of giant stalking poultry, but we'd like to note that the name Kluk is common in Portage County. We didn't find any Kluks buried here, but we did encounter a Peck or two.

No chapter on graveyards would be complete without a few scary stories and ghostly legends. While people tend to associate cemeteries with wandering spirits, this connection does seem a bit suspicious. After all, isn't the soul supposed to leave its host body at the time of death? Why, then, would the wayward spirit follow its former self, now a lifeless corpse, all the way to the graveyard and hang around after it was buried? It just doesn't make sense. Except, of course, in the case of Blood Cemetery, where the spectral apparition in question is said to have actually died right in the graveyard that it continues to haunt to this day.

Bloody Tales of Blood Cemetery

The name Blood Cemetery conjures images of sanguinary B-movies from the 1970s. Nevertheless, legend chasers expecting to encounter gruesome pools of crimson will be sorely disappointed. Stories about Blood Cemetery, officially known as Woodville Cemetery, vary tremendously. According to one legend, Calvin Blood committed suicide by hanging himself from one of the trees in the cemetery. If true, this would be the first time we've heard of someone offing themselves in a graveyard by hanging. It would certainly save on the cost of a hearse to transport the body.

Other tales allege that Calvin Blood deserted his fellow soldiers during the Civil War and was subsequently tracked down to Stevens Point. There, his former mates exacted revenge by hanging him from the tree that now overlooks his grave. Reputedly, however, neither leaves nor other debris ever obscure Calvin Blood's grave. Some people report seeing pools of blood forming on the flat tombstone. Others insist that the grave oozes blood. Still others claim that blood drips from the trees surrounding the grave.

As with many haunted spots, cars experience inexplicable electrical failures in the vicinity of Blood Cemetery, and strange lights flit through the graveyard gloom. People have even encountered hellish dogs that have chased them out of the cemetery. We'll let a researcher who has investigated the cemetery over a long period of time have the last word.

Woodville (Blood) Cemetery is a very small burial ground located just outside Stevens Point. A Civil War veteran named Calvin Blood is buried there. There are many local legends associated with Woodville Cemetery. A tree in the cemetery bleeds when bark is torn off it. Bodies can be seen hanging from the same tree. An apparition of a man from the waist up is seen roaming the cemetery, and there are a number of other stories.

I talked to many people who had heard these stories or gone out to the cemetery, but I could never locate anyone who had been out there and seen any of the phenomena reported.

Today, the bleeding tree has been cut down, and the cemetery has been vandalized so often that all but two of the headstones have been broken off. A fence surrounds the place, and signs warn of video surveillance. There's a caretaker who lives next to the cemetery. His dogs will alert him to anyone visiting the place, and he will come out to investigate.

In the past, there has been so much traffic on Halloween night that the county police have stationed a car at the cemetery to keep thrill seekers out. One Halloween, after a story about the cemetery appeared in a local newspaper, over one hundred people were turned back by the police.—*Todd Roll, Wausau Paranormal Research Society*

More Blood

Tucked in a remote corner of Appleton's Riverside Cemetery, the grave of Kate Blood has long attracted thrill seekers. The most commonly told story is that Kate murdered her husband and three children, then took her own life. The crime was so horrific that officials buried the entire family in a hidden-away spot so as to not remind townspeople of Kate's gruesome deed. People point to the three smaller tombstones located in front of the larger stone as evidence that Kate's three children are buried there.

According to legend, if you visit Kate's grave at midnight, blood will ooze from her headstone. This "liquid," however, is dry to the touch. Others are said to have witnessed orbs of light moving around her grave or have seen hooded figures moving in the shadows and trees. Screams are said to echo through the night. People feel watched.

In reality, many of these tales can be resolved by the simple act of reading for comprehension—a concept that seems to elude most thrill seekers. The larger tombstone has three names inscribed on its various sides: Kate Blood's name; the name of her husband, George M. Miller; and the name of Miller's second wife, Mary Moulton Hutchinson. George married Mary after Kate's death, a singular feat for a murdered man! Indeed, Kate passed away in 1874, while George lived on until 1916, some forty-two years after her death. The three smaller headstones are inscribed with the initials of these three individuals, not of any children. This is easily checked by matching the initials to the names on the larger tombstone. After thorough archival research, two investigators, Chad Lewis and Terry Fisk, reported that they discovered no evidence that either Kate or Mary ever bore any children.

Nevertheless, cemetery walkers continue to report paranormal events in the area of Kate Blood's grave. Clearly, even though the murderous legends are untrue, some phenomenon continues to trigger otherworldly activity there.

Creepiest Cemeteries

What are the creepiest cemeteries in Wisconsin? I would have to go with the little cemetery next to Lake Dubay in Marathon County. It's small but hilly and has that out-of-the-way creepiness to it. In the back is a large pine tree that shades a group of about four graves. Because of the tree, the temperature is always a few degrees cooler back there. A natural cold spot, if you will.

Also there is a graveyard next to the campgrounds in Peninsula State Park in Door County. The graveyard had been overgrown by the woods, so you have these little paths through the underbrush with headstones scattered here and there. I was there about ten years ago, and I don't know if the place had been fixed up or not. Story was that a ghost of a little boy haunted the place.–*Todd Roll*

Drive at Your Own Risk

I work with an older lady named Emma. I would not say she is a liar; she is very sweet. Emma left work early one morning—we work the night shift, and she lives way out in the country. It was raining, but not stormy or anything like that, just raining and still dark out. There have always been stories about a ghost in this part of the county, supposedly seen only when it's raining. I asked Emma about it, half jokingly, since I never thought anything like that really happens. Still, I was interested.

The answer I got shocked me. At first, I couldn't believe it; then I remembered that this lady does not lie. Emma said that once, as she passed the cemetery, something got in the car with her. She said, "I just froze and gripped the steering wheel very tightly."

She could see this ghostlike thing sitting in the passenger side of her car. She said it looked like a woman, but she really wasn't sure. She was too afraid to look for too long. Emma said as long as she has lived out that way, this is the first time she had ever seen anything like this. She's lived in the area for over forty years and has driven through many storms and rain showers in the early-morning hours, while passing the cemetery. This was the first encounter for her.

This story about the ghost appearing in the rain has been around for eighty years, as far as I can tell. I did a little investigating, asking everyone I knew about it. I came up with one more person this happened to, except they didn't see anything, only felt something. Whatever it was, it was trying to strangle the woman who was driving. Her mother, who was sitting in the passenger seat, didn't know how to drive, but was trying to help her daughter steer the car while her daughter was trying to unclasp whatever was gripping her throat.–*Punkstertn*

(Unfortunately, Punkstertn vanished before we could learn the name of the cemetery or where it was located. It was raining the day we received her last e-mail.)

Forest Home Cemetery

Long whispered to be one of Milwaukee's spookiest cemeteries, Forest Home is also one of the most spectacular. Massive white marble monuments and ornate crypts, oversized but graceful statues, and rolling terrain accented with a pond and a concrete bridge make Forest Home a gorgeous place in which to spend eternity. Unusual headstones abound, such as the one topped by a concrete replica of a boat, or the giant monument of an elderly couple with their portraits sculpted in realistic relief. The couple's faces lurk at eye level, seeming to pop right out of the stone and stare at those who walk by. The cemetery also features a Hall of History, a giant mausoleum where the founding fathers of Milwaukee are memorialized. The whole place is done in pink marble and pink carpet, a soothing color for eternal slumber.

A hill adjacent to the pond on the north side of the cemetery has been said to cause strange reactions in some people who walk on it, making them feel sick and fearful. One person reported experiencing visions of splintered coffins and shredded corpses, followed by headaches and bloodshot eyes. The report was posted online and received this reply.

I read what you wrote about Forest Home Cemetery. That reaction is very common among people who go there—in fact, that exact spot you're talking about! I am the Director of SEWPI (South East Wisconsin Paranormal Investigations), and we heard about Forest Home Cemetery. We went there and talked to a groundskeeper and also the assistant day manager of the place, and they both told us odd stories about that area in question. We went out there (in the day) to take a look, and there was a woman and her teen daughter walking by. Our eyes met, and we smiled at each other. We took some pictures and got an odd outcome; all three control pictures were bleached out. But the two afterwards, in a different area, turned out okay. What was interesting was when we went back to our car, a couple cars away was this lady and her daughter. She must have seen our ID's. Anyway, she asked if we were a "ghost-hunting group." I said yes, and she said, "My daughter told me to ask you if it means anything that she feels ill every time we come to see my father." I said, "Well, it could be just that the whole cemetery thing maybe upsets her or freaks her out, as it can some people." And she said, "That could be, but it's only in a certain area." And guess what area she described?—*Heidi*

La Belle Cemetery

The cemetery is the home of a large granite statue reported to be the focal point of a number of eerie phenomena, including the presence of a very dismal ghost that's often observed inside the graveyard. The statue stands over the graves of the Nathusias family. It depicts a sad woman gazing down at the ground; she holds a bouquet of flowers in her hands and stands in front of an imposing cross. For years, people have come to the cemetery to visit the statue, leaving coins and flowers in the woman's cupped hands. Many of those visitors have noticed odd things about the statue. Some have said that the woman cries blood, while others have seen blood dripping from the palms of her hands. Most intriguing, perhaps, are reports that the statue itself has from time to time been seen walking away from the cross toward the shore of nearby Fowler Lake.

This lake is also the centerpiece of another enduring legend of La Belle Cemetery. Many nighttime visitors have come to visit the Nathusias family plot, only to find a young girl in the vicinity of the statue. When approached, she walks to the shores of Fowler Lake, then jumps in, drowning herself. It is uncertain who this troubled, suicidal ghost is, but over the years the disturbing image of her drowning has shocked many nocturnal visitors at the cemetery.

Ghost Girl Poses for Pix at La Belle

We've been to La Belle Cemetery maybe ten times or so. The first time, we were in two groups of two. I was with Carlos, and Ted was with John. We were walking down the path near the water, and Ted and John went in the opposite direction. We stopped before we reached the small wooded area by the secondary entrance. We then walked farther down the path, and some strange things happened. One camera started malfunctioning, and we noticed that both digital batteries were dead. When we got back to the car, we found the two passenger doors open. We snapped some pictures, and one of them has what looks like it might be a young girl standing near the driver's door. Unfortunately, it was a disposable camera, and it isn't the best picture, but it's pretty clear to us what it is.

When we went back to the cemetery, we saw that we were parked near the grave of an eleven-year-old girl. Then one camera went berserk. The autofocus wouldn't work, and the flash wouldn't come up. We left the area, and the camera worked again. When we went back to the area, it again stopped working. I started seeing faint orange lights in the corner of my eye, and we were all filled with a distinctly odd feeling. We left when we couldn't take it anymore.

Some people, including myself, have noticed a distinctly calm, contented feeling fairly near the statue.—*Dan*

"There is no doubt but there are many people buried alive, and the awful suffering and strain of mind they surely must pass through is too sad to think of."

Buried Alive

As far as most people are concerned, the creepiest type of cemetery tale involves those desperate souls who were buried alive. The Victorians, in particular, were fixated on these stories, and Wisconsin has its own tragic example. On March 30, 1898, the *Pardeeville Crank* reported a gruesome discovery at Rosedale Cemetery, which is next to the Rosedale Presbyterian Church on Highway 33, a few miles east of Pardeeville.

On Wednesday last, at the Rosedale cemetery, the grave of Mrs. Sarah Smith, daughter-in-law of John Smith, formerly of this place, was opened for the purpose of removing the remains to an adjacent lot, and on opening the coffin, it was found that she had been buried while in a trance, as she must have come to after being interred, for she had partly turned over and the right hand was drawn up to the face and the fingers indicated having been bitten in the agony of finding herself interred alive. She had been buried thirteen years.

There is no doubt but there are many people buried alive, and the awful suffering and strain of mind they surely must pass through is too sad to think of. Persons have been known to have lain in a trance for the period of six weeks and then revived. All should be very careful and sure that their friends are not buried under these conditions.

INDEX
Page numbers in **bold** refer to photos and illustrations.

A

Ancient mysteries, 24–37
Angel of Death, 20
Angel hair from the sky, 92, **92**
Ape-men, 107, 114
Appleton Pond, screams of
    drowned girl in, 21
Appleton's Cemetery, 259, **259**
Ashland Road, running-board ghost of,
    221, **221**
Atkins family, 251
Atlantis, pyramids of, 29, **29**
Auto and toy museum, 199, **199**
Automobile, first, 138
Aztalan, mystery woman of,
    26–29, **26, 27, 28, 29**

B

Badger statue, 78, **79**
Barbershop, world's most beautiful,
    176, **176**
Bavarian-themed Kappel Park, 73, **73**
Beast of Bray Road, 110–113, **110–111,
    112, 113**, 177, **177**
Bee museum, 260
Beaumont, Dr. William, 201, **201**
Bigfoot, 107, 114, **114**, 119–121, **119, 121**
Bioweapons workshop, 138, **138**
Birdman, 107
Bizarre beasts, 104–121
Bjorn's Fine Clothing Store and Museum,
    189–190, **189, 190**
Black Point ghosts, **228**, 229–230, **230**
Black River boulder, 36, **36**
Black swirling thing in basement,
    96–98, **97, 98**
Blood, Kate, 158, **158**
Blood Cemetery, Stevens Point, 258

Blood-oozing graves, 258–259, **259**
Blue ice ball, 95
Boltonville, ghosts of, 218
Bong Heritage Center, 194, **194**
Boobooshaw, 21
Boscobel Hotel, ghosts of, 236
Boulder gravestone, 251
Bourgo ghost, 42–43, **42**
Boyd, Belle, 250, **250**
Bray Road, beast of, 110–113, **110–111,
    112, 113**, 177, **177**
Brumder Mansion, 238–239, **238, 239**
Buckeridge, Byron, 184–185, **184, 185**
Bruno, Ralph, 49
Buffalo, white (Miracle), 60–61, **60, 61**
Buffalo's mythical Northwoods creatures,
    152–153, **152, 153**
Bunyan, Paul, 68–69, **68, 69**, 164
Burials, Native American,
    32–34, **32, 34**, 252–253, **252, 253**
Buried alive, 263, **263**
Burlington Liars Club, 49
Burrows, Robert, 134

C

California raisin house, 159, **159**
Campbellsport, ghost of, 236
Carhart, John Wesley, 138
Car on a silo, 76, **76**
Carousel, world's largest, 185, **187**
Caryville, legends of, 211, **211**
Cemeteries, 40–41, 245–263
Chapelle de St. Martin de Seyssuel,
    37, **37**
Charlie (elephant), 131, **131**
Charron, Father Louis, 42–43
Cheese hats, 48–49, **48**
Chevy on silo, 76, **76**

Chicken, headless, 257
Circus animals,
    75, **75**, 129–131, **129, 130, 131**
Circus graves, 254–255, **254**
Claire de Loon, 78, **78**
Cleopatra of the South, 250, **250**
Coin found by lightning, 95, **95**
Collections and museums, 183–201
Concrete Park,
    164–165, **164, 165, 166, 167**
Concrete statues, **162–163**, 163–174,
    **164, 166, 167, 168–169, 170, 171,
    172, 173, 174–175**
Concrete wigwam grave, 252, **252**
Concretion museum,
    184–185, **184, 185**
Corkscrew statue, 78, **79**
Cornucopia Yacht Club, 50, **50**
Cow headstone, 255, **255**
Cow statues, 74, **74**
Culvert Man, 80, **80**
Curse of T. B. Scott Mansion,
    18–19, **18–19**

D

Dahmer, Jeffrey, 144–145, **144, 145**
Dead, visualizing living people as, 47
Delavan, statue, 175, **175**
Dice, giant fuzzy, 157, **157**
Dickeyville Grotto, **168–169**, 169, 170
Diehnelt, Walter, 200
Dinosaur bones, 196–197, **196**
Disappearing man of Highway 12, 218
Dixon, Jeane, 47, **47**
Doglike creatures, 115, 177
Dollhouse grave, 246, **246**
Don Q Inn, 88–89, **88, 89**
Dragon burial, 30–31, **31**

E

Eden, Garden of, 61
Edgerton, ghost of, 236
Ekiega, 33
Elephant statue, 75, **75**
Elkhart Lake monster, 116
Elkhorn, smiley-face house, 156, **156**
Elk Lake Dam, ghosts of,
 222–224, **222–223, 224**
Elk Mound Tower, 30–31, **31**
Elmer's Auto & Toy Museum, 199, **199**
Elm Grove, ghosts of, 237
Elson, Edward Ben, 124–125
Emmert, Frank, 48, **48**
Endres Manufacturing, 73, **73**
Engelbert, Nick, 172, **172, 173**
Erbstoesser, Daniel, 158, **158**
Evermor, Dr., 148–150, **148, 149,
 150–151**
Exorcising priest of Lake Superior,
 42–43, **43**
Exorcism tools, haunted house
 purchased with, 231, **231**

F

Fabled people and places, 38–63
FAST Corp. (Fiberglass Animals,
 Shapes & Trademarks Corporation),
 66–67, **66, 67**
Fence, extraordinary, 158, **158**
Fennimore Cheese, 71, **71**
Flying fish, 93, **93**
Foamation, Inc., 48, 49
Food statues, 77, **77**
Foote Mansion, 22, **22–23**
Forest Home Cemetery, 261, **261**
Forest sculpture garden,
 160–161, **160, 161**

G

Forevertron, 148–150, **148, 149,
 150–151**
Frog statue, 80, **80**

Gagnier, Marie Regis, 51, **51,** 52
Gambrinus, King, 83, **83**
Garden of Eden, 61
Gein, Ed, 141–143, **141, 142, 143**
Ghost ball, 99
Ghost Road, 220, **220**
Ghosts, 227–243
Giant corn, 77, **77**
Giant Indians, 33–34
Giant pumpkin, 77, **77**
Giraffe statue, 75, **75**
Glarner, Stube, 87, **87**
Glovchaski, Mary, 249, **249**
Gobbler restaurant,
 84–85, **85–86**
Grandview, 172, **172, 173**
Grave and a ghost in a soap-store
 basement, 233–235, **233–234**
Gravity Hill, Shullsburg, 225, **225**
Great Spirit Washbowl, 35
Green Bay, ghost of, 237, **237**
Grotto culture, **162–163,** 163–174, **164,
 165, 166, 167, 168–169, 170, 171,
 172, 173, 174–175**
Gump, Andy, 69–70, **70**

H

Halfway Tree, 219, **219**
Hall, Colonel George "Popcorn,"
 129–131, **129, 130, 131**
Hartland, ghost of, 238
Haunchyville, 56–59, **57, 58**

Haunted bridges of Stevens Point,
 216, **216, 217**
Headless nun, 16–17, **16**
Hell's Playground, 21
Hilbert Road ghost, 219
Hill of the Dead, 32, **32**
Hobbitt House, 132–133, **132, 133**
Honey museum, 200
Horse burials, 256, **256**
Houdini Historical Center, 198, **198**
House on the Rock, 185–187, **186, 187**
Humpback ship, world's last, 81, **81**

I

Ice ball, 95
Igor, 71, **71**
Indian baby grave, 253, **253**
Indian Bill Cemetery, 253, **253**
Indians, *see* Native Americans
Inventors, 134–137, **134, 135, 136**

J

James Tellen Woodland Sculpture
 Garden, 160–161, **160, 161**
Joan of Arc stone, 37, **37**
Jurustic Park, **178–179,** 179–181, **180, 181**

K

Kangaroos, 12–15, **13, 14**
Kappel Park, 73, **73**
Kemper Hall's headless nun, 16–17, **16**
Kempfer, Jean and David,
 233–235, **233, 234**
Kirschnik, Marv, 177, **177**
Kohoutek Comet, 124–125, **124–125**
Kuehner, Bob, 101–102

L

La Belle Cemetery, 262, **262**
La Crosse nursing home, 20, **20**
Lake monsters, 116–117, **117**
L'Allemand, Pauline, 128, **128**
Lawyer, loony, 124–125, **124–125**
Leahy, Thomas, 138, **138**
Letter of the alphabet, world's largest,
    79, **79**
Liars Club, Burlington, 49
Lightning, coin found by, 95, **95**
Little Lord Fauntleroy, grave of, 248, **248**
Little witch of New Berlin, 43–44
Local legends, 11–23
Local notables, 123–145
Lodi's blue mystery thing, 106
Lombardi, Vince, 237, **237**
Loon statue, 78, **78**
Lost boy, 53
Lost pyramids of Atlantis, 29, **29**
Louis XVII, 54–55, **54–55**

M

Madison, ghost of, 238
Mars Cheese Castle, 71
McKeeth Road (ghost road), 220, **220**
Medical Progress, Museum of, 201, **201**
Metal chunks from the sky, 94
Meteorite, 94
Midgets of Haunchyville, 56–59, **57, 58**
Millard Dinosaur & Taxidermy Store,
    196–197, **196**
Milwaukee, ghost of, 238–239, **238, 239**
Mississippians, 26, **27**
Moccasin Bar, 200, **200**
Mona Lisa smile, 36, **36**
Mouse statue, 71, **71**
Muffler Man, 68, 69

Museums, 182–201
Mystery woman of Aztalan,
    26–29, **26–29**

N

National Fresh Water Fishing
    Hall of Fame, 197, **197**
Native Americans
    burials, 32–34, **32, 34,**
        252–253, **252, 253**
    curse on T. B. Scott Mansion,
        18–19, **18–19**
Neeve, Jean, 247, **247**
New Berlin, little witch of, 43–44
Nicolet, Jean, 8
"Nine Angels" memorial, 247, **247**
Novel, worst, 134
Nursing home's little boy of death,
    20, **20**

O

Oakes, Russell E., 135, **135**
Old Man Weary, 204–206, **204–206**
Orange ghost ball, 99
Outagamie Museum, 198, **198**

P

Paradise Road, 207–209, **207, 208, 209**
Peace Monument, **170**, 171, **171**
Penny statue, 78, **79**
People and places, 38–63
Perry, Michael, 47
Personalized properties, 147–181
Petit Butte des Morts, 32, **32**
Phillips, Ernest and Chester, 33
Pipe, ghosts of, 240

Poison Widow, 139–140, **139, 140**
Polonia's roadside shrines,
    212, **212, 213**
Popcorn, 129–130
Port Washington's Boobooshaw, 21
Prairie Moon Sculpture Gardens,
    174, **174–175**
Presley, Elvis, 51
Presley, Elvis Aron, 126–127, **127**
Price, George E., 251, **251**
Pyramids, submerged, 29, **29**

R

Rammer, Edward F., 136–137, **136**
Red Cedar Lake monster, 117
Red snow, 95
Reptile man, 106, **106**
Roadside oddities, 65–89
Roads less traveled, 203–225
Rock in the House, 188, **188**
Rock Lake, 29
Rock Lake monster, 117
Rotter, Rudy, museum of sculpture,
    195, **195**
Running-board ghost of Ashland Road,
    221, **221**
Rusch, Herman, 174, **174–175**

S

Sawdust Factory, 132–133, **133**
Sawyer County, ghost of, 240
Scalped lady, 51–52, **52**
Schaude, Myrtle, 139–140, **139, 140**
Schettl's Freight Sales, 72, **72**
Schlais, Mary, 222–224, **223, 224**
Scott Mansion, 18–19, **18–19**
Sculpture museum, 195, **195**

Seven Bridges (Grant Park), ghost of, **214**, 215
Seven Bridges Road (Boltonville), ghosts of, 218, **218**
Shrines, roadside, 212, **212, 213**
Shullsburg's Gravity Hill, 225, **225**
Six-pack statue, **82**, 83, **83**
Sky, objects falling from, 92–95, **92–95**
Smiley-face house, Elkhorn, 156, **156**
Smith, Nelva Jean, 247, **247**
Smith, Rudolph (Rudi) 176, **176**
Space junk, fallen, 94, **94**
Spinning Top Museum, 191, **191**
Spiritualists, 45–46, **45, 46**
Spook Hill, spiritualists of, 45–46, **45, 46**
Spook Temple, 40–41, **41**
Sputnik, fallen piece of, 94, **94**
Squirrel and chipmunk museum, 192–193, **192–193**
Statue that will not die, 69–70, **69, 70**
Stevens Point, haunted bridges, 216, **216, 217**
Stone Elephant, 35, **35**
Strommer, Christiane, 233, **233**

T

Tall Tales Trail, 49
Tellen, James, 160–161 **160, 161**
Three centuries, grave of woman whose life spanned, 249, **249**
Thunderbirds, 108–109, **108–109**
Tree gravestones, 251
Truck in tree, 76, **76**

U

UFOs (unidentified flying objects), 100–103, **100, 102, 103,** 136–137, **136** landing port, 154–155, **154, 155**
UFO Bob, 101–103, **102**
Unexplained phenomena, 90–103
Urinal, Midwest's largest, 87, **87**

V

Vampire Valley, 210
Van Hoof, Mary Ann, 62–63, **62, 63**
Vienneaux, Bill, 132–133, **132, 133**
Virgin Mary, vision of, 62–63, **62, 63**

W

Waukesha
    kangaroos in, 12–15, **13, 14**
    Wily Wizard of, 135, **135**
Wausau, ghosts of, 241–243, **241, 242**
Weary Road ghost, 204–206, **204–205, 206**
Wegner, Paul and Matilda, 171, **171**
Wells Hall, 40–41
Werewolves, 114, **114,** 177
Whaleback ship, world's last, 81, **81**
Whatsit, Central American, 118, **118**
White buffalo (Miracle), 60–61, **60, 61**
Whitewater, mysterious goings-on in, 40–41, **41**
Wildlife Museum, 200, **200**
Williams, Eleazar, 54–55, **54–55**
Wily Wizard of Waukesha, 135, **135**
Witches' tunnels, 40–41
Witch of New Berlin, 43–44
Witch Road, 210, **210**
Wizard of Waukesha, 135, **135**
Woodland Indians, 27
Woodville Cemetery (Blood Cemetery, Stevens Point), 258
Woolley, William, 14
Worm shower, 93

Weird Wisconsin

By
Linda S. Godfrey and Richard D. Hendricks
Edited by
Mark Moran and Mark Sceurman

CONTRIBUTORS

Jennifer Lauer is a paranormal researcher and a founder and director of the Southern Wisconsin Paranormal Research Group (www.paranormalresearchgroup.com) based in Janesville, Wisconsin.

Elaine A. Roberts is an avid doll collector with a strong interest in antiques. She is also author Linda S. Godfrey's mother.

Joe Schackelman of Racine is a former newspaper editor and the author of the book *God Lives.*

John Scherf is an investigator of all things strange who runs two Web sites on Milwaukee weirdness: http://www.geocities.com/milwaukeemadness2u/mainpage1.html and http://www.geocities.com/wisconsinfreakylinks2u.com.

Julie Von Bergen is copy editor for a national association based in Chicago and works in her spare time as a freelance writer and editor. She lives in Lake Geneva, Wisconsin.

Tony Woiak is a Washburn writer and historian who has authored five local history books and several documentary films. He also writes radio commercials and newspaper articles, as well as a history column.

Daniel J. Wood is a Michigan-based researcher who has published articles on history, religion, archaeology, and the paranormal. He is a frequent contributor to *FATE* magazine.

Publisher:	Barbara J. Morgan
Assoc. Managing Editor:	Emily Seese
Production:	Della R. Mancuso
	Mancuso Associates, Inc.,
	North Salem, N.Y.

ACKNOWLEDGMENTS

Too many individuals and organizations deserve a tremendous amount of thanks for their influence and help with research, photos, and fieldwork. To name them all would take pages, so we'd like to offer up a universal thanks to everyone. If you ran across one of us somewhere along the way, chances are, some piece of you has rubbed off and is included here—thank you very much.

Our special thanks go to that great state treasure the Wisconsin Historical Society and its library and archives, underappreciated and underfunded; to libraries and historical societies across the state and the dedicated women and men who work in them; to the many people who have shared weird stories and news tips over the years; to Steven A. Godfrey, for his work as weird field agent and for taking weekend "vacations" to places like the town of Poland; to Michelle Gerise Godwin, just because; to Richard Heiden, for news clippings galore; to Chad Lewis, Terry Fisk, and Unexplained Research for loads of research and assistance; and to Todd Roll, raconteur.

Thanks also to *The Anomalist;* to Bonnie at the Fifield grocery store; to Charles E. Brown, Dorothy Moulding Brown, Robert Gard, Walker Wyman, and Dennis Boyer, unsung folklore heroes; to Capital Brewery (Middleton) and Sprecher Brewing (Glendale), for inspiration and award-winning microbrews; to Christopher D. Claus and the Wisconsin Paranormal Research Center; to our adventurous e-mail reporters from everywhere; to Richard Fanning; Charles Fort, John Keel, Loren Coleman, and Patrick Huyghe, the Four Horsemen of Weird Inspiration; to *The Fortean Times;* to L. J. Jones, who rocks; to Jackie Loohauis, ace reporter; to Janet Marcuccio, roadside recorder; to the Media Mavens Breakfast Association; to Kevin Nelson, tiki god; to John Scherf, Milwaukee Madman (this prediction came true!); to Terri Schlichenmeyer, who has more books than God; to all the folks at *Wisconsin Today;* Daniel J. Wood, for comic relief; and to R. W. Wolff, for Reptile Man. And most important, thanks to all the people of unusual talent, deed, and accomplishment who have enlivened and made this book possible.

PICTURE CREDITS

All photos and illustrations by Linda S. Godfrey and Richard D. Hendricks
except for public domain art and as listed below:

Page 2 bottom right © Larry Harris; 3 bottom © BURCH TINA/CORBIS SYGMA; 6 © Ryan Doan; 13 © Martin Harvey/CORBIS; 20 © Ryan Doan; 21 © Mark Tuschman/CORBIS; 22 courtesy of the Cuff family of Hortonville; 23 courtesy Omro Historical Society; 26 inset © Don Schuler; 32 © Historical Picture Archive/CORBIS; 35 courtesy of the Palmyra Historical Society; 38–39 © Ryan Doan; 42 © Philip James Corwin/CORBIS; 47 © Bettmann/CORBIS; 48 © BURCH TINA/CORBIS SYGMA; 50 © James O. Keyes; 52 © Bettmann/CORBIS; 55 © Bettmann/CORBIS; 57 © Ryan Doan; 60 © David and Valerie Heider; 68 © Lin Schmidt; 87 © The Glarner Stube; 91 © Ryan Doan; 92 © Philip Gould/CORBIS; 93 © Thomas Hartwell/CORBIS; 97 © Ryan Doan; 105 © Mark Moran; 106 © Tom Mandrake; 107 © Joe Oesterle; 108–109 © Jim Bliss; 112 © Marv Kirschnik; 114 © Underwood & Underwood/CORBIS; 117 © Ryan Doan; 118 © Michael & Patricia Fogden/CORBIS; 119 © Mark Moran; 121 © Brian Quinn; 122 bottom left courtesy The Waukesha County Historical Society and Museum; 128 © Linda S. Godfrey; 129–131 courtesy Evansville Eager Free Public Library; 134–135 courtesy The Waukesha County Historical Society and Museum; 138 © *The Janesville Gazette;* 139 courtesy the *Palmyra Enterprise;* 140 © Joe Oesterle; 141, 142 © Bettmann/CORBIS; 144, 145 © Reuters/CORBIS; 161, 162–163, 165 inset, 166 bottom, 168, 170, 171 top, 172–173, 174–175 © Larry Harris; 176 courtesy Palmyra Historical Society; 183 © Kay Shaw Photography; 186 left, 187 © Mark E. Gibson; 194 top, 195 courtesy Karen Rotter; 198 top courtesy Outagamie Museum; 198 bottom left Library of Congress, Prints & Photographs Division; 198 bottom right courtesy Outagamie County Historical Society; 199 © Kay Shaw Photography; 201 top © Bettmann/CORBIS; 202, 203, 217 © Ryan Doan; 218 © John Bartholomew/CORBIS; 221 © CORBIS; 227 © Brian Quinn; 228, 231 © Ryan Doan; 237 © Bettmann/CORBIS; 241 © Benjamin Rondel/CORBIS; 244 © Ryan Doan; 246 © Elaine Roberts; 252 © Dawn Benrud; 257 © Alison Wright/CORBIS; 262 © Ryan Doan.

SELECTED BIBLIOGRAPHY

BOOKS AND PERIODICALS

Balousek, Marv. *Famous Wisconsin Inventors and Entrepreneurs.*
Oregon, WI: Badger Books, 2003.

Beckwith, Albert Clayton. *History of Walworth County.*
Indianapolis: B. F. Bowen & Co., 1912.

Birmingham, Robert A., and Leslie E. Eisenberg. *Indian Mounds of Wisconsin.* Madison: Univ. of Wisconsin Press, 2000.

Federal Writers Program. *Wisconsin Indian Place Legends.*
Madison: Univ. of Wisconsin Press, 1936.

Forbes, Don. "White River Polygamy, the King James Version."
Lake Geneva Magazine, vol. 1, issue 6, December 1988.

Gard, Robert. *This Is Wisconsin.* Spring Green, WI: Wisconsin House, 1969.

Gard, Robert, and Elaine Reetz, compilers. *The Trail of the Serpent: Lore and Legend of Fox River Valley.* Madison: Wisconsin House, 1973.

Gard, Robert, and L. G. Sorden. *Wisconsin Lore: Antics and Anecdotes of Wisconsin People and Places.* Ashland, WI: Heartland Press, 1987.

——. *The Romance of Wisconsin Place Names.*
New York: October House, 1968.

Gilpatrick, Kristin. *Famous Wisconsin Film Star.*
Oregon, WI: Badger Books, 2002.

Godfrey, Linda S. *The Beast of Bray Road: Tailing Wisconsin's Werewolf.*
Black Earth, WI: Prairie Oak Press, 2003.

——. *The Poison Widow: A True Story of Sin, Strychnine, and Murder.*
Black Earth, WI: Prairie Oak Press, 2003.

Gollmar, Robert H. *Edward Gein, America's Most Bizarre Murderer.*
Delavan, WI: C. Hallberg, 1981.

Hall, Jane. "Would You Believe?" *Landmark* (Waukesha County Historical Society), vol. 13, no.1, Winter 1970.

Hollatz, Tom. *Gangster Holidays: The Lore and Legends of the Bad Guys.*
St. Cloud, MN: North Star Press of St. Cloud, 1989.

Holmes, Fred L. *Badger Saints and Sinners.*
Milwaukee: E. M. Hale & Co., 1939.

Howard, L. "Wisconsin Is Talking." *Newsweek,* vol. 116, issue 2, July 9, 1990.

Jaeger, Richard, and M. William Balousek. *Massacre in Milwaukee: The Macabre Case of Jeffrey Dahmer.* Oregon, WI: Waubesa Press, 1991.

Jensen, Don. *Kenosha Kaleidoscope: Images of the Past.*
Kenosha, WI: Kenosha Community History Committee, 1985.

Kabitzke, Donald. "The Mysterious Tombstone." *Landmark* (Waukesha County Historical Society), vol. 38, no. 3, Autumn 1995.

Lake, Rena. *Fifield: Her People and Their History.* Fifield, WI: 1972–1975.

Lapham, Increase A. *Antiquities of Wisconsin.*
Madison: Univ. of Wisconsin Press, 2000.

Leary, James P., ed. *Wisconsin Folklore.*
Madison, WI: Univ. of Wisconsin Press, 1998.

Lesy, Michael. *Wisconsin Death Trip.* New York: Random House, 1973.

Lewis, Chad, and Terry Fisk. *The Wisconsin Road Guide to Haunted Locations.*
Eau Claire, WI: Unexplained Research, 2004.

Martin, Joe. *Mister Boffo: Unclear on the Concept.*
Boston: Little, Brown & Co., 1989.

Mason, Philip P., ed. *Schoolcraft's Ojibwa Lodge Stories: Life on the Lake Superior Frontier.* East Lansing: Michigan State University Press, 1997.

Masters, Brian. *The Shrine of Jeffrey Dahmer.*
London: Hodder & Stoughton, 1993.

Menn, Esther. *Wisconsin Footsteps.* Wisconsin: privately printed, 1989.

Mielke, Delores Chilsen. *T. B. Scott Mansion.*
Merrill, WI: Merrill Historical Society, 1989.

Morse-Kahn, Deborah. *A Guide to the Archaeology Parks of the Upper Midwest.* Lanham, MD: Roberts Rinehart Publishers, 2003.

Paprock, John-Brian, and Teresa Peneguy Paprock.
Sacred Sites of Wisconsin. Black Earth, WI: Trails Books, 2001.

Phillips, Charles R. "Little Lord Fauntleroy." *Landmark* (Waukesha County Historical Society), vol. 6, no. 3, Summer 1963.

Pohlen, Jerome. *Oddball Wisconsin: A Guide to Some Really Strange Places.* Chicago: Chicago Review Press, 2001.

Roberts, James P. *Famous Wisconsin Authors.*
Oregon, WI: Badger Books, 2002.

Schackelman, Joseph A. *God Lives: Stories of Extraordinary Spiritual Experiences.* Philadelphia, PA: Xlibris Press, 2001.

Schechter, Harold. *Deviant: The Shocking True Story of Ed Gein, the Original "Psycho."* New York: Pocket Books, 1989.

Schwartz, Anne E. *The Man Who Could Not Kill Enough: The Secret Murders of Milwaukee's Jeffrey Dahmer.* New York: Carol Publishing, 1992.

Simonson, Harold P. *Zona Gale.* New York: Twayne Publishers, 1962.

Thieme, John B. *Fantastic Stories.* Phillips, WI: privately printed, 2001.

Tutton, Mary. "An Unabashed Artist." *Palmyra Historical Society Newsletter* (Palmyra, WI), Winter 2000.

Wagner, Herbert. "Wisconsin's Monsters of the Deep."
Wisconsin Outdoor Journal, August 1993.

Waldenberger, Dina. "Tales of UW-W Spooks: Legends Live On."
The Royal Purple (University of Wisconsin–Whitewater), October 21, 1987.

Westover, Ruth. "Twins First Dwelled in Dream House."
Oshkosh Daily Northwestern (Oshkosh, WI), July 26, 1969.

Whyte, Bertha Kitchell. *Wisconsin Heritage.* Boston: Charles T. Branford, 1954.

Woiak, Tony. "Spooks Afoot in Washburn."
The Lake Superior Sounder (Ashland, WI), October 2004.

Wolf, Wayne. Earl Chapin's *Tales of Wisconsin.*
River Falls, WI: Univ. of Wisconsin River Falls Press, 1973.

Wyman, Walker D. *Wisconsin Folklore.* Madison: Univ. of Wisconsin-Extension Department of Arts Development Grass Roots Book, 1979.

WEB SITES

Civil War Home, "Belle Boyd, Cleopatra of the Secession"
http://www.civilwarhome.com/belleboyd.htm

Ruth Ann Montgomery Evansville History Pages
http://mywebpage.netscape.com/ruthannmontgomer/2circus.html

This Rock online magazine
http://www.catholic.com/thisrock/1998/9810drag.asp

Miracle the White Buffalo Home Page
http://www.homestead.com/whitebuffalomiracle

Richard D. Hendricks' Web site, *Weird Wisconsin*
http://www.weird-wi.com

Linda S. Godfrey's Web site, http://www.cnb-scene.com

SHOW US YOUR WEIRD!

Do you know of a weird site found somewhere in the United States, or can you tell us about a strange experience you've had? If so, we'd like to hear about it! We believe that every town has at least one great tale to tell, and we're listening. It could be a cursed road, haunted abandoned site, odd local character, or bizarre historic event. In most cases these tales are told only in the towns in which they originated. But why keep them to yourself when you could share them with all of America? So come on and fill us in on all the weirdness that's lurking in your backyard!

You can e-mail us at: Editor@WeirdUS.com,
or write to us at:
Weird U.S., P.O. Box 1346, Bloomfield, NJ 07003.

www.weirdus.com